NOT GUILTY

NOT GUILTY

The Case in
Defense of Men

▲

DAVID THOMAS

WILLIAM MORROW AND COMPANY, INC.

New York

It is the policy of William Morrow and Company, Inc., and its imprints and affiliates, recognizing the importance of preserving what has been written, to print the books we publish on acid-free paper, and we exert our best efforts to that end.

Library of Congress Cataloging-in-Publication Data

Thomas, David, 1959–
    Not guilty : the case in defense of men / David Thomas.
        p.   cm.
    Includes bibliographical references.
    ISBN 0-688-11024-X
    1. Men—Psychology.   2. Men—Mental health.   3. Men—Social
conditions.   4. Feminism.   I. Title.
HQ1090.T49   1993
305.32—dc20   93-517
                                                               CIP

Printed in the United States of America

First Edition

1 2 3 4 5 6 7 8 9 10

BOOK DESIGN BY GIORGETTA BELL MCREE

*This book is dedicated to the memory of
Nigel Thomas, 1948–1993*

"Who would be a man must be a nonconformist."

—RALPH WALDO EMERSON

CONTENTS

CONTENTS

AUTHOR'S NOTE
AND ACKNOWLEDGMENTS

This is a book about men, but it would not have been possible without the efforts of two women, Allegra Huston and Lesley Baxter, my editors at Weidenfeld and Nicolson, in London. Their encouragement, advice, good humor, and the rigor with which they challenged any arguments that were slack or loosely expressed were as inspiring as our conversations were enjoyable.

In New York, I owe a similar debt of gratitude to Adrian Zackheim, whose patient guidance—along with that of Suzanne Oaks—was an essential aid to the process of translation from one side of the Atlantic to the other.

That we were working together at all was due to three men: Lord Weidenfeld, who commissioned this book in the first place; Anthony Cheetham, who published it in Britain; and Howard Kaminsky, who brought it to the United States. My thanks go to them, too.

En route, I received an immense amount of help from people who spared me their time and the benefit of their own work and experience, including (in approximate chronological order) Dr. Brian Novack, Cloy Morton, Carey Kennedy, Douglas Thompson, Dr. Irene Kassorla, the staff of Gold's Gym, Sue Peart and Jean Carr at *The Sunday Express Magazine*, Steve Smethurst, Neil Lyndon, Sally Ann Lasson, the production team at BBC2's *Fifth Column*, Paul Whyte, Charles Kreiner and all the men of the Sydney Men's Festival, Lindsay Foyle and Lyndall Crisp at *The Bulletin*, Mark David, Steve Panazzo, Stephanie-Anne Lloyd at Transformations, Professor Steve Jones, Dr. Robin Skynner, Myriam Medzian, Claire Rayner, Melvyn Bragg, Maureen Rice at *Options* magazine, Mike Sharman at *Punch*, Peter York, Dr. Malcolm George, Trevor Berry and Bruce Liddington at Families Need Fathers, Lucy Jaffe of Relate, Anne-Marie Hutchinson, Andrew Gerry, Renate Olins and the staff at London Marriage

Guidance, Susan Faludi, Andrew Harvey at *The Times*, Dr. Liam Hudson, Bernadine Jacot, Stephanie Jeavons, Jenni Manners, Detective Chief Inspector Crozier of the Metropolitan Police, Detective Inspector Aston of the West Midlands Police, Misha Hervieu, Joel Mahabir, Mr. Hugh Millington at Charing Cross Hospital, Robert Hart at the Everyman Centre, Cathy Lever at Move, Erin Pizzey, the staff of the American Humane Association, George Gilliland and the members of the Domestic Rights Coalition, Craig Bromberg, Eleanor Alter, Jeannette Benny at *New Woman*, the librarians at the American embassy in London, and all the many men to whom I spoke about their experiences of domestic violence and/or divorce, who must remain anonymous. Finally, my thanks go to all the various commissioning editors at newspapers, magazines, radio stations, and TV channels dotted around Britain who have, over the years, allowed me to write the articles and scripts that were the first rehearsals for the ideas that appear in these pages.

One of the themes that run through the chapters that follow is the vital importance of a secure family background. No man could have asked for a more supportive family than my own. Conversations with my mother started me thinking about sexual politics when I was a teenager . . . and I haven't stopped since. My father was not only my inspiration when I was a boy, but also an eagle-eyed editor of the earliest drafts of this book. My wife, Clare, was, as she has been since I first started out as a journalist, a constant source of support, encouragement, and love. And my two daughters, Holly and Lucy, have not only brought a special joy to my life, but also provided the financial incentive necessary to keep an idle writer at his word processor.

A word about the title of this book. Some British critics interpreted the words *Not Guilty* as a denial of all male wrongdoing. Let me state for the record that I do not pretend that men do not harm and abuse other people, male and female, adults and children. Nor do I condone or excuse acts of oppression or violence. This book is so called because it aims—among other things—to show that men are not guilty by definition, and that there is not some fatal flaw in masculinity that causes males to be inherently violent or dysfunctional. In other words, we are, like anyone else, innocent until *proven* guilty.

Finally, let me pass on an observation from another writer. Just before I settled down to write these words, I was talking to P. J. O'Rourke, the American satirist whose work I had the great pleasure of publishing in *Punch*. I told him that I was trying to write about the situation in which men find themselves today. "Tell me," I said, "what is the solution to our problems?"

The great man paused for a moment and then replied, "I think that the answer is to be found in a bottle of Dewar's."

"Is there an answer which does not involve getting smashed on Scotch?" I asked.

"No," he said. "We're surrounded by women. We'll just have to drink our way out."

So if the book that follows becomes too depressing at any point, or too much like hard work, just remember . . . there's always an alternative.

INTRODUCTION

M en stand accused. As everyone knows, men earn more money than women. Men run all the world's governments and fill the vast majority of seats on the boards of its major corporations. Men are generals, bishops, judges, newspaper editors, and movie studio heads. To make matters worse, men—if we are to believe the campaigns waged by women on both sides of the Atlantic—oppress women to the point of open warfare. They beat them, rape them, and attempt to control their powers of re-production. They stereotype them sexually and enslave them to ideals of beauty that lead thousands of women to undergo surgery or starve them-selves half to death. And every time women look as though they are making any progress, men knock them back down again.

That's what we've been told. So here's a simple question: If men are so much better off than women, how come so many more men kill themselves?

According to the *1991 Statistical Abstract of the United States,* the most recent edition available at the time of writing this book, 30,400 Americans committed suicide in 1988, the most recent year for which full figures were available. Of these, 24,100 were male, and 6,300 were female.

So 79 percent of all suicides were male. For every dead woman, there were nearly four dead men. And the gap between the sexes is widening. Since the 1970s, the rate of female suicides has dropped by more than 30 percent, from 6.8 to 4.7 suicides per 100,000 women per annum. Meanwhile, the rate of male suicide has gone up by approximately 8 percent, from 17.3 to 18.7 suicides per 100,000 men.

Similar patterns apply to Australia and Great Britain. Wherever you look, male suicides are rising, while female suicides decline. We should be glad that women no longer feel driven to end their own lives as often as they once did. Were I a feminist I would consider that to be a concrete sign of achievement. But let me ask two questions, starting with:

1. Aren't all these suicides telling us something about the real state of men's lives?

And:

2. If women comprised four fifths of all suicide victims, don't you think we'd have heard about it by now?

Western society is obsessed with women to the point of mass neurosis. While researching this book I spent some time in the library at the United States embassy in London. It is an invaluable source of information, a repository of books and magazines that are otherwise difficult to find in Britain. One morning I was searching through the *1991 Index to The New York Times,* which lists every article published in America's most famous newspaper. The *Index* is published in four quarterly sections, and as I flicked through one of them I happened to notice that the list of articles under the heading "Women" was far longer than that under the heading "Men." Although individuals males—politicians, celebrities, and sportsmen, for example—were written about very frequently, their sex as a whole was not.

Intrigued, I started to count. Between July and September 1991, *The New York Times* published 20 articles about men, including fashion pages, and 135 articles about women. I wondered whether this was an anomaly. So, with the zeal of the natural obsessive, I resolved to go through the entire index and count up the articles published on men and women for the year as a whole.

The final tally was: Men, 104 articles; Women, 679 articles.

Many of these were simply news stories. And some were listed under both headings. Even so, not only were women written about nearly seven times as often as men, but they were also the subject of far more editorial "think" pieces. Readers of *The New York Times* were regaled with opinions about the liberation of women in Africa and the alleged slaughter of tens of millions of unwanted girls in southeast Asia. They pondered the meaning of the film *Thelma and Louise* and considered, contrariwise, the reasons why women went to see movies that degraded them. Acres of newsprint were devoted to contemplating sexual harassment, date-rape, and the significance of the latest books to come rolling off the feminist presses.

Men were mentioned. They were the Africans who couldn't cope with women's liberation and the Americans who felt threatened by *Thelma.* They were the Chinese who were killing women, and the Hollywood directors who were making violent movies. And then, of course, they were the office bullies and fraternity-house rapists. They were William

Kennedy Smith, Mike Tyson, and Judge Clarence Thomas. They were, in short, the bad guys.

The Manhattan White Pages illustrated the point, too. Under "Men" I found five entries, including a store called Men Go Silk and the Men Women Modeling Agency. Not one of the entries was a men's organization or self-help group. The section for "Women" contained 128 entries, ranging from Women Against Rape, to the Women's Republican Club, and including Women in Need, Women in Data Processing, Women's Health Care, Women's Counseling, and the Women's Bar Association.

Looking through the directory, I was reminded of a conversation I had had with Dr. Liam Hudson, a psychologist at London's prestigious Tavistock Clinic, and a member of the Institute for Advanced Study at Princeton, whose work is discussed at some length in a later chapter. I had asked him, as I did a number of my interviewees, "What are men?"

Dr. Hudson smiled and said, "What's left over when you've finished talking about women."

Along with his wife, Bernadine Jacot, Dr. Hudson had written a book called *The Way Men Think*. The subject matter of the book is exactly summed up by its title. It is a book about men. And yet, said Dr. Hudson, when it came out it was reviewed as if it were really all about women. "People seem to be in the grip of some necessity to talk about women," he said. "They don't know how to stop themselves. We weren't wholly surprised when it came from feminists in their twenties, thirties, and forties. But some of the people who did it to us were men in their seventies, who were in no way part of that movement."

Men certainly feel under attack. During the two years I spent working on this book, I was repeatedly told that men were not interested in the question of what it means to be male today, and that they were completely untouched by all the arguments over the ways in which men were allegedly mistreating women. And then, again and again, I had conversations that demonstrated this was not the case: Increasingly, men felt as if they stood accused. They felt as if they had been put in the wrong. And they didn't like it.

Of course, it can be a dangerous business for a man to tell his side of the story. In November 1991, David Fletcher, a forty-year-old British aerospace engineer from Preston, Lancashire—an industrial town in the north of England—wrote a letter to his local paper. In it he observed, "I have never encountered a more pampered and selfish set of people than today's so-called modern young housewife. I am left with a feeling of shame when I stand back taking in the sight of so many young men, many in their working clothes, pushing trolleys round supermarkets and hurrying about the market."

This was not the most brilliant argument ever committed to paper. But it wasn't really all that different from the many letters, articles, reports, and so forth that purport to show what an idle, good-for-nothing slob the British (or American, Australian, French, Italian, and, for all I know, Balinese) husband is. But Mr. Fletcher found himself on the end of a hurricane of abuse. To quote an awestruck London *Daily Mail*, "His furious wife Linda and daughter Laura, 15, stopped speaking to him. Women at work shunned him. He received hundreds of angry letters and phone calls. . . . Mrs. Fletcher was incandescent with rage. 'I paint, fix hinges, do a little plumbing, put on plugs, decorate, act as nurse to the children, attend their parents evenings and do the laundry. How dare he moan about being sent to do a week's shopping?"

At first, Mr. Fletcher was defiant. He told the *Mail*, "Modern women are whingeing about nothing. My grandmother worked in the cotton mills all day from the age of 14 and, at the same time, brought up children and kept her house spotless." Nor was he any less scathing about modern men: "They are just wimps who have got men into this mess."

This unapologetic stance did not last long. Overwhelmed by the rage that his letter had unleashed and unnerved at being ostracized by his family, friends, and coworkers, Mr. Fletcher spoke to the *Mail* again a few days later. He produced a series of self-loathing apologies whose groveling tone, complete with admissions of guilt and promises of new thinking, reads like a confession at a Chinese communist show trial: "I'll say sorry as many times as necessary to get myself out of the hole I dug myself into. I never believed my observations would upset women so much. That letter was the biggest mistake of my life.

"I sat down before Linda and apologised. I asked her to please start talking to me again and, thankfully, she has. I am forgiven. I've also stirred up a hornet's nest among the women at work. But when I go back tomorrow I'll apologise to them, too. I hope they forgive me.

"I don't suppose I appreciated the vast amount of work my wife, and other women do. It is said a woman's work never ends. Now I agree. It has been spelled out for me in capital letters—down the phone and in domestic silence. My big mistake was that in trying to make a point with humour and emphasis, I went over the top and paid dearly for it. I had the choice—to see the light or be a social leper with at least half the population. I rethought my views and decided, for sanity's sake, on the first."

Just to show what a great sport she was, Mrs. Fletcher added, "I have accepted his apology. Life is getting back to normal. I don't know what possessed him to write that letter, but there will be no more."

The most bizarre aspect of the whole affair was that no one, for one moment, considered that Mr. Fletcher might have had a point. Or even, if he actually was in the wrong, that he had a right to voice his opinions. Just imagine the situation in reverse. Imagine—why not?—that it happened in America. Only the surface details would change. A woman writes a letter to the local newspaper of a traditional, blue-collar town in Pennsylvania, observing that all men are sexist pigs. Her husband, who believes that he is not a sexist pig, refuses to talk to her. So do the equally outraged men at work. Eventually she confesses her sins and confirms her repentance to a writer from *People* magazine. Her husband smugly remarks, "There'll be no more letters from my Linda."

It's inconceivable, isn't it? Because if a woman did write that letter, the response would be one of anguished self-examination on the part of the men concerned. And no man would dare respond as Mrs. Fletcher did. That would be unacceptable. Instead he would be quoted by *People* agreeing with his wife, accepting responsibility for his faults, and promising to do better next time.

The reason for our double standard is that men, being so much better off than women, are expected to remain silent. Women, being so much worse off, are thought to have every right to complain. If I have learned anything at all, however, during the writing and researching of this book, it is that unhappiness and oppression are far more evenly distributed than we have been led to believe.

In saying that, I have no desire to heap accusations on women in the same manner that they have been heaped on men. I have two daughters, whom I love beyond all measure. I want them to grow up to be cherished, respected, and admired. I want them to be able to work in any job they choose and raise a family with men they love. The last thing I want to do is add to the sum of hatred in the world.

There's enough of that already. There are too many gender politicians with their self-righteous theories packed away in their cases. I for one have had it with isms and ideologies. This century's been crippled by them. Their adherents all think that they, and they alone, know the answers. And every time a new one comes along, another set of victims is prepared.

We are faced, as a society, with a series of devastating social problems that hinge upon the relationship between men and women: rape, child abuse, domestic violence, the material and emotional chaos wrought by the breakdown of the traditional family unit. But none of these problems, including those which involve male assaults upon women, will be solved unless we look at the situation as a whole and consider the point of view of both sexes equally.

Too often in recent years, gender-based issues have been presented purely in terms of woman as helpless victim, man as evil protagonist. Not only is man seen to be oppressive, but he is also held to possess a set of inherent moral and psychological weaknesses amounting to inferiority.

It is almost impossible for a man publicly to discuss any of the positive qualities of men or masculinity without being accused of sexism, on the grounds that he is, by implication, demeaning women. He must, on the other hand, accept full responsibility for a wide range of failings that are held to result, automatically, from his gender. This grossly distorts our analysis of social issues, denies men a voice in areas that are of concern to us, and is having a catastrophic effect on the self-image of an entire generation of young men. And, incidentally, it has a powerful negative effect on the struggle for women's equality into the bargain.

Are we to believe, then, that men are simply born bad? Or is there something that happens to men that makes them more likely to act in destructive ways than might otherwise be the case? Are women, fundamentally, any better than men?

The casting of the two genders into the roles of male oppressors and female oppressed ignores the possibility that the balance of power may be far more complex and flexible than that. The undoubted strength and privilege that some men have in the public world should not blind one to the fact that their private selves may be very much less privileged.

Just think about your father. He may be alive, he may be dead. He may have been a decent man who did his best, he may have been a monster. But did he look like an all-powerful patriarch? Did he seem to be someone who was getting any benefit from all this male power that we hear so much about? What was in it for him?

My dad epitomized all the privileges of his class and gender. His parents sent him to a smart private school. There he distinguished himself academically and was picked for the school track, rugby, and diving teams. He then spent two years in the army, winning the Sword of Honour at his officer training academy. On completing his national service, he went to Oxford University, where he was awarded a First Class honours degree in history—the highest grade possible—before coming second in the Civil Service examinations, the nationwide tests for future staff of government departments. He joined the Foreign Office, serving in both Moscow and Washington before being appointed British ambassador to Cuba at the age of forty-eight, at which time he was the youngest ambassador in the Diplomatic Service.

Along the way, my father married his college sweetheart and raised three children. At fifty-nine, he is fit, handsome, and has a full head of hair. So why is his life a wasteland? Why does this charming, intelligent man, who has friends in every corner of the globe, feel that his life is essentially purposeless and empty? The answer, I believe, is that he has spent so long being a good son, a good husband, a good father, and a good employee that he has no sense of who he actually is underneath all those obligations.

Now, this is no different from the type of complaint made on behalf of women by the feminist movement. Women, it was said—and with good reason—were so busy fulfilling their duties as daughters, lovers, wives, and mothers that they had no space to be themselves. This was an entirely valid and well-justified complaint. But men, for all their supposed power, are facing exactly the same problems. And they may be paying an even heavier price than women in return for all their public privilege.

Although men are presidents, generals, and chairmen, they also constitute the bulk of alcoholics and prisoners. They display a far greater propensity than women for sexual perversion, fetishism, and dysfunction. They form the vast majority of the homeless beggars who line our city streets: In America, for example, 86.5 percent of all people arrested for vagrancy are male.

Is this because men are naturally prone to fecklessness? Or could it be that there are other contributory causes—such as, for example, divorce laws which tend, overwhelmingly, to leave women in possession of the family home when a marriage breaks down? Similarly, is the incidence of alcoholism among men due to their inherent weakness? Or is it that alcohol is an acceptable way for men to drown their sorrows in a society that is not prepared to listen to their problems and insecurities?

Men live, on average, lives that are about 10 percent shorter than those of women. They are more likely than women to suffer heart attacks, lung cancer, cirrhosis of the liver, and strokes. Indeed, they are more prone to a whole range of physical and mental illnesses, some of which—hemophilia, for example—are manifested only in the male.

Trouble is, people are so busy looking at the men on top of the heap that no one notices them when they fall. The willful ignorance of men's issues arises from three apparently contradictory sources. In the first place, since orthodox feminism has convinced the vast majority of academics, writers, broadcasters, and legislators that the relationship between men and women is inherently oppressive, and in only one direction, it follows that any problems faced by the oppressor should be regarded as being worthy not of sympathy, but of derision.

Equally significant is the stupidity of traditional male machismo, which leads men to refuse to admit to any of their problems, lest they be accused of weakness or—worst of all—effeminacy. Middle-aged men, in particular, are famously reluctant to give in to any form of frailty. In the recent past, at least three men of my acquaintance have refused to see a doctor when suffering from serious medical complaints. Only when they actually collapsed would they agree to be admitted into a hospital. Once there, each was discovered to be suffering from a potentially life-threatening condition (to wit, two heart attacks and one case of stomach cancer). Yet so conditioned were they by countless generations' worth of upbringing in which boys were told that it was unmanly to give in to pain or illness that they risked their own lives rather than threaten their fragile masculinity.

Such apparent indifference to physical suffering is matched by a willful blindness to psychological disturbance. The very fact that so many men drink themselves to the point of oblivion, thereby causing irreversible long-term damage to their health, indicates that all is not well. Yet they remain obstinately convinced that they have no need of special treatment.

One example of this phenomenon (the obstinacy, that is, not the alcoholism) was a man I met at a business dinner. He was a highly successful attorney in his mid-fifties. Over the course of a long meal with our respective spouses we discussed the subject of the fledgling men's movement. He couldn't see the point of it all and said that for men of his generation it was impossible to conceive of what men's issues might be. A little later on he told a story about his childhood. His mother, he said, used to take an ice-cream scoop and flick it at his genitalia whenever he was naked— when he had just gotten out of the bath, for example.

I asked him whether he liked this.

Of course not, he said. He found it acutely embarrassing. He hated it. But, he added, as if to correct any misgivings we might have, it was just a family game.

Was it a game his sisters played?

No, he was the only player.

A little later on he was talking about his father. He had left home for twenty years and when he returned, his father was extremely ill in the hospital. One day, sitting by his father's bed, the attorney leaned over, took him in his arms, and kissed him. "I'm sorry, Dad," he said, "but I just had to do that." When he looked again, he saw that his father's face was wet with tears. He was stunned. Here was a hard man, the rock of the family, and he was crying. Then the father spoke: "I've always prayed that one day you would do that," he said.

When the man finished his two stories, I pointed out that he had just given a perfect justification of the need for a men's movement. His childhood had contained casual brutality of the sort meted out to boys in the hope of toughening them up. So "tough" had he become that he was unable to show his feelings to his own father until the man was on the point of death. He had, in other words, been crippled by his upbringing.

The truth is that all of us carry wounds that we spend most of our lives trying to cover up. We dare not reveal them for fear that if we do we will be considered unmanly, even by those who appear to hold manliness in contempt. The self-hatred that arises from the deception we all practice leaves us defenseless before accusations that we are, in some way, bad people who must be blamed for what is wrong with the world.

The third limitation on effective action on behalf of men comes from men who have been imbued with the worst of both worlds. Brought up with the traditional male stereotypes, they have at some point internalized the feminist critique of men. The result is an overriding determination to prove that they are truly penitent, that they are more willing than any woman to criticize the wrongdoings of men. Faced with evidence of male wrongdoing, they will report it in tones of the utmost loathing. Faced with a man who is attempting to redress the balance, they will react with the utmost contempt. Male feminism has almost become a perverse badge of machismo. But self-hatred is as poor a basis from which to start an argument as hatred of anyone else.

So let's get positive. It is possible to be strong without being oppressive. It is possible to be assertive without being domineering. And it is possible to possess energy, determination, and even aggression without being violent or bullying.

The last thing that the world needs now is another bunch of whining, self-proclaimed victims, and no one should close this book thinking that I spend my whole time feeling miserable about being male. I have been privileged in every aspect of my life. The work I do, the family I love, the friendships I have made, the football, the sex, the laughs, the beers . . . all of that, from the profoundest feelings to the most trivial pursuits, has been affected by or dependent upon my gender, and most of it has been just fine. But that doesn't mean that I don't get angry or hurt or perplexed about some of the things that I see happening to the men around me. Nor does it alter my conviction that men, and the whole concept of masculinity, are passing through a time of crisis.

If we are to emerge from this crisis with any sort of grace, we have to know ourselves as we really are: neither the heroes of old, nor the villains of modern mythology. We have to get to a point where we can find some common ground with the women we live with, work with, and love— even if that common ground merely consists of an agreement to differ. I hate the conflict and tension that permeates so much of the relationship between men and women. This book is not intended to be yet another battle in the sex war. It's one small stage on the way to a peace settlement, a Geneva Convention of the genders.

One final note: I once interviewed one of the producers of *Studs,* the late-night TV dating game. He told me that if ever a woman made a jokey, but negative comment about a man, the audience laughed. If the man made a similar remark about her, the audience booed. It's a fine metaphor for the double standard we all apply to discussion of the two sexes: We are made uneasy by apparently negative remarks about women in a way we are not when those remarks are directed at men.

Now, at several points in this book, I will demonstrate that women are capable of committing acts of abuse or violence normally thought of as being exclusive to men. Some of these claims may seem surprising and even shocking. Please do not suppose that I use them in an attempt to denigrate women. On the contrary, my hope is that I can emphasize our shared humanity. We are all fallible, and it makes no more sense to suppose that one sex has the monopoly on harmful behavior than it does to suppose that one race is better than another. Men and women are equal. But whether we are the same is quite another matter.

CHAPTER 1
For What Is a Man, What Has He Got?

SPOT THE DIFFERENCE

The question of gender identity is one of the most controversial and divisive issues of our time. Many people feel that men and women are quite different from one another, but in what ways? And what effects do those differences have? When James Morris, the soldier, reporter, and writer, became Jan Morris, the woman, she discovered that the gap between the sexes was still vast. In *Conundrum*, the story of her journey from man to woman, she remarks that, having seen life from both sides of the sexual divide, there is not one moment of the day, one event or one experience that is not different for a man and a woman.

Although *Conundrum* was first published in 1974, it is hard not to feel that Morris's observations still hold true today. Yet the endless debate between nature and nurture continues to swing back and forth: Are the sexes born different, or are their differences merely the result of social conditioning?

From the start of the women's movement, this has been a vital issue. Women's leaders have needed to be able to establish that women had a right to work at the highest level in every profession. Yet research carried out in the early 1970s among large numbers of Americans and cited by Dr. John Nicholson, then a lecturer in psychology at Bedford College, London, in his 1979 book *A Question of Sex*, showed that more than three-quarters believed that the sexes were fundamentally different. Furthermore, the majority felt that the so-called male qualities, such as leadership, assertiveness, objectivity, logic, competitiveness, self-confidence, and so forth were superior to supposedly feminine characteristics of kindness, gentleness, tearfulness, and emotional subjectivity. Clearly, if women were to get anywhere in this man's world, it was vital to prove that they could, if properly brought up, be just as competitive, analytical, and so forth as men.

To this end, academic researchers sought to establish the essential sameness of men and women. So strong was their desire, in fact, that vast amounts of research from the sixties and seventies are now having to be reconsidered as the biases that lay behind them become increasingly apparent.

More recently, as I and other writers on men's issues have pointed out, sexism has to some extent been reversed. Open any women's magazine or newspaper women's page and you will read generalizations about the superiority of female qualities over male. There's a nice bit of dialogue from an episode of *Roseanne* that sums up the situation. Dan, the great big lunk of a husband played by John Goodman, has just made an insensitive remark to one of his daughters, causing her to dash upstairs in tears. *"Oh, Dan, you're such . . . a man,"* exclaims Roseanne, before leaving to see what she can do to help. Dan Junior, their son, is puzzled, and has a brief conversation with his father, which proceeds as follows:

DJ: Dad, why did Mom call you a man?
DAN: Because she's mad at me.
DJ: I thought it was good to be a man.
DAN: Oh, no, son, not since the late sixties.

It gets worse. Deborah Phillips, a behavioral therapist from Princeton, with a private practice in Hollywood, was quoted in the London *Evening Standard* in March 1990, as follows: "If we just look at the female orgasm, it does not occur in the rest of the animal kingdom. It only occurs in human females. It's a much more highly evolved response than the male. . . . It can be multiple. I know there are reports about multiple male orgasms, but it's nothing compared to the female. So if we just look at that, and the female's ability to communicate, I think that the female is a more highly-evolved species than the man."

One often reads similar statements of female supremacy, statements which would immediately be condemned as the most grotesque sexism if they were ever made about men. It is, for example, rapidly becoming a cliché to state that women make better managers than men because they are more caring toward their staff, are less concerned with pointless status symbols, and possess superior communication skills. Man's apparent propensity for violence and aggression is also contrasted unfavorably with more conciliatory female qualities.

The most obvious 180-degree turn has occurred in perceptions of friendship. It used to be said that women could never be friends in the way that men were, because they were too busy competing for male attention. Now it is said that men cannot be friends in the way that women are, since they lack the emotional honesty to enable them to bond with one another.

I shall be dealing with some of these generalizations in more detail elsewhere in this and other chapters. Suffice it for now to note that, for reasons exactly comparable with those of the early feminists—i.e., the need to demonstrate moral and intellectual equality—some male authors have recently been as vociferous in their refusal to accept gender-based stereotyping as their female predecessors. The women did not want to be typecast as tearful, fluffy-headed sex objects. The men do not want to be thought of as insensitive, muscle-bound hooligans.

The problem arises, however, that many of the theories that seem ideologically desirable have little basis in scientific fact. This century has seen many recipes for social justice that begin with the instruction: "First, change your human being." Human nature, however, does not take kindly to being changed, and many authorities in genetics, physiology, neurology, psychology, and a whole bunch of ologies besides are coming to the conclusion that there really are differences between the sexes that are innate and ineradicable.

These differences, however, must be qualified by a number of provisos. There is a feminine side to most men, and a masculine side to most women: It's just the proportions that vary from one person to another. Preexisting differences of a minor nature may be greatly exaggerated by social conditioning. Worst of all, many individuals may be socialized to behave in ways that correspond to the natural tendency of their sex as a whole, but do not suit their personal aptitudes or inclinations.

Social policies and legislation are in a state of utter chaos for want of any certainty. A company, for example, that was considering employing a woman would be accused of gross sex discrimination if it inquired into the interviewee's susceptibility to premenstrual syndrome. Yet that same woman, were she in court on a murder charge, might very well be able to prove that her PMS was so bad that it rendered her, effectively, temporarily insane. Few companies wish to employ people who go legally mad for a few days every month, so does PMS have a significant effect upon a woman, or not? Which are we supposed to think is the most enlightened attitude?

In the sexual realm, as in so many other areas of our lives, our attitudes are struggling to catch up with the staggering speed of technological change. An innovation like the contraceptive pill, for example, not only has an immediate physiological effect, but throws into confusion social attitudes that have all presumed an entirely different reproductive situation.

Meanwhile, scientists are increasingly discovering convincing biological or chemical explanations for human characteristics that have previously been thought of as moral or psychological. If a man, for example, is accused of committing an act of violence against a woman, is he evil, as traditional moralists would say? Is he the product of his upbringing, as a psychologist or sociologist might maintain? Is he, as feminists like Marilyn French claim, merely a pawn in the continuous war waged by all men against all women? Or is he the helpless victim of his brain chemistry? Finally, could it be that he is not the guilty party at all, but merely the fall guy for a society conditioned to see men as baddies and women as their helpless victims?

The moment one starts to try and explain human behavior, one is deluged with theories and manifestos. It soon becomes clear to anyone who tries to look at more than one approach to the subject that few of the experts in one field have any idea at all about what is going on in the others. On the rare occasions when they are conscious of the findings of workers in different disciplines, they seem to feel honor bound to despise them.

I have attempted to explore some of these separate approaches. My aim is to come to some sort of understanding about the nature of masculinity and the consequent differences between men and women. Having tiptoed my way as best I can through a number of intellectual minefields, I have ended up with the simple, unscientific, commonsense belief that men and women are the same . . . but different.

We're the same because we share the human condition. We are born, we live, and we die. We need sustenance and shelter to survive. We need love and companionship truly to live. We share our intelligence and we share our anger, even if we may express both of those qualities in different ways. When it comes to questions of moral worth, men and women are equal. Neither sex is more or less evil than the other, nor is the value of a man's life any greater or less than that of a woman.

On the other hand, men and women are shaped differently and sized differently. They look different, they sound different, they feel different, and they taste different. Looked at that way, it's hard to believe that they are not, in fact, different.

It sounds, I know, completely obvious, but the simplest way of solving an enormous number of the problems that divide men and women is to accept that their differences are differences of type, rather than of quality. In other words, just because we may express ourselves in different ways and may be motivated by different impulses does not mean that one way, or one impulse, is better than another. They're just . . . different.

Once we grab hold of that simple truth, then it becomes possible to understand that males and females may, in some areas of their lives, need to be treated in ways that recognize the needs that are specific to their gender. Boys, for example, may benefit from being taught their school lessons in a highly structured, well-disciplined, and competitive environment that is geared toward one-shot examinations. Girls may do better with less formal methods that recognize their greater aptitude at and preference for continuous assessment. There are biological, psychological, and sociological reasons for these particular differences, and they are echoed throughout our lives.

This does not mean biology is destiny, or that women should immediately be corralled within their kitchens and nurseries making babies, while their men bring home the bacon. I want to free both sexes from the prejudices by which they are dogged. But it helps to do that if we know where we are actually starting from. For far too long, we have enslaved ourselves to political theories that have, at best, a misguided view of human nature, and are, at worst, deliberately deceitful.

So let's try, at least, to uncover the truth, starting with a spot of science.

WHY, OH, Y?

To any scientist, the political battle between nature and nurture is a futile endeavor. According to Professor Steve Jones of University College, London, one of Britain's leading geneticists, "The mistake is to suppose that there exists a cake of human behavior that can be cut into slices called 'genetics' and 'environment.' But every genetic attribute has some environmental component, and vice versa."

Think of a finely woven carpet. Imagine that all the genetic influences are the warp, running in one direction, and that the environmental factors are the weft, running in the other. These are intermingled with such subtlety that it is no longer possible to tell which is which. All that one can see is the pattern they produce together.

The phenotype of any given species—i.e., what it actually is—is the product of its genotype, or characteristic DNA sequence, acting in a particular environment. The Siamese cat, for example, can have either a predominantly black or cream-colored coat. The difference looks like a straightforward genetic mutation. But the DNA stays the same and the color difference occurs because of changes in temperature. The hotter the environment, the lighter the coat. Same DNA, different phenotype.

Environmental factors can alter an individual's physical nature during his own lifetime. Studies carried out with tropical fish, for example, show that the dominant male in any school of fish possesses a number of disproportionately swollen cells in the area of his hypothalamus (an organ linked to the brain) that is responsible for controlling sexual functions.

But should he lose his dominance to another fish, that area shrinks back. Is his behavior influenced by his hypothalamus, or vice versa?

Even when links between behavior and physiology appear obvious, sexual politicians should hesitate before using them as the basis for value judgments. Studies have shown that testosterone levels in children, both male and female, can influence their behavior. Crudely speaking, the more testosterone the child possesses, the more likely he or she is to be aggressive, irritable, and boisterous. Such children, particularly the girls, do not necessarily translate their behavior into actual violence, but it is tempting nevertheless to link testosterone, which is a male hormone, with levels of antisocial or aggressive behavior in men so as to suggest that masculinity is, inherently, a violent phenomenon.

Except that there's a catch. Laboratory experiments suggest that when testosterone passes through a mammalian brain, it is metabolized into estradiol, which is a female hormone. From which one might—assuming that one wanted to rush to hasty and unsupported conclusions—deduce that violence is actually a female phenomenon.

In other cases, misguided conclusions can be drawn from seemingly straightforward evidence. Take the question of determining human sex. This is done by two chromosomes, the X and the Y. A baby born with two X-chromosomes will be female. A baby born with one of each—i.e., XY—will, unless anything goes wrong during pregnancy, be male. Sometimes, however, boys are born with an extra Y-chromosome and thus have a pattern that reads XYY.

Researchers noticed that the inmates of institutions for the criminally insane tended to show an unexpectedly high incidence of additional Y-chromosomes. So, too, did prisoners jailed for violent offenses in regular jails. This observation was irresistible to those who sought to show that men were inherently more violent and criminal than women. The more male your chromosomes, the more psychopathic your behavior. Ergo masculinity was once again, by definition, violent.

The chromosomal view of violence has obviously reached as far as Hollywood. Movie buffs may remember that the prison colony upon which Sigourney Weaver, alias Lieutenant Ripley, lands in *Alien 3* is comprised of violent men, who are specified as being double-Y. The same belief may have spread to Washington, D.C., too. Professor Jones tells the story—which may well be the scientific equivalent of an urban myth—of how Richard Nixon wanted to start a program to screen children for XYY patterns at birth. Any boy found to possess the condition would then be followed for life by the FBI to prevent his doing anything too shocking to the American electorate.

Before we get too carried away, however, it is worth observing one other even more obvious side effect of an additional Y chromosome. It makes people much bigger and stronger. So if they hit someone, they do far more damage than they would have done if they were small. As they say in boxing, "A good big 'un will always beat a good little 'un." But there is little evidence to suggest that they have a greater predisposition to hit anyone in the first place. Mr. Nixon might just as well have had the XYY kids followed by coaches from the Washington Redskins: They would make excellent football players.

A similar confusion explains much of the apparent difference in male and female criminality. By all conventional measurements, men commit much more crime than women, a fact to which our overflowing jails pay testimony. But is that because men are actually worse than women, or simply that—when it comes, for example, to acts of violence—they are simply more effective? In any fight between a man and a woman, the man is usually the big 'un. He may well land the final blow. And he will almost certainly be the one who ends up in jail. But that does not necessarily mean that he started the fight in the first place.

Consider the matter of intention, and a very different picture emerges from the one to which we are accustomed. Women are just as capable as men of feeling anger, hatred, and hostility. They are just as prone to feelings of resentment or the desire for revenge. Just because women do not always express those feelings in the same way that men do—although they do so more often than is commonly supposed—that does not mean that they are free from the need or desire to harm other people. They may be different, but, once again, they are also very much the same.

That, however, is to get ahead of ourselves. We cannot leave genetics just yet. If he looks at a human cell under a microscope, Professor Jones can tell within seconds whether it comes from a male or female body. Given time, he could also determine the racial origins of the cell. But the difference between black and white is tiny compared to that between male and female.

What Professor Jones cannot do, however, is to tell us why there should be any such thing as a male at all. Because, as he explained to me, no one can. There is—and this is a sobering thought for those of us born to pee standing up—no necessary or sufficient scientific reason for the existence of the male sex. The most efficient form of reproduction, parthenogenesis, occurs within a single sex. Given that this single sex produces offspring, it is, essentially, female, rather than either neuter or male.

So why does Nature complicate matters? Well, it is possible to argue that the existence of two sexes, pooling their genes in an infinite range of combinations, offers an opportunity for diversity, flexibility, and adaptability. But one might also say that it doubles the number of things that can go wrong, too.

Similarly, it might be argued that the struggle that some male animals go through before being able to mate sorts out the weak from the strong, thereby ensuring the survival of the fittest and enriching the gene pool. Among deer, for example, stags fight among themselves, thereby establishing a hierarchy and—or so it has always been assumed—reserving all the most attractive young does for the Prince of the Forest. But as Professor Jones explained to me, it doesn't necessarily work like that. Scientists have recently discovered that the sex life of deer (and some other combative male mammals) follows a rather different pattern.

With modern techniques of genetic fingerprinting, it is possible to follow bloodlines with extreme accuracy, so that one can determine exactly which stag in a herd fathered a particular fawn. What has become clear is that while the dominant male of the herd is off fighting other males, digging up turf with his mighty hooves and bellowing his masterful cries throughout the whole length and breadth of the forest, other, altogether more wimpy males are having it off with compliant does behind their master's back. This is known, with all the calm, considered categorization for which the scientific community is renowned, as the Sneaky Fucker Theory.

Funnily enough, the same theory applies to human life as well. Much aggressively male behavior is predicated on spending as much time as possible apart from females, except for brief periods of sexual activity. Traditionally, men who spent too much time in the company of women, talking to them and taking an interest in their affairs, have been considered to be effeminate. The fact that they may actually have enjoyed a much higher sexual success rate does not seem to have reduced the opprobrium they faced for not concentrating on more appropriate activities, principally killing other men in the service of one's country.

But the question still remains: What's the point of fucking in the first place? Or, to put it another way: Why does the fuckee have to be put to so much trouble when she could manage perfectly happily on her own?

Were there only one, female sex, it would exist—biologically speaking—in an atmosphere of calm, peaceful stability, adapting gradually to its circumstances over long stretches of time. On the other hand, life would not, in all probability, be particularly exciting. Camille Paglia has remarked, much to the fury of many of her fellow feminists, that if the world were run by women, we'd all still be living in grass huts. So one might think of the male sex as the irritating bit of grit in the great oyster we call life. But is this really a valid justification for its existence?

Could there, perhaps, be an explanation based—appropriately enough —on the screw-up, rather than the conspiracy, theory? Maybe masculinity is an accidental side effect of some other process, rather than an intended part of Nature's plan. One possibility is that she had no choice. Professor Jones suggests that man might be a form of genetic parasite. The idle male layabout, slumped in front of the tube with can in hand, expecting to be waited upon hand and foot by an overworked woman, may not be merely an indolent dork who could use a kick up the backside. He may be expressing a fundamental truth about human genetics.

The process works as follows: We are now discovering that many human diseases, from hemophilia to certain types of cancer, are caused by viruses that have infiltrated the human genome—that is to say, the genetic blueprint for the human race, which is carried within every cell of every human being on this planet. These viruses are a bit like secret agents, dispatched into enemy territory, living lives of apparent normality, but just waiting for the signal that will order them into battle against the host community. In the same way that we all are threatened by external viruses, to which we all have varying degrees of resistance, so we all possess a number of parasitic, genetic viruses, which we "caught" at our conception. Whether or not they ever act upon us is determined by our environment, stress, general health, and so on.

In 1990 teams of scientists led by Dr. Robin Lovell-Badge of the British Medical Research Council and Dr. Peter Goodfellow of the Imperial Cancer Research Fund announced that they had found the actual DNA trigger that sets off the chain of genetic events that leads to the formation of a male fetus. It is a substance known as SRY and it acts as a sort of switch, sending development along a new, male pathway. This crucial piece of genetic material is tiny. If one imagines the human genome as being the distance between California and Maine, then the critical section deter-mining masculinity would cover less than one footstep.

It is Professor Steve Jones's suggestion, made partly—but only partly—in jest, that SRY may well have started life way back in the mists of time as a microscopic viral organism, which wormed its way into DNA at an early stage of evolution, long, long before *Homo sapiens* arrived on the scene. If this is the case, then this was a spectacularly successful little bug, since vast numbers of species now have male members. On the other hand, since men may yet pollute or explode most life off the face of this planet, the male virus may yet find itself restricted to the cockroach family, which might seem like something of a comedown. Or, then again, perhaps not.

There is certainly a case to be made for the proposition that this genetic virus, if that is what it is, has a harmful effect upon the human body. Because one of the reasons scientists wonder why the male sex should exist is that it is, in many respects, much weaker and less likely to survive than the female. Some people, indeed, see masculinity as a weak, second-rate mutation of a superior female form.

All human fetuses start out female. The presence of a Y-chromosome, in conjunction with a series of hormonal reactions during the mother's pregnancy, determines that the previously female embryo will develop as a male. The first thing to note about this process is that all sorts of things can go wrong.

This partially explains why many more male than female fetuses are miscarried. It may also help to account for the much greater number of men than women who suffer from conditions such as transsexualism: In the journey from female to male there are, as it were, occasional stragglers. In some cases, the fetus will be born hermaphrodite, with both a penis and a vagina, or with a greatly exaggerated clitoris. In such cases, the child is surgically given the appearance of a little girl and grows up to be a normal-looking, though frequently infertile, woman.

So prone to misfunction are baby males that 120 of them are conceived for every 100 females. By the end of pregnancy the ratio is 110:100. Since more male babies miscarry or are stillborn, the ratio of surviving births is 106:100. Mother Nature knows that little boys will suffer more diseases than their sisters and experience appears to have taught her that those who survive to puberty will then devote much of their considerable physical energy to the business of mutual self-destruction.

This leads us on to the two physical characteristics of men that appear to be an inherent part of their physical makeup. They are stronger than women, but their lives are shorter: As a sex, their motto appears to be, "Live fast, die young."

MATTERS OF LIFE AND DEATH

By and large, men are some 30 percent larger than women. They have more muscle and less fat as a proportion of their body weight. They can lift greater weights, run faster, and jump further than women. Until recently these would all have been considered to be uncontroversial statements. Whatever drawbacks the male may have, his physical power was his one incontrovertible advantage and was bestowed on him by his natural physiology, rather than any social conditioning.

This belief has, however, been brought into doubt recently. Doctors in America who have studied world records in athletic events over recent years have noted that women's performances have been improving at a rate far greater than those of men. From this they have concluded, by extrapolating those improvements forward into the future, that women will soon catch up with and possibly even overtake men.

These findings caused considerable news interest when they emerged in 1991, but they did not convince many women athletes, who appeared to be less confident of their chances of beating their male peers, and they should, I believe, be taken with several grains of salt.

In the first place, one might question whether women really are improving at such a staggering rate. Before me as I write these words is a copy of the *Guinness Book of World Records*, 1992. From it I can glean the following pieces of information. During 1991, five new world records were set in men's track and field. This was an improvement on 1990, in which only two were set, although 1989 had seen five new records. Turning to the women's records, I see that only one world record was broken in 1991 (the Russian athlete Inessa Kravets set a new triple-jump record of 14.95 meters in Moscow). None at all were set in 1990 and only one in 1989. In fact, performances at major championships by female athletes have been showing a decline of between 5 and 10 percent.

It does not take long to work out two reasons why there should have been such a sudden halt to female sporting progress at the end of the 1980s. The first is that the testing of athletes for drug abuse became progressively tougher. And the second is that the sport's major pushers found themselves kicked out of business.

The vast majority of female track and field record holders are, or were, citizens of countries that used to lie within the Soviet bloc—Russians, Bulgarians, East Germans, and so forth. When the Berlin Wall collapsed in 1989, so did the state-run sports teams of the East. As they did so, details emerged of the extraordinary lengths to which they had gone in order to improve the performance of their athletes, particularly the female ones.

Young women were routinely made pregnant and then forced to undergo abortions shortly before major championships—women possess their greatest powers of strength and endurance during or shortly after pregnancy. They were also injected with massive doses of steroids and male hormones. This policy increased their muscle bulk, diminished their fat ratio, turned them into pseudomales, and perfectly, if repellently, illustrated the old axiom that if you can't beat them, join them.

That said, if training methods that have been hitherto reserved for men are applied for women, the gap between the sexes can be narrowed. But though the differences may be diminished, the only way that they can be removed is by turning women, artificially, into men. Until that happens, it might be worth remembering Arnie Bolt, gold medal winner of the men's one-legged high jump at the 1992 Paralympic Games, the world's greatest tournament for handicapped athletes. Mr. Bolt's personal best of 2.04 meters, set back in 1981, when he was twenty-four—achieved, remember, with the use of just one leg—was two centimeters higher than the winning jump in the women's high jump at the 1992 Barcelona Olympics.

What, then, of life expectancy? This, surely, is an immutable female advantage. As Professor Steve Jones remarked to me, "That is one biological difference that is absolutely clear. Men live shorter lives than women. If you castrate them, they live longer—or, at least, it just seems longer!" This last fact is based on research done among American mental patients in the days when troublesome patients were castrated in the hope of calming them down. Once deprived of their testes, and more significantly, their testosterone, the patients lived, on average, thirteen years longer than those who were still entire.

This differential, if accurate, would mean that castrati also live longer than ordinary women. So, for anyone keen on longevity, the thing to be is a eunuch. Judging by an informal poll I took among my former staff at *Punch* magazine, however, 100 percent of all male respondents felt that life was not worth living sans balls, so let us proceed on that assumption.

One of the reasons for the shorter lives of men is that the period of their lives in which they are fittest is also that at which they are most likely to destroy themselves, or be destroyed by other young men much like them. Self-destruction is a trait that is found among males of many species. The male fruit fly, for example, attempts to have sex with as many as one thousand females, all but one of whom reject his advances. Having finally found a compliant female, he mates . . . and then he dies.

We may consider ourselves to be a few rungs up the evolutionary ladder from the humble fruit fly, but sometimes you have to wonder. Old men may start wars, but it is young men, of all nations, who fight and die in them. Oppressed by poverty and corrupted by drugs, young African-Americans buy guns and shoot one another on the streets with such regularity that murder is the most common form of death for young men in the inner cities. It is also true that, all over the world, young men buy or steal cars and then drive them at high, often fatal speeds.

Middle-aged men are little better, except that they choose different means of annihilation. Men have traditionally drunk more than women and smoked more. So they score high marks for liver diseases and smoke-related lung and heart conditions. One of the reasons that they turn to nicotine and alcohol is that they need an emotional anaesthetic. They feel unable to express their fears or worries to others. This tendency not only has addictive side effects, but also adds to stress and is harmful to their health.

Finally, men work too hard. In Japan, the country whose white-collar workers work longer hours with fewer holidays than anywhere else in the developed world, they are beginning to recognize a condition called *karoshi,* or death through overwork. More and more of their clerks, accountants, and junior executives are devoting excessively long hours to jobs offering little prospect of creative satisfaction or self-determination. The result is that they drop dead at an early age, thereby ensuring that the famous Japanese system of a job for life ensures a job for death, too.

Even if one discounts man's self-destructiveness, the ravages wrought by nature have always been thought to be enough to ensure that women aged seventy would continue to outnumber men of the same age by a factor of two to one. Dr. John Nicholson cites research done among forty thousand American monks and nuns. Both sexes were leading low-stress lives with minimal physical danger and no smoking or drinking (apart, presumably, from communion wine). The results showed that the men still died an average of five-and-a-half years before the women.

Researchers such as Dr. Nicholson felt that the fundamental reason for this weakness surely had to be our old friend the Y-chromosome. Compared to the X-chromosome, it is a sorry creature, and does little but make a man male. The X-chromosome, however, carries a wealth of information. Some of this may, like a faulty piece of computer software, become corrupted. It may carry a tendency for genetically linked diseases, such as diabetes, rickets, or hemophilia. A woman, however, always has a failsafe, since she possesses two X-chromosomes, and the odds against both being identically flawed are extremely long. For the man, lumbered with his useless Y-chromosome, he is left with what he's got on the one, faulty chromosome.

That said, I do not think that one need assume that the differences between the sexes will always be as pronounced as they are at the moment. Just as women can become stronger, if not quite as strong, so men can live longer, if not quite as long. Funnily enough, that is just what they appear to be doing—in some parts of the world, at least. The British life expectancy figures, issued in June 1992 by the Office of Population Censuses and Surveys, showed that the gap between men and women had narrowed. Between 1980 and 1992, the life expectancy for women had increased by a little less than two years, from 76.6 to 78.5 years. But the male figure had jumped by more than two-and-a-half years, from 70.4 to 73 years.

If, like those scientists who extrapolated athletic performances, we project those trends into the future, then by the year 2088, British male life expectancy, which will then be 93.8 years, will have overtaken the female figure of a mere 93.7. The odds are that I will predecease my wife. But if I ever have a grandson, he may be given one lonely month in which to mourn the premature demise of his nonagenarian spouse before he too finally kicks the bucket.

In the United States, the pattern is less clear. In 1960, men could look forward to a life of 66.6 years, while women could expect 73.1, a difference of 6.5 years. Ten years later the gap had widened to 7.6 years (67.1 to 74.7). But by 1990, men had closed up once again. Their figure had risen to 72.1, while women were up to 79.9—an extra 6.9 years.

Women might care to consider the possible reasons for the narrowing of this hitherto-immutable gap. Although increased living standards, improved nutrition, and breakthroughs in medical technology are giving us all a prolonged stay on this planet, women, it could be argued, are benefiting from these improvements less than men. Perhaps, now that they are entering more of the world that was once reserved for men alone, they are also managing to kill themselves with a near-masculine efficiency.

The rate of smoking among women, formerly much lower than the male rate, is converging with it. Teenage girls seem to be more susceptible than their male peers to the lure of cigarettes—perhaps because they believe that smoking will keep them thin. And, as more and more women work, so they go out for more early-evening drinking sessions. At these they will encounter another physical difference between the sexes: A man's greater bulk and lower fat ratio enable him to handle and process much more alcohol much more quickly than the woman sitting next to him at the bar. Tough, I know, but there it is.

Before women throw away one of their greatest natural advantages, they should consider one important fact that sober, health-conscious, emotionally open men have cottoned on to: The traditional male lifestyle is hazardous to your health. It doesn't carry a government warning, but it should. Once women start to behave like men, and work like men, and earn like men, they may well start to die like them, too.

THE MIND OF MAN

An old calypso song states that "Man Smart, Woman Smarter," but it is generally agreed by most researchers that men and women are indivisible in terms of their average overall intelligence. In *A Question of Sex,* Dr. John Nicholson summarizes the history of research into intelligence, much of which had presumed the intellectual superiority of men. He concludes with a sentence from which there has been little subsequent dissent: "The most important fact is that men are not more intelligent than women— the average man's IQ score is indistinguishable from that of the average woman's." Yet, as Dr. Nicholson points out with the aid of a few simple experiments, the sexes do differ in the types of mental tasks at which they excel.

In the words of a *Time* magazine cover story, published in January 1992, "Psychology tests consistently support the notion that men and women perceive the world in subtly different ways. Males excel at rotating three-dimensional objects in their head. Females prove better at reading the emotions of people in photographs. A growing number of scientists believe the discrepancies reflect functional differences in the brains of men and women . . . some misunderstandings between the sexes may have more to do with crossed wiring than cross-purposes."

If shown drawings of several three-dimensional shapes, seen from different angles and perspectives, men will generally be able to spot the ones that are identical more accurately than women. On the other hand, if women are given two minutes in which to come up with as many synonyms as possible for a series of words, they will, on the whole, score better than men. In both of these tests, however, some individuals will do much better or worse than their sex suggests that they "ought" to do.

In the same *Time* feature it was revealed that Janet Hyde, professor of psychology and women's studies at the University of Wisconsin at Madison, had "discovered that overall gender differences for verbal and mathematical skills dramatically declined after 1974." Hyde was quoted by *Time* as follows: "Americans have changed their socialization and education patterns over the past few decades. They are treating males and females with greater similarity."

This apparently reasonable and noncontroversial remark seems to make perfect sense. But it begs two questions. Are differences really diminishing? And, whether they are or not, are we educating our young—of both sexes—in ways that fail to take account of their particular abilities or disadvantages?

Coeducation of both sexes in the same classrooms and laboratories, using the same teaching methods, has many advantages. There is a lot to be said for giving boys and girls the experience of working and socializing together as a normal part of everyday life, and the overwhelming number of school pupils are taught in that way. Yet there is a price to pay for bringing the sexes together. Educationalists have long believed, for example, that mixed high school classes tend to favor boys, whose assertiveness causes them to receive the lion's share of attention. But there are reasons to believe that there may be comparable prejudices operating against boys at other stages of their education, by which they in turn are disadvantaged.

Whatever their inherent differences, environment can have a dramatic effect upon the academic performance of males and females, by no means always for the best. A look at educational standards in the United States and Britain (two nations that have in common the distressing characteristic of producing much lower standards of performance than are found in the best Asian and European nations) demonstrates what I mean.

In the United States, scores in Scholastic Aptitude Tests have declined markedly since the 1960s, although, to be fair, the graph has begun to point upward again. Within that decline, however, the differentials between males and females have varied markedly. In 1967, the average scores in verbal SATs were 463 for males and 468 for females. That is what one might have expected, given the female superiority over males in verbal IQ tests.

Except here's a funny thing: Since the early 1970s, male high school students have been opening up an ever-widening lead over their female contemporaries in verbal SAT scores. In 1970 the scores were males 459, females 461. By 1980, males had slumped to 428, but the females had fallen even faster, to 420. By the end of the decade there had been a revival of sorts. Males scored 434 and females 421. But the male lead had widened to 13 points.

For all Professor Hyde's optimism, there does not appear to be any evidence that young women are enjoying an equal advance in the subject that had always been their weak suit—math. Between 1967 and 1989, the male lead in mathematical SATs declined from 47 points (514 to 467) to 46 points (500 to 454). Any narrowing is due less to female improvement than to a fractionally faster rate of male decline. So far, then, the news is bad for women.

However, despite the fact that males outscore females on their SATs, young women are increasingly more likely than young men to go on to college. In 1970, 55 percent of college freshmen were male. Since then, that figure has fallen consistently, dipping below 50 percent in 1980 and dropping to 46 percent by 1989. No wonder the very term "freshman" is increasingly coming under attack on politically correct university campuses—it simply isn't an accurate description.

What has happened to eighteen-year-old men between their last summer in high school and the following fall? Why don't they want to go to college? Could it be that so much effort has been made to make university education attractive and relevant to women that men have been forgotten? Could it be that the image (however distorted) of college as a place where the women's studies faculty dictates the ethical and political tone of the campus; where men have to watch their behavior, their words, and even their opinions, for fear of being labeled offensive; and where the male contribution to culture is actively derided has persuaded young American men that they'd rather be somewhere else?

That much is pure speculation. What is certain is that it is no more healthy for a disproportionate number of college graduates to be female than it was for them to be male. We cannot afford to waste the talent and enthusiasm of either sex. So when will we see programs designed to attract men back into college?

The manner in which children are taught and then tested can also have a marked effect on their performance, starting at a very early age, and again this may not always be advantageous to young males. For example, is the whole culture of teaching—particularly at kindergarten and elementary levels—so fundamentally female that boys are bound to get off to a poor start?

The British kindergarten and primary school education, reading and math tests, show that little girls outperform boys by a huge margin. This has been assumed to be a result of accelerated female development. Yet, at these same schools, the vast majority of teachers are female. (This is equally true in the United States, where 97.8 percent of kindergarten teachers are female.) Surveys by the now-defunct Inner London Education Authority showed that women teachers consistently praised girls more than boys, and equally consistently criticized the boys' behavior, often regarding it as a serious problem requiring remedial treatment.

In the words of Tony Mooney, a secondary school headmaster, writing in the London *Independent on Sunday,* "Women teachers find boys too noisy, too aggressive, too boisterous. Unconsciously or not, they consistently reinforce and reward more 'feminine' behaviour. If all this is true, it is understandable that boys should not be as advanced as girls in the hands of women junior school teachers. There is a direct relationship between a child's academic achievement and a favourable response from the teacher."

Mooney was first alerted to this possibility by the behavior of his own son, whose performance and self-confidence at school altered markedly when he was taught by a woman, rather than a man. When the boy's mother asked him why this should be so, he replied, "Because the men teachers never shout at me as much as the women teachers."

Research evidence from an experiment at the University of California, Los Angeles, appeared to support Mooney's anecdotal experience: "Seventy-two boys and 60 girls at kindergarten . . . learned reading with a self-teaching machine. There were no differences between the sexes in their reactions to the mechanical gadgetry. Yet when the girls were tested on their reading progress they scored lower than the boys. Then the children were placed under the normal classroom instruction of women teachers. The children were tested again on the words they had been taught by the teacher. This time the boys' scores were inferior to the girls'."

Mooney noted that boys' exam results at secondary school were declining just as the number of women secondary school teachers was increasing. Boys, however, continued to outperform girls in scientific and technical subjects where teaching was still dominated by men. The issue here is not just the favoritism that teachers may show to pupils of their own sex, but the instinctive understanding that an adult will enjoy with a child who is going through a process he or she went through too.

One of the few generally accepted differences between boys and girls is that boys are, across all cultures, much more boisterous and overtly competitive than girls. Boys enjoy games of rough-and-tumble. They play with guns, real or imaginary. They seek out physical competition, whether through sports or informal bouts of playground warfare.

This makes them harder to control than girls, particularly if they are being taught in an open-plan classroom. Janet Daley, writing in the London *Independent,* has observed that "Anyone who visits an open-plan infant-school classroom, where the children organise much of their own time, will notice a pattern. Groups of little girls will be absorbed in quite orderly work or play . . . requiring little supervision. A few of the boys will be engrossed in solitary creative or constructive activity. A large number of children will be noisily participating in some loosely directed project which needs guidance and some of those will be boys who are persistently disruptive and out of control."

Daley ascribes this behavior to the fact that boys develop neurologically at a slower rate than girls, and are thus "physically and mentally unstable for much of their childhood and adolescence." Are they? Or does Ms. Daley share a prejudice—unintended, no doubt—with the boys' teachers, who are trained to define the relative maturity of their charges by their ability to sit quietly and be attentive? By those standards, boys may appear backward, troublesome, and even threatening. But all that has happened is that we are criticizing little boys for their failure to be little girls.

If girls do better in single-sex education, where their particular needs can be catered to exclusively, does the same apply for boys? Having spent ten years in single-sex boarding-school education, I have mixed feelings about its benefits, but I am absolutely certain that boys need specially tailored treatment to at least as great an extent as their sisters (a point with which, I might add, Janet Daley concurs).

In Britain during the 1970s and 1980s educationalists reacted against the strict traditions of the past, in which brutality was routine and competitive sports mandatory, by banning corporal punishment, relaxing discipline, and removing sporting activity from many of the nation's schools. American writers seeking a cure for the apparently compulsive violent behavior of youthful males have sometimes suggested similar cures.

Looking at the machismo and the obsessive competitiveness of a typical high school football team, it is hard not to sympathize with that point of view. But beware: Far from pacifying young Britons, the removal of sports from the curriculum has merely left them frustrated, undisciplined, and increasingly unfit. Some 60 percent of British teens now suffer from being overweight. Scarcely 20 percent are fit enough to complete a simple set of physical tests. And violent crime among young males—who comprise the vast majority of all offenders—is on the rise.

Boys whose lives are led without structure and discipline do not become liberated. Instead they become bored, frustrated, and maladaptive. They

fight. They misbehave. And they perform badly both at school and thereafter. However much it might want boys to change, any society that wants
to limit the antisocial behavior of young men should start by accepting
the way they are. Then it should do everything possible to make sure that
their energies are directed toward good, rather than evil. When Yoda sat
on his rock in *The Empire Strikes Back* and told Luke Skywalker that he
had to choose between the dark force and the light, he knew what he
was talking about.

WOUNDED PEOPLE

There is one educational characteristic of young British men that does
bear further examination. Once they get to university, the pattern of their
examination results is observably different from that of female undergraduates.

British degrees are ranked—from the top down—as Firsts, Seconds
(subdivided into 2.1 and 2.2), and Thirds. Roughly speaking, women
receive the bulk of second-class honors degrees, while men get the firsts
and the thirds. Why? Taking the thought a stage further, why is it that
there are certain fields of academic and intellectual endeavor—typically
those concerned with engineering, architecture, mathematics, music, and
abstract thought, whether scientific or philosophical—in which women
are almost entirely absent from the highest ranks? Most educated people
could name at least one great female author, but a female composer? Or
philosopher? Or architect?

The obvious reason for this disparity is to be found in the social conditions prevalent throughout history. Women were barred from entry into
the universities at which scientific research was conducted. Nor would
they have been given the opportunity to carry out works of building or
engineering, even if they had been trained and even if—in an age before
effective birth control—they were not hampered by the demands of pregnancy and motherhood. By contrast, a novel can be written in private. It
does not require the support of an academy or institution. It was, in other
words, the one field in which women could excel . . . so they did.

Nowadays, some women claim to be similarly disadvantaged at universities. Arguments for this proposition have included the suggestion that
the effect of examinations upon female students is disproportionately
stressful; the unwillingness of women to articulate or have confidence in
their own opinions; the lack of female role models; and the additional
social pressures faced in college by female students.

Yet it is hard to avoid the conclusion that there really is something
different about the ways in which men and women like to work that goes

deeper than mere conditioning. Certainly, the way we are treated will exaggerate differences, but if similar trends are at work at every stage from kindergarten to Ph.D. and on into the outside world, there must be more to it than that. This is another pattern whose threads run in more than one direction.

Despite the vast and continuing growth in the number of female students as a whole, it is still proving very difficult to attract women into certain academic fields. You find women throughout medicine, genetics, psychology, and sociology. They make up the majority of legal students in both Britain and America. But you still do not find them in quantum physics or mathematics to anything like the same extent. So are there inherent reasons why men are so dominant in certain subjects? What does this have to do with their passion for baseball cards? And what has it got to do with Mozart, Jack the Ripper, and victims of domestic violence?

The answer may be found in a deeply repressed psychic agony known as the "male wound." This is a concept whose effect is comparable in psychological terms to that of the Y-chromosome. It gives men some qualities of undeniable strength. But it may also leave them fatally flawed.

The idea of the wound is much in vogue among men's movement gurus like Robert Bly, but the most level-headed account of its development is to be found in a book called *The Way Men Think*, by Dr. Liam Hudson and his wife, Bernadine Jacot.

In their view, the wound arises from the fact that, at a very early age— approximately eighteen months—boys make a psychological transition away from the female norm, which echoes the genetic and physical transitions they made as fetuses in the womb. In order to establish a sense of their identity as males, they are impelled to move away from their mother toward a suitable father-figure, who, with any luck, actually is their real father to boot.

If this transition happens successfully, in a loving family with a stable, well-adjusted father and a caring, but not overpossessive mother, the boy experiences what Dr. Hudson describes as "a dislocation"; he has gained a sense of his male self, but the price is a loss of some of the comfort he derived from his mother. This dislocation, Hudson believes, may act as a motivating force as emotional energy that might have been spent on the mother is reassigned to other areas of the boy's life.

The tremendous emotional commitment that boys and men have to abstract ideas, or inanimate objects or institutions, is an example of this phenomenon in operation. Boys collect stamps or baseball cards and support football teams in a way that most little girls do not. Having learned at an early age that profound feelings toward other people may carry with them a heavy emotional cost, they choose to direct their emotions toward nonthreatening targets.

If the wound is little more than a dislocation, this tendency may not be particularly marked, and it may even give males part of their externally directed sense of drive or purpose. But what if it goes wrong? The mother may hold on to the child too long. The father may be absent or dysfunctional in some way, so that the child learns to associate masculinity with violence or alcoholism. The father's image additionally may be tarnished by the mother's hostility or bitterness after a divorce or breakdown.

The whole process may even prove so painful for the child that he decides that deep emotional attachments to people are simply too painful to be risked. Instead, he sublimates his emotions completely, transferring all his energies away from people and into areas of his life that are more open to control.

Although women are quite capable of possessing immense ambition, few possess the single-minded, almost manic energy that is characteristic of those men who build great fortunes or conjure up towering academic theories. These men—who must, I believe, be regarded as suffering from profound imbalance (how often the biographies of great men reveal massive emotional or familial dysfunction)—are often prepared to take much greater risks than women in order to achieve their ends.

Men are, by and large, the great entrepreneurs, and they are also the great bankrupts. As academics, they can be characterized by a desire to stamp their theories upon the world, forcing the evidence to fit, whereas women scientists tend to let themselves listen to the evidence and go where it wishes to lead them. So men come up with the most spectacular discoveries, which may turn out, on further examination, to be spectacularly wrong, while the more reticent approach of a woman may lead her, in the longer run, to knowledge that is more secure. (In this context, of course, the development of feminist theory may turn out to be the exception that proves the rule.)

Sexually speaking, the wound's distortions mean that men are much more likely than women to become sexually fetishistic or perverse. Nervous about genuine intimacy, not only do they turn people into sex objects, they also turn objects into sexual beings, be they high-heeled shoes or inflatable dolls. Intellectually, they are often fascinated by abstract concepts, rather than human ones. Some fall in love with mathematics, music, or theoretical physics, fields in which relationships between numbers, notes, or particles are predictable, beautiful, and unable to cause pain.

Hudson and Jacot cite research conducted among scientists in the 1950s by the American psychologist Anne Roe and followed up a decade or so later by David McClelland. They noted that the successful physical scientist tended characteristically to be male; to come from a puritanical family background; to avoid personal relations, preferring to work with great single-mindedness; to avoid complex emotions; to prefer music (which is based on rational harmonic patterns) to painting or poetry (which are not); and to develop a strong interest in analytical thought by no later than the age of ten.

Men of extreme genius—including Newton, Descartes, Schopenhauer, Tolstoy, Kierkegaard, Goethe, Ruskin, and George Bernard Shaw—share a common desire to retreat from human intimacy in the direction of formality and abstraction. They tend, too, to be sexless, since sexual activity, with its threat of engulfment by the woman, is too painful to contemplate. When there is a strong sex drive it is often, as in Beethoven's case, acted upon in as basic a way as possible, so that brief encounters with prostitutes or servants take the place of any deeper, more troublesome relationships. One of the most interesting aspects of real brilliance in abstract thought is that it is not passed on. Newton, Locke, Pascal, Spinoza, Kant, Nietzsche, Wittgenstein . . . you could fill an encyclopedia of philosophy with the names of men whose children were their ideas, rather than any human offspring.

Finally, there are those such as Freud or Skinner, the Harvard behaviorist, who believed that all organisms, including humans, could be manipulated by means of systems of punishment and reward. They resolve their difficulties with personal and sexual relationships by attempting to master them by means of their intellect. For them, understanding—or, more to the point, organizing according to their own theories—is a form of control. In its most extreme form, this need to sublimate sexual fears by means of control leads to that uniquely male creature, the serial sex-killer, who transfers his own pain onto his victim, terminally.

In her book *Sexual Personae,* Camille Paglia makes an observation whose concluding sentence is destined to be one of those quotational clichés, along the lines of Andy Warhol's dictum about fifteen minutes of fame, to wit: "Serial or sex murder, like fetishism, is a perversion of male intelligence. It is a criminal abstraction, masculine in its deranged egotism and orderliness. It is the asocial equivalent of philosophy, mathematics and music. There is no female Mozart because there is no female Jack the Ripper."

Before one leaps to any conclusions about the implications of the male wound for sexual politics, a few caveats are in order. It may be that campaigners who are hoping to increase the proportion of female physicists, architects, and engineers are, to some extent, wasting their time. If the characteristics required of them may be described as on the extreme, male end of the spectrum, there will never be a high proportion of women—or even of emotionally sensitive men—among them. On the other hand, there may be other areas of research—genetics and psychology are two that come to mind—whose human component is attractive to female academics. The key thing is to make sure that no one is excluded from a field just because he or she does not conform to the sexual norm.

Another vital point is this: The male wound may cause what Hudson describes as "the depressing side of men—the behavioural perversions, the driven promiscuity and the eruptions of violence." But whatever Camille Paglia may say, men have no monopoly on antisocial behavior.

In Hudson's words, "There is an argument that says that women are locked into a relationship with their mothers in a way that men are not, because they haven't taken the step away by identifying with their fathers. That means that all the beneficial elements of that relationship become part of themselves and so do all of the grim bits—all of the rage and anger and frustration and rivalry are carried into the growing girl and become part of her personality."

Hudson believes that there are "powerfully perverse elements" in both men and women. However, he notes, "Men tend to act out, especially aggressively, their perverse needs. Women create perverse situations."

In interviewing men who had been in relationships that had gone badly wrong, often violently so, I found Hudson's observations being repeatedly borne out. Men from a wide range of backgrounds whose wives had either been abusive, or exceptionally vindictive—over the issue of child custody, for example—repeatedly told me that their wives had intense, highly problematic relationships with their mothers. Some had inherited personality disorders. Others passed on to their partners pain that had been inflicted on them in their childhood. Often, the mothers still exerted enormous influence over their daughters' lives. The wives were bitterly resentful of their mothers' suffocating attention, but were unable to direct their anger toward its actual source. They transferred it instead to their partners.

They did this by means of verbal, psychological, and even physical harassment, filling their homes with an atmosphere of anger and tension. This was the "perverse situation." The man might be driven to a point at which he was faced with a choice between leaving the relationship or lashing out—the "perverse act"—but his violence would merely be the physical expression of a hostility that was common to both partners. Indeed, marriage guidance counselors now see some acts of domestic violence as fulfilling a mutual need. In this scenario, the woman satisfies her need for violence, not by enacting it, as a man might do, but by drawing it upon herself.

There are three lessons one can draw from all of this. One is that in Hudson's words, "Women are different. Sometimes they're different in a complementary way to men. And sometimes they're just plain different."

The second is that while such a difference may be manifested in practical ways, it does not mean that women are incapable of violence. They may simply choose different methods. After all, there has never been a female

Jack the Ripper, but thirty years before he made his bloody way through the streets of London's East End, Mary Ann Cotton poisoned some fifteen victims, including her husband, her lover, and her child, in the mining towns of County Durham.

Finally, if the boy has to travel from the mother to the father, he has to have a father to whom he can travel. Rocketing rates of extramarital births, divorce, and deliberately chosen single-parenthood are rapidly making the conventional father an endangered species. The net effect of that, in Hudson's view, will be that one can expect to see consequent increases in rates of delinquency and behavioral disorders among young men. This is by no means the only evidence that we will uncover of the relationship between paternity—or its absence—and delinquency, but this is as good a time as any to set that particular ball rolling.

It has a long way to go.

NO COMPRENDO

At one point in our conversation, Dr. Liam Hudson observed that "one would like to feel that there are two clear lines of argument: one, what men get up to, and two, what women get up to." But communication between the sexes is rarely that simple or that easy to understand: "Some sort of deal is done, but the rewards and the costs are mutually inscrutable. Even if you live with someone for a long time, they're still slightly inscrutable."

We had been talking about the psychological background to date-rape and the possible causes of a situation in which both parties sincerely believed their own stories. In other words, the woman was certain that she had been raped, while the man truly thought that she had consented. This is an issue that will be gone into at much greater length anon, but what Hudson said about it was relevant to so many of the disputes between the sexes.

Describing this hypothetical couple, he said, "Both might have had romantic and pragmatic systems of need at work, but they were in some way differently deployed. The ingredients may be alike, but the brew is different. It's a bit like the relationship between two languages—an act of translation has to take place. You could translate the boy's feelings into the girl's feelings and elements would be alike, but often you would be stuck for a translation."

The linguistic analogy is apt, because different languages do more than substitute one word for another—they embody entirely different systems of thought. English, for example, may be distantly related to Italian, since they both share a common ancestor in Latin. Yet the character of the two languages could hardly be less similar. Here is a translation, printed in the London *Times*, of the introduction to an Italian comic book, written by the Marchesa Marina Ripa di Meana, wife of the European Community's environment commissioner: "Only recently I learned that comics represent the dimension of adventure for me, the true possibility of continuous hyperbole. . . . I feel exactly like a comic character: dilettante, exhibitionist, excessive, making continuous incursions into the sacred gardens of the arts, where severe priests see me as smoke in their eyes."

I am quite certain that the original passage made perfect sense to any Italian reader. I am also sure that every word in it has been accurately transferred from Italian into English. The result, however, is gibberish. Exactly the same process applies in the gulf between men and women.

In her best-selling book, *You Just Don't Understand: Women and Men in Conversation*, the American academic Deborah Tannen takes a close look at the differences in the ways that the two sexes communicate and the difficulties that this may cause. It is a scrupulous, even-handed, and admirable book. In no way would I wish to describe it as deliberately biased or distorted, and I am hesitant to comment upon what is obviously the product of many years of study and research. Even so, there were times when, reading the book as a man, my reaction was, "But Professor Tannen . . . you just don't understand."

Her basic point, which is echoed by other researchers such as Michael Argyle, is that female-to-female communication is essentially affiliative, whereas male-to-male communication is essentially competitive. So when two girls or women talk, they are seeking intimacy and inclusion. They will look one another in the eye. The nonspeaker will nod in agreement. Their bodies will be aligned with one another. And they will swap experiences as a means of establishing empathy. That is not to say that women do not compete, or fight, or have intense rivalries, but they do so in ways that do not overtly threaten that sense of intimacy—hence the catty remark disguised as a compliment, or the looks that flash between one woman and another.

Men, however, learn from boyhood that the subtext of all their conversations is a competition for status and control. Unless they are very close to one another, or very secure in their hierarchical relationship, they do not look one another in the eye, since such an invasion of the other person's space might be seen as a challenge or threat. They sit with their bodies at angles to one another. They do not reinforce. And their conflicts are overt and clearly displayed.

This means that, for example, men will frequently miss 90 percent of the communication that goes on between women, or even between women and men. A couple return from a dinner party. The wife says, "Did you see the way that Margaret was looking at Emma? She was furious with Jack. He could hardly keep his eyes off Emma's body all night." And the husband replies, "Really? They seemed all right to me."

To be fair, this is not necessarily men's fault. The English journalist and author Celia Brayfield went on assignment for the *Mail on Sunday*'s *YOU* magazine, armed with a false beard and a man's suit, to see life from the other side. Sitting in a London cocktail bar, "I discovered why men always fall for blatantly obvious girls. They don't notice the others. From the receiving end girls put out such extraordinarily low-key signals to a man they want to know that most of the time the fella probably never notices. A come-hither glance is very hard to spot, even if you know exactly what you are looking for. . . . The kind of behaviour which feels outrageously bold and provocative to a girl still looks faint and covert to the man whose attention she is trying to attract."

Tannen gives several examples of the confusion that our different patterns of communication can cause. For example, if a woman is talking to a friend who is going through hard times, she may very well say, "I know just how you feel. I had exactly the same thing happen to me once . . ." and then start into an anecdote. She is thereby endorsing her friend's experience and empathizing with it.

As a consequence, says Tannen, when a woman is faced with a man who is down in the dumps, she may employ the same tactics, only to be rebuffed, whereupon she feels hurt and rejected. What she does not know, however, is that the man has interpreted her anecdote as a form of challenge. He does not hear "I am sharing your sorrow." Instead—attuned as he is to competition—he hears, "My story is much more powerful than yours." The result is mutual incomprehension and anger.

Looked at in reverse, a man may greet a friend's depression with a brisk "Never mind," followed by a joke or story about an altogether different subject. To a woman, that sounds like callous indifference. To a man, it is an attempt to lift his friend out of depression by reminding him of the positive side of life. Again, the consequence is confusion.

But I wonder whether there is a sort of Heisenberg effect that applies to this form of psychological and sociological research. Just as the very existence of a scientific experiment affects the nature of the phenomenon it is designed to study, so any study of gender is bound to be influenced by the identity, the sex, and the preconceptions of the researcher who is attempting to study it (a fact that, of course, applies to this author as much as to anyone else). At one point in *You Just Don't Understand*, Professor Tannen describes her own experiences as a lecturer. When she has spoken before students, she says, women's questions have tended to be supportive, asking for clarification or personal explanations, but not challenging her hypothesis. Men's, on the other hand, are challenging, demanding that she justify her ideas. "The women's questions seemed charming to me, but the men's seemed cheeky," she remarks.

Tannen then reports that, in conversation with her husband and other men, they saw the men's questions as a form of respect. By being tough they were taking her seriously. But, concludes Tannen, "I liked the women's questions better: I felt they reinforced my authority. I didn't even mind the intrusive one about my marriage, which allowed me to be wry and amusing in response. . . . I doubt whether I am unusual among women in seeing challenges as somewhat more real than ritual, and to take them personally as attempts to undercut my authority rather than to bolster it by 'grappling' with me."

Tannen is making an honest attempt to give a personal example of the confusions that can arise between the sexes. But it is hard, when reading the whole section from which these extracts have been taken, to avoid the conclusion that she feels there is something fundamentally wrong, or unpleasant, about the male approach. I suspect that she is right when she says that her feelings would be echoed by many women, and I think that the implications of that fact go to the heart of many of the workplace and political quarrels between the sexes. More than that, I think that she has hit upon a fundamental distinction in the ways the sexes view the world and their place in it.

Professor Tannen believes that, having achieved authority, she deserves automatic respect. Well, up to a point, of course, she's right. But, in a democracy, authority must always justify itself, and the way that it does so is by proving its right to power on the basis of achievement. We continue to vote for governments because their policies stand up to time and interrogation. We should continue to respect professors on exactly the same basis.

One might ask how much the cause of academic understanding is advanced by cozily supportive questioning and mumsy gossips about married life? I am pleased that Professor Tannen should be "wry and amusing," but I am surprised that she should feel so outraged by male questions such as "Doesn't much of the material in your book fall more easily into the realm of rhetoric and communication than linguistics?" which she cites as examples of competitive behavior.

That doesn't sound particularly offensive to me. On the contrary, the student might well have thought that he was helping to develop understanding by moving the debate forward. One of the most enjoyable elements of speaking before university audiences is precisely the fact that carefully nurtured ideas are going to be challenged by bright, youthful minds intent on tearing them apart. It is a form of conflict, but one from which the supposedly senior partner should emerge invigorated. Professor

Tannen's desire for the quiet life seems to me to be a worrying one, since it leads inexorably to Camille Paglia's vision of placid women living in grass huts, unwilling to face up to the challenge of working in stone.

This, admittedly, is a typically male response. I see competition and challenge as part of the natural order of things. And, if one looks back through human history, and across at other species, it is hard to avoid the conclusion that this is a universal male experience. The leader of a political party, the head of a tribe, and the dominant male in a pack of chimpanzees all share the knowledge that their leadership is always subject to threats from below. Sooner or later, a younger male will take their place. The king must die.

The archetype of female power, however, is very different. The matriarch can never be deposed, since her authority derives from the fact that she has given birth, an event that cannot be undone. Every father will, sooner or later, be eclipsed by his son, if only over a game of tennis, or a round of golf. But Mother will always be Mother, and neither her sons nor her daughters can ever overthrow her in quite the same way. Women, therefore, do not expect their authority to be under threat in the way that is automatic for men. Tannen felt that her male students' attitudes were inappropriate in part, I would suggest, because they were so unexpected.

Given this paradigm, daughters are not brought up in the expectation that they will have to fight and compete for the things they want. Even now, they are still raised by parents who are much more gentle to them than they are to male offspring. They are not given the training of casual brutality and emotional suppression that are the lot of most young boys.

When they grow up, however, young women have to go to work in professions that are still run along male lines. They encounter the challenge-driven systems of masculine culture. Cocooned in a communication system whose values are so different, and inclined to perceive intellectual attacks as personal affronts, is it any wonder that some women are ready to see themselves as victims of harassment and discrimination? Equally, however unpleasant it may be, we should hardly be surprised if men treat women with crudeness. That, after all, is how they have been trained to treat each other, too.

There is one final observation I would make about Professor Tannen's remarks: Her picture of docile, helpful female students, ever eager to support their elders, turns a blind eye to the manner in which feminism itself was propagated on the campuses of the Western world. The challenge that successive generations of young women have made to the established, patriarchal authorities is like a large-scale version of the student who challenges his or her professor.

This process has had a massive impact upon the way that people think, and for that it deserves applause. But here's the rub: Feminist orthodoxy has since become as touchy as Professor Tannen. It is no more happy to have its authority challenged than she is. Men are constantly being told to express their feelings, but woe betide them if those feelings do not fall within the politically acceptable norm. The result is that men, and, for that matter, many women, feel themselves to be excluded from the debate, and little real progress is made toward either advancement or a common ground. Still, who knows? Maybe we men are simply speaking the wrong language. Perhaps the professor is right, after all. Perhaps we just don't understand.

THE BRAIN MACHINE

It would be nice to think that the two sexes could become, as it were, bilingual. Certainly, there is a lot to be gained for both sides from making the attempt to see the other's point of view. But there may be biochemical roots to this particular problem that render it fundamentally insoluble.

Neurologically, it has recently been suggested that women link the two sides of their brains more effectively than do men. It is thought that the corpus callosum, the bundle of nerves that links the left and right halves, much like a cable links the units of a stereo system, may be as much as 23 percent thicker in women than in men. As a result, women may be able to "access" much more of their brain at any one time, bringing a wider range of intellectual and emotional faculties to bear on a problem. This might account for feminine intuition and also for the traditional female trait of adding an emotional element to problems that men believe are purely rational.

This effect is reinforced by small-scale differences within the cortex of male and female brains. The brain works on the basis of excitation and inhibition. You need to excite nerves and muscles to make them work, but you need to inhibit that activity in order to control the work that they do. After all, we want our arms and legs to move, but only when we tell them to do so.

The inhibition is performed by Gamma Amino-Butyric Acid receptors, otherwise known as GABA-urgic cells. They filter and inhibit brain activity, eliminating extraneous "noise" in order to concentrate the required "signal." Men have a higher density of GABA-urgic cells than do women, so their brains are thereby more inhibited. One of the effects of this may be that the fabled inability of men to get in touch with their emotions arises not from their conditioning, but from their brain chemistry. The brain filters out emotional noise so as to concentrate on the intellectual signal.

Of course, this can be greatly exaggerated by the way in which a boy is brought up, and one would not want to encourage the idea that men are inevitably devoid of emotions. The current obsession with getting men in touch with their feelings, however, may not be a desirable form of progress so much as another example of the way in which an increasingly feminized society makes futile and counterproductive demands upon men to make them more like women.

Even allowing for any problems that may be caused by their brain chemistry, men's real problem has got nothing to do with an insufficiency of feeling. Most men feel quite enough as it is. Their problem is that they can't express themselves. Again, this may have less to do with inability than with prohibition. Men are convinced that if they reveal their fears or weaknesses, they will be perceived as unmasculine. The cure lies in letting men be the people that they know they are, not the people they think they are supposed to be. They don't need improving. They need freedom.

In any case, the current idea that women are superior to men as a result of their greater emotional sensitivity is less an objective judgment than a reflection of social fashion. If you value male qualities, then you will see men as superior. If you value female ones, the situation is reversed. Neither judgment is valid. In *My Fair Lady,* Professor Higgins asks, "Why can't a woman be more like a man?" Nowadays, Higgins wears a skirt. Now she wonders why men can't be more like women. Both questions are equally foolish.

One way of looking at the male and female brains might be to imagine that they are two different types of computers—an IBM and a Macintosh, for example. Overall, they perform roughly similar functions, but they do so in different ways and each has particular strengths and weaknesses. The basic principles that govern them are the same. The actual wiring, however, is different. Nor can they read one another's software—at least, not without a great deal of trouble.

The only trouble with this analogy is that one cannot update and improve the human brain quite as easily as one can a computer. Man has been around for a long time. The earliest primates appeared about seventy million years ago. Remains found near Salonika in Greece indicate that hominoids, which may be the link between men and apes, were present ten million years ago. The earliest tools yet found—simple sharpened stones—are some 2.5 million years old. And the oldest known example of *Homo erectus,* the ancestor of *Homo sapiens,* found near Lake Turkana, Kenya, by Kamoya Kimeu in 1985, is thought to be about 1.6 million years old. Brain-wise, not a lot has happened since then.

We are probing the Big Bang and creating artificial genes using brains that were designed for simple tasks like hunting and gathering. Men are characterized by powers of high concentration, focusing on a particular task for a limited period, because that is the kind of ability required by the successful hunter. Women are characterized by emotional sensitivity, less intense concentration, but greater powers of mental endurance over time, because that is what a mother needs if she is to perceive and tend to her child's needs. Men are able to analyze three-dimensional objects moving in space, because that is what a huntsman has to do with his target. Women are able to recall the arrangement of objects because that is what a gatherer, searching the ground for edible plants, needs to be able to remember from one harvesting trip to another. Modern men find it easier than women to drive a car through a narrow opening. But, unlike women, they can never remember where anything in the house is kept.

These differences suggest a biochemical cause for one of the most pervasive causes of misunderstanding between men and women. From the male point of view, women seem to require a phenomenal amount of attention. I can remember when I first went out with girls being amazed by the amount of constant communication they seemed to expect. My male friends didn't behave like that. You could do something with a guy—whether it was building a model airplane or going off to a football match—but he didn't expect you to talk to him all the time.

I'm sure my girlfriends were equally baffled. They, like most other women, would be infuriated by the male habit of disappearing behind a newspaper or sitting silently in front of the television. They wanted more active companionship.

This social pattern fits exactly into the biological pattern described a little earlier. Men, being built for short bursts of high concentration, seem, to women's eyes, to alternate between sexual frenzy and indifference. Women, being built for long-term, low-intensity activity, seem, to men's eyes, to want too much chatting and cuddling, and not enough basic sex.

I am both simplifying and exaggerating. Everything that one says about women applies to some men, and vice-versa. And all of us contain individual mixtures of male and female characteristics. Just to take my final point, many sex therapists point out that their biggest problem these days is that men seem unwilling to have as much sex as their female partners require. But maybe if the therapists spent less time making men behave unnaturally by getting in touch with their feelings, they might start behaving a bit more like men again, instead of spending all their time moaning and groaning . . . like a bunch of old women.

ARTIFICE AND INITIATION

The picture that has been emerging of men to this point is by no means entirely positive. For every advantage they appear to possess—every one of which is itself open to considerable debate—there is an evident disadvantage. And the very fact that scientists cannot come up with a convincing reason for the existence of the male sex in the first place suggests that there is, at the very heart of man's existence, a fundamental insecurity.

My mother always used to say that a woman knew *that* she was female, and *why* she was female, every time she had a period. It was put to me another way at a men's group I attended at which one of the men remarked that women were the trunk of the tree of life, whereas men were just the branches. By this he meant that there was an unbroken flow of life through the female sex as one generation gave birth to another. Men, on the other hand, were left on the side. They served a function, but they certainly weren't the main event.

This observation may help to explain one all-pervasive aspect of being male, which is that sense of being slightly cut off, or alienated, from the rest of the world. This feeling is, I am sure, explained by the sense of prohibition referred to earlier. Men cannot be themselves for fear of ridicule or even emasculation. So they put up a barrier between themselves and the outside world. Once again, the problem is not that they do not have feelings, but that they repress and deny such feelings as they actually possess.

The poet John Donne wrote that "no man is an island, entire of itself," but sometimes it can seem that he is. In the words of the American writer Don Hanlon Johnson, "Alone, we ache for contact. That ache, we now know from various medical studies, is a major factor in male patterns of illness, addiction and death. Even in groups working, hunting, drinking, or playing cards, we men often feel alone. We talk a lot, but from a distance. With only a handful of men do I experience the presence of eyes, transparency of facial expression and punctuating touch that show that we are truly listening to each other."

My personal belief is that men do not need to imitate female speech patterns in order to free themselves. As anyone who attends a men's group soon discovers, just saying what's really on your mind, as a man, will do the trick. But, in general, Hanlon is surely right. Men are engulfed in a sea of uncertainties. They cannot afford to let their guard drop with one another for fear of compromising their continual need to define and prove their masculinity. The most obvious example of this, of course, can be found in the sex act itself. The man has to display his potency, visibly and tangibly, in a way that has no parallel for a woman. "Getting it up" is the absolute sine qua non, and an inability to perform that feat strikes at the heart of a man's sense of being male.

His performance anxiety is fully justified, to judge by a two-part feature entitled "What Women Want" published by *GQ* magazine in October and November 1987. The piece was a transcript of a ten-hour talkathon in a Manhattan hotel room, conducted by a sex therapist, Stephani Cook, and six women aged twenty-five to thirty-three, five of whom were single or divorced.

At one point, Cook asked her panel, "What happens if the guy has everything else going for him but is temporarily lacking an erection?"

To this, answers included:

"It makes me feel unwanted and so I lose my desire for him."

"Good luck and good-bye. That's his job and he's failed."

"I would have to regard any erectile failure as crucial. It would be very important to do something about it." And:

"If a man wasn't consistently potent, I'd think he was pulling something on a woman, and that's not fair."

Once a man has successfully penetrated a woman, he faces a further uncertainty. A mother needs no reminding that she has given birth and her offspring are unquestionably her own. But how can a father be sure of his paternity? Nowadays, the answer is by conducting DNA tests, but until recently, artificial codes of naming and inheritance had to be established to enshrine a succession from father to child that could equate with the natural descent from the mother.

Men have constantly to create, by the force of their own will, what is naturally self-evident in women. Femininity is automatic, but masculinity is a concept that requires active definition. Nowhere is this more clear than in the initiation rites with which male societies, from jungle tribes to college fraternities, test and greet their new members.

Again, the comparison with women holds true. Girls pass into womanhood by the simple act of menstruating: The process may be a mysterious one and surrounded by mythology and taboo, but the evidence is clear to see. For males, however, the transition from boy to man is not a matter of growing pubic hairs or acquiring the ability to ejaculate. Instead, it has always been marked by a series of artificial, ritual experiences. These mostly attempt to confirm the boy's departure from the soft, oversensitive world of women into the hard, fearless, active world of men.

As if to prove that an obsession with the phallus is common to men everywhere, many of these rituals involve circumcision, a practice made all the more agonizing by the fact that this is physically, as well as psychologically, the most sensitive part of the male anatomy. Coming-of-age ceremonies often also include elements of separation, isolation, starvation,

pain, and, thereafter, learning. As any good torturer will tell you, starvation, solitude, and sleep-deprivation are all aids to extracting information, or replacing it with ideas you wish to impress upon your subject.
In the course of initiation, boys learn the tribal lore that will enable them
to become fully—even if artificially—male.

A few examples follow of the ways in which young males around the
world are expected to prove their manhood. Men may wish to cross their
legs at this point.

The Gisu, from Uganda, expect young men aged in their teens or early
twenties to stand perfectly still while their foreskin is cut and the flesh
peeled away. This proves that they can conquer pain and fear through
inner strength and it gives them the status of *Basani*—or men—as opposed
to *Basinde*—or boys—a term that is also applied to all members, as it
were, of uncircumcised tribes.

In the Sudan, certain tribes cut concentric circles around the shaved
heads of their young men. Once again, no sign of pain may be shown.
The resulting scars are then a sign of the adult male.

The Iban of Borneo take their young men away into the forest, where
their teeth are blackened and holes drilled through them. Brass plugs are
inserted into the holes and the teeth are filed down to sharp points. The
resulting piece of cosmetic dentistry is regarded as the very height of
fashion and beauty.

It is, however, to the Aborigines of Australia that one must look for the
most fully developed use of agony as a fire in which the male steel is
forged. Once village elders have determined that a boy has reached an
appropriate level of maturity, he will be taken away from the village, to
the accompaniment of the wailing of tribal women, who physically resist
his removal. His teeth or penis will then be mutilated in ways similar to
those described above, ways that reach a peak of sadistic sophistication
among the Mardujara Aborigines.

Their initiates go through a five-stage process which begins with the
initiate (who is already fasting) eating a dish of nettles cooked in bamboo
with pork fat. This unappealing recipe induces a painful stinging in the
throat, accompanied by swelling. Two days later, a nosebleed is induced
by hammering sharp pegs into the nostrils with a mallet. Small wedges
of flesh are then cut from around the tip of the penis, producing deep
lacerations which penetrate the urethra. The penis is then beaten, repeatedly, with the handle of the circumcision knife. And finally, the penis
is rubbed vigorously with salt and nettles.

This mutilation represents the killing off of the Aborigine's old life, after
which he is ready to enter his new existence. He is then taught his tribal
lore for a period of six to eight weeks, whereupon he is ready to return,
as if from death, to his village, where he is treated with the respect owed

to a man who has displayed both his courage and his commitment to his tribe.

Before one mocks these apparently primitive and outlandish customs, it is worth considering the degree to which they mirror our own experience. After all, Christianity is based upon a story of suffering, followed by resurrection, redemption, and ascent into a better life that is an uncanny parallel of the narrative enacted in almost all ritual initiations. And, on a far less elevated plane, boys of all sorts are put through tests by their peers to confirm their right to the status of full group member.

Wherever you find groups of men, be they sports teams, motorcycle gangs, college fraternities, or army regiments, there you will find rituals whose purpose is to solidify the unit and distinguish its members from outsiders. A September 1992 *Rolling Stone* feature on Alpha Delta, the Dartmouth College frat on which *Animal House* was based, revealed that AD pledges could expect to suffer rites such as the Rack of Gnarl, "which entails the chugging of up to a dozen twelve-ounce cups of various cocktails (blue cheese mixed with diet Coke and Listerine is a favorite) designed to make an already drunk pledge boot (Dartmouth slang for vomit)."

Other pleasures to which aspiring pledges could look forward on Hell Night included interrogation about sexual experiences and the Circle of Death, in which they marched around a dank basement, alternately chugging and booting. At another Dartmouth frat, Alpha Chi Alpha, pledges fondled a frat brother "dressed as a bleeding, post-mastectomy woman." In the British army, soldiers would regard that as kids' stuff. The Coldstream Guards once blowtorched a new recruit's testicles.

At Eton College, Britain's most famous public school, boys carry out much of the disciplinary action of the school via a series of self-electing bodies. Every house has a group of junior prefects, known as Debate, and above them a senior group called the Library. The school as a whole is governed on a day-to-day basis by the Eton Society, or Pop, whose members wear special braided coats, colored waistcoats, and sponge-bag checked trousers. In each case, the members of the group elect new members and initiate them into the ranks by means of well-planned acts of ritual humiliation.

When I attended Eton in the 1970s, boys had their pubic hair sprayed silver, were thrown into hot baths, or stripped naked and smeared with potions whose recipes do not bear repetition in public. Over the next few decades, these boys will go on to become cabinet ministers, generals, bishops, bankers, and pillars of the establishment in quantities unmatched by any other school in the country. So perhaps the initiation is more effective than may at first appear. Or perhaps our establishment is even more perverted than has ever been imagined.

Even in groups that appear to be anarchic, clear patterns of ritual will exist, which reinforce the hidden structure and hierarchy of the group. In Britain, young boys going to football matches, for example, will often devote more time to watching older supporters than the game itself. They learn the rules of their "firm" or "posse," along with their chants, gestures, and songs. Within the crowd, there are clearly defined power positions, such as chant leader, or aggression leader. Only once they have the support and confidence of their tribe are individuals allowed to initiate chants or acts of aggression against rival supporters.

Masculinity has to be confirmed by outside approval, and men will go to great lengths to construct social groupings that give them a *raison d'être*. Men have exploited their advantages—physical strength; their pack instincts; their ability to exclude emotion and even humanity from their considerations; and, most significant of all, the fact that they do not spend any time either being pregnant or nursing—to establish patriarchal structures in which they feel safe from the threat of women, whose inherent powers remain much stronger and more mysterious than their own. Men, in other words, have constructed a world that justifies their own existence.

PAYING THE PRICE

The price men pay for their power is a heavy one indeed. Faced with the need to stay within the boundaries of masculinity and to preserve the patriarchal status quo, little boys are brought up to conform to rigid guidelines of acceptable masculinity. A simple illustration of this occurred to me when my little daughter first started to watch Walt Disney videos. Entranced by *Peter Pan* and *Robin Hood,* she took to making herself jaunty caps, with paper feathers stuck in the rim, arming herself with a sword made out of a drumstick, and setting off to fight baddies (most notably her little sister). Then a craze for Batman swept through her kindergarten, so she had to have her black cape and mask and yellow belt.

A little girl wandering around in a Batman outfit is cute. And given the extreme care with which—at the age of five—she styles her hair and chooses her dresses in the morning, not to mention her professed intention of marrying her favorite little boyfriend, I have no doubt at all about her essential femininity. But imagine that I had a son who dressed up as Maid Marian, Wendy, or Catwoman—what would I think then? Here I am, a child of the glittering, glam-rock 1970s, a teenage David Bowie fan whose rebellion took the form of shocking my elders with mascara rather than motorbikes, but I'd still be worried if my little boy started bending his gender too avidly. For all that I know the harm it does, I'd still want the poor little chap to be a man.

The truth is that masculinity can't take the strain. It is so fragile and so delicately balanced that it cannot withstand the shock of nonconformity. A modern woman can, like my little daughters, play any number of roles in her everyday life. Her persona is as flexible as her wardrobe. But you do not have to venture far from the beaten path of masculinity before becoming trapped in the thickets of what society sees as effeminacy or perversion. Men have to keep any internal deviations from the straight and narrow locked up within their psyches. It is no surprise that so many men, unable to express themselves in normal circumstances, turn instead to deviancy and perversion. Countless broken lives, and careers cut short by scandal, testify to the damage that is done as a result.

A man has freedoms that a woman does not. He can walk into a bar or restaurant without being propositioned. He can go out alone at night without the fear that accompanies a woman who walks alone down a city street (even if he is actually at much greater risk of attack). But he lacks one vital freedom. He cannot be himself.

I do not think it is possible to exaggerate the degree to which male behavior is motivated by the fear of other people's disapproval or contempt. All over the world, there are millions of men acting in overtly macho ways in order to demonstrate a form of masculinity which they personally find alien and even repugnant. Yet none of them dares let down his guard for fear of losing face, even though the person whose scorn he dreads probably, if he did but know it, feels exactly the same as he does.

Sometimes, men can use praiseworthy activities as a smokescreen for emotions that might otherwise be disallowed. Sports, for example, is a vital component of the mythology of masculinity. Irrespective of the efforts of female athletes, sports simply does not play as important a role in female life as it does in male. It is, if you like, the mirror image of fashion. All men wear clothes, but very few of them read *Vogue*. Many women exercise, but very few could give a damn about the contents of the sports pages.

Every winter, the men of America's two finest football teams run out onto the field of whichever stadium has been chosen for the Super Bowl, cheered on as they go by pom-pom-waving cheerleaders. The men wear tight pants and huge shoulder pads, which exaggerate their physiques to an almost comic degree. The women wear leotards, lipstick, and sequins. This is the single event that, more than any other, unites the most powerful nation on earth, and it is sex-role-stereotyped to the nth degree.

At its worst, sports exemplifies the least appealing aspects of men in general and its host culture in particular. Football is materialistic, hyper-aggressive, territorial, and competitive to the point of inflicting permanent physical harm on almost everyone who plays it professionally or even in college. But it is also noble, creative, graceful, and dignified.

Sports, any sport, deals with the issues that are at the heart of a man's being. A true sportsman—be he golfer, football player, grand prix driver, or jockey—works to make the best of what he has got, fighting against the ravages of nature, time, and his fellow men. He fights to impose his will on his surroundings. He must be as gracious in victory as in defeat (in public, at any rate). The writer Colin Welland, Oscar-winning script-writer of *Chariots of Fire,* a movie that celebrated the Olympic ideal, once wrote an obituary of a rugby hero of his youth. He observed that no matter how old a man gets, he always feels younger than the men he sees on the sports field: Their genius makes him look with the eyes of a boy once again.

Sports may be, as others have observed, a pursuit as trivial as it is magnificent, but it allows men to free their emotions. In 1990, the England soccer star Paul "Gazza" Gascoigne made headlines around the world when he broke down in tears during the World Cup semifinal, but no one thought him any less of a man. Some newspaper columnists dived in to announce the arrival of the New Man in sport, but a man more unreconstructed than Gazza it would be hard to imagine.

Here was a young man who came from the barren working-class housing estates of northeast England, where extreme, self-conscious masculinity is the sole defense left against forces of technological and social change that are making the traditional unskilled working man as redundant as the carthorse. Being "hard" is everything. Yet within his sport he could express creativity, sadness, joy, loss, even tears . . . and still remain a man.

In the world from which Gazza emerged, lads walk around Tyneside bars on freezing nights in February dressed only in sleeveless shirts. In that world, no man would dare cry if he lost his job, or his wife, or his kids. But if his football club was eliminated, he would weep buckets and everyone would understand. Sports justifies his tears. Sports is masculine, therefore anything connected with it is masculine too. So men who would sneer at poetry will go into raptures about a move on the football field.

Many people like to sneer at sports and men's passion for it. They feel that it is indicative of men's essential childishness that they should care so deeply for something so unimportant. I would argue against this on both counts. In the first place, the expressive powers of sportsmen (and women) at their best rival anything that any actor or dancer could come up with. They produce a magic that expresses the very best that a human being can be. But even as the powers fade, the tragedy of the declining Muhammad Ali, or the stubborn refusal of Jimmy Connors to give in to the passing years, expresses a struggle against time which all of us must share. More than that, however, sports does not illustrate the comedy of man's immaturity. It illustrates the tragedy of his imprisonment. We are trapped by the demands of masculinity. Sports offers the illusion, at least, of escape.

Those individuals who have made the journey, whether permanently or just temporarily, from one sex to another, tend to tell similar traveler's tales. Some readers may find the observations of people who have had a sex change, or lived temporarily in the guise of the opposite sex, to be unreliable, even distasteful testimony. Some—including, perhaps, anyone who concluded from *The Silence of the Lambs* that all transsexuals were psychotic, woman-hating mass-murderers—may even consider such people to be freaks, whose opinions are not worthy of serious consideration.

Other, perhaps more sophisticated, observers might ask how anyone who was brought up as a man and who has never, for example, had a period, can truly understand what it means to be female. They could claim that male-to-female transsexuals—those people whose original, masculine body is at odds with the female gender to which they feel they actually belong—are merely conforming to a fantasy of femininity to which they have chosen to aspire, rather than its reality. They might protest that there is, therefore, a sort of sexism about her, or their, opinions.

I can only beg for your tolerance, both for the very existence of transsexuals, and for the stories that they have to tell. They are, after all, the only people who can speak from experience of the view from both sides of the sexual fence. There is a lot to be said for firsthand experience: The observations of one sensitive human being may be worth more than all the theoretical textbooks in the world.

Stephanie-Anne Lloyd began life as a boy called Keith. By his midthirties, Keith was a balding man in a suit. He worked as an accountant, was married, and had two children. Within him, however, he harbored a conviction that there was something profoundly wrong with his life. He began to suffer from near-total sexual impotence. Other men seemed to him like aliens, rather than members of the same sex. Eventually, he was diagnosed as a transsexual. Following a gender-reassignment operation, dull, mousey Keith became the flamboyant Stephanie-Anne. The suits and bare scalp made way for dresses and luxuriant locks. Strapped for cash, she was, for a while, a prostitute, servicing at least one Tory cabinet minister as a regular client (he liked, she said, to be spanked), before founding her own business, Transformations, which caters to the needs of male transvestites.

Stephanie and Keith may have been the same person underneath, but they were treated very differently. As a nondescript but efficient executive, Keith was used to being taken seriously at business meetings. But in the commercial world of the north of England, Stephanie was looked on as an accessory, rather than a protagonist: "I went to a meeting when I first formed Transformations. I went with a man and we walked in and they immediately started talking to him, thinking that he was in charge. They automatically assumed that I was his secretary or assistant because I was female. I found it quite amusing, but I can understand women getting very, very cross about that."

On the other hand, Stephanie says, "Society does put a lot of pressure on the male species from all sorts of different points of view. Life is hard for men. Career-wise, work-wise, it may be much easier in most professions for a man. But on an emotional level, life is much, much richer for a woman. Women can let down barriers and can get much closer to people. Men have to maintain barriers. As a man, you can't go and cry on a best friend's shoulder when things go wrong. The first thing he'd do is edge away if you touch him."

Toward the end of her book *Conundrum*, Jan Morris describes the ways in which her life altered as a result of her change of sex. She remarks that the more she was treated as a woman, the more woman she became. She found herself more and more in female company and she discovered that she preferred women's conversation and the sense it gave of belonging to a school of thought that was quite distinct from male-dominated society. As a man, Morris had enjoyed all the privileges of upper-middle-class male life. James was a public schoolboy, who served as an officer in the 9th Queen's Royal Lancers before going up to Oxford and then becoming a correspondent for *The Times*. He was a member of the Travellers' Club, one of London's snobbiest gentlemen's clubs. Had his personal identity allowed it, a glittering establishment career awaited him.

As a woman, however, Jan was treated very differently. Men assumed that she was their inferior. They expected her to be less well informed than they were and they presumed that she would wish to remain quiet while they took the lion's share of the conversation. By and large, like so many women before her, she found it simplest to oblige them.

Jan Morris calls this "the subtle subjugation of women." But she discovered that there were compensations. People were more courteous to her than they had been to James. They treated her more kindly and with greater tolerance. In a sentence whose relevance will become ever more evident as this book progresses, Morris remarks of womankind, "Her frailty is her strength, her inferiority is her privilege."

Tellingly, Morris found that the differences were more than merely social. The physical changes in her had dramatic effects. The loss of her penis and the softening of her body made her, she says, more passive and more willing to be led by others. She became more emotional and more easily moved to tears. Even her interests changed. She lost her fascination for the great, impersonal sweep of history, preferring instead a smaller, more personal scale upon which to focus.

What of those who journey in the other direction? Celia Brayfield, living temporarily as a man while on assignment for *YOU* magazine, found that the male world gave its inhabitants greater respect, but exacted a heavy toll in return. She found that, as a man, other motorists would give her more room on the road. Complaints to waiters were dealt with more promptly. Policemen were respectful, rather than flirtatious. But, she remarked, part of the reason that she was granted space was out of fear. People resisted contact in case it should lead to an implication of intimacy, or a provocation of violence.

"I began to have a distinct sense of isolation. Without the rapidly exchanged, insignificant glances to which I was accustomed I had a greater sense of distance from the people around me. . . . Living as a man was rather like living in a plastic bubble as far as relationships were concerned. A man's world seemed a harsh, lonely place where most relational behavior was mysteriously taboo. I felt cut off from other people, distanced from them simply by the assumptions they made about manhood. As a person I had a sense of pitching from further back, needing to be louder and tougher in order to be acknowledged."

However the sexes start out, they end up by living lives that are differentiated by gender at every possible juncture. Stephanie-Anne Lloyd remarked to me that "Men and women are so different that they could have been designed for different planets. But maybe, the very fact that they can't understand one another is what keeps them interested."

How much longer, though, must men put up with concepts of masculinity that diminish them as individuals? Why, for example, should we sacrifice so much of our lives upon the altar of work? It is to that central experience in a man's life that my attention now turns.

CHAPTER 2
This Working Life

"Every man's work," wrote Samuel Butler in *The Way of All Flesh*, "whether it be literature or music or pictures or architecture or anything else, is always a portrait of himself." Butler knew what he was talking about. Work is how a man defines himself. Of course, work matters to women too, and a woman may also be judged by her professional status, or whether she has such status at all. But, as any cocktail party conversation illustrates, work is not such an overwhelmingly determining factor for the identities of women as it is for those of men.

The first question one woman asks another may very well be, "What do you do?", but even before they begin to talk, the two women will have judged one another in terms of their appearance, their clothes, and their accessories. Later on in a conversation, they may exchange information, which is, in its own way, as competitive as it is solicitous, about their lovers, husbands, and/or children. Men, however, exchange endless clues about their professional status, their earnings, and their access to power or information. Their anecdotes are designed as much to reinforce or establish status as they are to inform or amuse. They are positioning one another on a ladder. They want to know which one of them is really the chief monkey.

One illustration of this occurred several years ago to a show business reporter for a British newspaper. A friend of his was in London, on leave from his duties as a pilot in the Royal Navy. The reporter offered to take him to a big rock industry party, at which the two men ended up sitting next to a pair of superstars—legend (apocryphal, perhaps) has it that they were David Bowie and Pete Townshend. The pilot, overawed by the presence of these musical demigods, remained silent until one of them asked him what he did for a living. Somewhat reluctantly he confessed that he flew Harrier jump jets. In fact, he added, he had just returned from the war in the Falklands.

At this, the musicians' attitudes changed completely. This apparently insignificant person at their table was, in fact, a fighter pilot who had seen active service. His machismo ranking, therefore, was even higher than that of a rock star. In professional terms, at least, he had the biggest dick at the table. A man's work, after all, is his very identity.

More than that, it is a compulsion. Even now, many women regard work as something that will take a different role in their lives as time goes by. They may give up work altogether, either temporarily or permanently, in order to have and look after a family. They may work part-time or on a volunteer, charitable basis. Although the majority of women who work need to do so for the sake of their own or their family's finances, only 14 percent of working women in the United States are the sole breadwinners within a family. The great majority of women do not experience, or— perhaps even more important—expect the lifelong responsibility for the financial well-being of a family that is the expectation of every man.

An interesting indication of the differences in the male and female perceptions of work as an element in family life was given by the *Connecticut Mutual Life Report on American Values in the '80s*, a survey conducted by Research and Forecasts in 1981. Its findings are now more than a decade old, but they give a sense of personal priorities that would not, I believe, have changed out of all recognition were the same questions to be asked today.

The researchers asked more than two thousand respondents about the career sacrifices they would make on behalf of their children. Eighty percent of women, and 75 percent of men, said that they would make at least one career sacrifice in the interests of their children. What would be given up for the children's sake, however, turned out to differ markedly between the sexes.

By and large, women's sacrifices involved doing less work, while men's involved doing more. Half of all women would work limited hours in order to help their children; 46 percent would work at home; 40 percent would quit work entirely; 36 percent would delay or suppress ambitions, while only 28 percent would actually work more. The men's responses were a mirror image of the women's. Forty-six percent would increase their working hours with the onset of children, while only 8 percent would quit work; only 22 percent would delay or suppress ambitions, and 32 percent would reduce their hours worked. The sense of obligation was clear: Women became good mothers by staying home and working less, while men demonstrated their paternal instincts by leaving home and providing more.

Men carry with them a form of gender-memory, handed down from grandfathers, fathers, and elders. It tells them that their work is the way in which they become fully male. But it also speaks of the price that must be paid. Most of us have seen our fathers go gray or even die in the service of their work. We know that we too will be enslaved by the tyranny of the paycheck. We know, in other words, that work is a burden as much as it is a benefit.

For all that women fight, quite rightly, for equality in the workplace, it tends to be equality of rights, rather than of responsibilities. The aim is to achieve a fair deal for those women who choose to take advantage of it, not to force it upon them, whether they like it or not.

Much as been said, for example, about the role of women in the armed services. In the wake of the Gulf War it is increasingly clear that the only way in which a woman is any less effective on the battlefield than a man is that she is unlikely to be able to carry the physical burden of weaponry, equipment, and supplies that is loaded onto the modern frontline infantryman. Where brute strength is less important—on a warship, for example—her performance will be as good as any man's. As a consequence, the demand has arisen for equal treatment for women within the forces. No one, however, has suggested that women be faced with the possibility of conscription. For men, the onset of an all-out war would entail the duty, if called upon, to die for one's country. For women, that peculiar privilege would only be an optional extra. To paraphrase Lord Byron:

> Woman's work is of woman's life a thing apart,
> 'Tis a man's whole existence

In her book *Backlash*, Susan Faludi reports on the Yankelovich Monitor Survey, an annual poll, as follows: "For twenty years the Monitor's pollsters have asked its [male] subjects to define masculinity. And for twenty years, the leading definition, ahead by a huge margin, has never changed. It isn't being a leader, athlete, Lothario, decision-maker, or even being 'born male.' It is simply this: being a 'good provider for his family.' "

Faludi cites this link between masculinity and bringing home the bacon as one of the major causes of the threat men feel from the presence, and success, of women at work. After all, if a man is not a worker—what is he? At a time when the combined forces of technological change and prolonged recession have devastated the traditional industries that have employed the bulk of the male labor force, replacing men's work in steel mills or coal mines by "women's" jobs in shops or silicon-chip manufacturing plants, men are being doubly emasculated both by unemployment and by their replacement in the work force by women.

Nor can men retaliate by migrating into female territory. However much a man washes dishes, shops, or takes care of the kids, he can never do what a woman can. He can never give birth. In these circumstances, it is hardly surprising that men might feel a sense of crisis. In fact, given the degree to which male power is threatened, the surprising thing is not that there has been a "backlash," but that it hasn't been infinitely more virulent.

What Faludi chooses not to mention in her book—although, to be fair, she has done so in subsequent interviews—is that there is plenty of evidence to show that the men surveyed by Yankelovich have every reason to stress the importance of their ability to provide. A five-year study of ten thousand men and women from around the world carried out by the American publication *Behavior and Brain Sciences* showed that while men in all cultures see beauty as the most important quality in a prospective mate, women base their decisions on their man's earning power and ambition.

Commenting on the survey's findings in the London *Daily Express* (May 1, 1989), Professor David Buss, a psychologist at the University of Michigan, remarked, "It appears women throughout the world, whether they be Zulu, Brazilian or British, look for the same traits when it comes to choosing a partner. In every case, women prefer their mates to be older and value the ability to provide very highly. A woman will tend to look for a strong, prosperous male because he will be better able to support a family."

A more specific view of the degree to which a man's profession can affect his desirability was provided in June 1991 by a survey conducted for the British edition of *New Woman* magazine. More than two hundred women, aged twenty to forty-five, were asked which profession their ideal man would work in and what traits they valued most. *New Woman* found that security, stability, and intelligence were seen as the greatest male virtues, and that the legal profession was judged most capable of providing them.

Lawyers were felt to have sex appeal, a good social background, and plenty of brains. More than two-thirds of the women sampled felt that their own status would be increased by dating a lawyer. "The idea of a man fighting for justice in the courts is powerfully sexy," one particularly idealistic woman remarked.

Second on the list came architects, who, it was reckoned, "dressed like Italian love gods," a gift that placed them narrowly ahead of doctors and designers. The survey was, however, strongly dismissive of politicians (they talked rubbish, dressed badly, had terrible haircuts, and cared only for themselves), "boring" librarians, and "brain-dead" bus drivers. In a neat parallel of the usual bimbo stereotype, women thought that male models were "drop-dead gorgeous . . . but thick as two short planks."

The main point here, apart from the institutionalized sexism and lighthearted misandry displayed so carelessly by *New Woman*'s respondents, is the degree to which their hopes and expectations are still those of the same old women of days gone by. Forget sensitivity, caring, sharing, and all the rest of the New Man package—a man's status and salary are still the keys to his attractiveness to women.

New Woman has not run a comparable survey in the United States. American women may feel that they have progressed further than their British counterparts and have moved beyond the point where their man's career is a major factor. But to anyone who takes that view I would merely observe that British women are as advanced as their American counterparts when it comes to going out to work. In both countries women form between 40 and 45 percent of the total work force, and at least as high a proportion of married women are in paid employment in Britain as in the United States. Nor is there any sign of greater conservatism among the British population as a whole. After all, they three times elected a female prime minister, and there is, as yet, no sign of a female president.

It's also worth quoting a story that *New Woman* did run in the United States, in a November 1991 section called "A Man's Life." In an article headlined "His Feelings," New Jersey writer Jon Katz told a story to which a lot of men could relate: "We are mighty confused about what is expected of us. 'For years,' an attorney confided to me recently, 'my wife fought with me because I came home from work so late—routinely eight-thirty or nine—and saddled her with the kids. Now, I've had two different jobs in less than a year. I make a third less money and I'm home a lot more. And she's pissed at me because we're broke. I truly don't know what I'm supposed to be.' "

At the same time that men are being asked to spend more time with the kids, but also make money and reach the top, they are also being told that they must abandon their grip on the upper ranks of the professions in order to let in more women. More than that: They are increasingly being told that they are, by definition, less well suited than women to the demands of modern management.

On January 8, 1992, the London *Guardian* opened its report on a conference on occupational psychology with the words, "Women are the natural business leaders of the future because they have personality traits which motivate and encourage staff, an occupational psychologist said yesterday." The shrink in question was Dr. Beverly Alimo-Metcalfe, of Leeds University. If she had said exactly the same thing about men, it would never have been reported with quite such unquestioning acceptance.

Put it another way. Suppose I said, "Men are often much more efficient than women and get things done quicker. I have always worked for women, which has been great because they tend to be on the lazy side. What they call delegating responsibility actually means getting somebody else to do the job for them. Another reason that there are so many successful men around is that they have far greater stamina. They're much stronger mentally and physically . . . women will take to their beds at the first sign of 'flu.' " I'd be hung, drawn and quartered.

I, however, have never said any such thing. The words above are taken from an interview given by the British television producer Linda Agran, speaking to the London *Daily Express* in February 1990. Except that she did not say them quite like that. She said, "Women are much more efficient than men . . . [men] tend to be on the lazy side . . . [women] have far greater stamina . . . men will take to their beds at the first sign of 'flu.' " This is female sexism at its most blatant, with Ms. Agran revealed as a classic female chauvinist sow. Yet her words were reproduced as if they were entirely reasonable and unobjectionable.

Mind you, there seem to be plenty of men willing to support the new stereotypes, which show their fellow males in the worst possible light. Here, writing in the London *Evening Standard* in August 1992, is the psychologist Oliver James, who believes that "Men are far more concerned about the size of their desk or office, the flashiness of their company car and the grandness of their organisation than their sisters."

Dr. James, however, has not spent as much time as I have in the magazine business, in which women bosses are the norm, rather than the exception. Had he done so, he would know that there are plenty of power-crazed, status symbol–laden female executives around the place whose demands for office redecoration, clothes allowances, chauffeur-driven cars, Concorde tickets, and endless designer freebies are at least as avaricious as anything a man would ever consider. Reread Dr. James's words. Now consider the following: Leona Helmsley, Fergie, Madonna. Think about their oh-so-modest, entirely unflashy lifestyles . . . see what I mean?

There is, in my experience, little to choose between male and female bosses. Some are good, some are lousy; others drive you crazy, but happen to be successful enough to be forgiven. They don't make your life better or worse in the same way, necessarily, but you end up at the same place, regardless. The drives that impel a man or a woman to the top may, as Dr. Liam Hudson suggests, arise from different sources. But the manically ambitious, of either sex, have much more in common with each other than they do with those of their fellow men or women who possess a more low-key outlook on life.

The reason that this is seldom said in the media is that balance is not the intention of the people who write and edit most articles about the two sexes, whether they are about working habits or anything else. These stories appear, by and large, on pages intended to attract female readers (even if they are given names like "Living" or "Style"). So, naturally enough, they support the female perspective.

This may seem strange, given the enormous publicity that has been given, over the past few years, to women writers who maintain that the media wage a war against their sex. I can only make this observation: If you want to show that the media are biased against women, you have to prove that articles that appear to be even-handed are actually sexist. You have to look at the subtext and the hidden agendas. But for those of us who want to demonstrate media prejudice against men, life is much easier. We just open the papers and there it is. Nobody bothers to hide it because no one thinks that it matters.

In the same edition of the *Evening Standard* that contained Dr. James's remarks, fashion editor Lowri Turner revealed that men are frightened of women who wear red lipstick—"They feel threatened"—while columnist Nigella Lawson announced that "Men, poor victims of testosterone, would be far better off out of the boardroom and safely in the bedroom, to which they are obviously more biologically suited."

So why do we not react to female sexism in the same way that we do to the male variety? Simple: We are convinced that women are society's victims. That being the case, they are entitled to complain. But are they really quite as hard done-by as we have been led to believe? Let's take a look at women's working lot.

MALE BOSS: FEMALE VICTIM

The assumption of female victimization is deeply embedded: so much so, in fact, that we take it for granted that women get a raw deal. After all, if they did not, why would we have all these organizations fighting to protect and enforce their rights? Clearly, since this phenomenon is true of society in general, and since the workplace is the font of male power, work must be the area in which women get the roughest treatment of all.

Endless magazine and newspaper articles have gone into the disadvantages faced by women as they seek to rise up the corporate ladder. The so-called "glass ceiling" is said to prevent women from rising to their rightful places in the boardrooms of America, and the number of female CEOs still remains woefully low. There is, however, an interesting fact tucked away within the pages of the *Statistical Abstract of the United States*, and it is this: 42.5 percent of the total U.S. work force is female. And 42.5 percent of all managerial and professional posts are female, too. So, even if they are not, as yet, making it to the very top (a position that is not, after all, reached by the vast majority of men, either), women are represented in management in exact proportion to their presence in the work force as a whole.

In this instance, as in many others, racial barriers are far higher than sexual ones. African Americans make up more than 10 percent of the work force, but occupy barely 6 percent of managerial posts. Hispanic Americans similarly have only half the professional positions that their numbers as a whole would suggest. For anyone who wants to get to the top, being black is much more of a handicap than being female.

In terms of employment as a whole, there is evidence to suggest that women are gaining an ever-greater chance of getting a job, relative to men. Between 1980 and 1985, 6.9 million new jobs were created in sectors of the U.S. economy traditionally considered the preserve of women—sales, services, and so forth. During the same period, only 500,000 jobs were created in occupations such as manufacturing, transport, and mining that are thought of as predominantly male.

Looking ahead, U.S. government projections suggest that the fastest-growing occupations in the last decade of the twentieth century will be—in descending order—medical assistants, home health aides, radiological technicians and assistants, and medical secretaries. All these jobs are the mark of a health-obsessed culture whose members are becoming increasingly geriatric. They are also, by and large, the preserve of women.

Now, it has been argued that this shift is not good news for women. The men's jobs that are being lost tend to be highly skilled, highly paid, and unionized. The new women's jobs are low-paying, often part-time, carry few benefits and little security, and are nonunionized. There is a lot of truth in that. But a bad job may be better than no job at all. And the sufferings of a struggling health care assistant, or a female executive on Madison Avenue, vexing though they may be, pale in comparison to those of an unemployed miner or autoworker whose family no longer has a breadwinner.

That is not, however, the impression given by media outlets obsessed with women's issues, nor by some of the women one meets. To them, men still have it easy. More than that, men still seek to push women down. Men are the bad guys.

I remember talking to a middle-ranking executive on an English national newspaper. She had just come from an editorial conference, which the paper's editor had interrupted to take a call from one of his children. "A woman could never have done that," she said. "The moment people saw her talking to her family, they'd stop taking her seriously as a boss."

As it happened, however, I used to work for the man's wife and had been present at several similar conferences or meetings during which she had taken family phone calls. No one on the staff had thought anything of it. The reason was very simple: The woman in question was an extraordinarily successful editor. Whether or not she chose to speak to her teenage daughter in conference was irrelevant. The magazine's circulation and advertising revenue were rising by leaps and bounds. The numbers told you everything you needed to know about her value.

Conversely, I suggested, had her husband been perceived as a poor boss (which, I might add, he was not), it would not have mattered if he had never interrupted a single conference in his entire life. His staff would still not have respected him. In the end, loyalty is earned by competence—gender does not come into it.

The same misconception applied in a rather different way to another woman I knew. Talented, ambitious, and energetic, she had deservedly become one of her company's youngest department heads. The problem was, she said, the other department heads would not take her seriously because she was a woman. If she made suggestions to them concerning their departments, they tended to dismiss them out of hand. This, she thought, would not have happened with a man.

As any man who has ever achieved a high position at an early age could have told her, it would have happened and it does. The issue here was not her gender, but her youth. Senior members of staff, whatever their profession may be, do not take kindly to being, as they see it, lectured by young whippersnappers, particularly if the whippersnapper happens to be right. Given the choice, middle-aged men may even be less inclined to react angrily to an attractive young woman, by whom they may well be charmed, than they are to a younger man, by whom they will undoubtedly feel threatened.

The culture of victimization, however, is hard to eradicate, once it has been put in place, and one could hardly blame those two women for their opinions. They had, after all, been brought up to look on themselves as victims of unjust social prejudice. Every magazine and women's page that they had ever read had underlined the fact of their oppression. But they might, perhaps, have been surprised had they known the results of a survey into attitudes at work that was to be conducted some years later.

Commissioned by, of all people, Royal Crest Dutch Bacon—whether on the grounds of chauvinist piggery, or the need to bring the bacon home, I do not know—it examined the way in which men and women were treated in the workplace. Four hundred British workers were interviewed, and, as a spokesman for Royal Crest told the London *Daily Express,* "We were frankly surprised at the results. We expected that workers throughout the country would experience the same sort of treatment but our survey clearly shows bosses are much tougher on their male employees."

Men were more likely to be bullied or sworn at in public; more likely to have rows with their boss; more likely to feel ill treated; and, as a consequence, far less likely to feel a sense of loyalty to their superiors. Respondents gave the following answers to a series of questions beginning with the phrase, "Do you . . ."

Question	Men	Women
Have rows	79%	33%
Swear/get sworn at	60	18
Get blamed in front of others	50	26
Feel no loyalty to the boss	17	5
Get treated well by the boss	41	58
Feel taken for granted	59	40

Looking at these findings, you would have to conclude either that men are inclined to exaggerate their problems, while women minimize theirs, or that men are demonstrably treated with less kindness than women. Since it is the case that, from their earliest babyhood, males are given a rougher ride than their female sisters or playmates in the hope that this will make them the tough, forceful, independent men of the future, it would not be at all surprising to see the same disregard for their humanity displayed when they are adults.

MONEY: HOW IT'S EARNED

The worst sin committed by the male worker is that he earns more than his female counterpart. Here, at least, is one area in which gender out-weighs race. On average, white women in the United States earn about fifteen bucks a week less than black men. I have no desire to argue that this is a laudable state of affairs for either party. If two people do the same job, working for the same number of hours, at the same level of seniority, and to the same degree of competence, then they should get the same pay, irrespective of gender, race, sexual proclivities, shoe size, or anything else. The market, however, may take a different view. Sometimes those examples of unequal pay that appear to be discriminatory merely reflect the simple laws of supply and demand, rather than any evil, masculine conspiracy.

Over the next few pages, I will attempt to demonstrate the reasoning behind one apparently discriminatory situation, to question the apparent steps toward equality in another, and to give an example of a third profession in which the traditional male/female pay differentials are reversed. In all three cases, the activities that I look at—acting, professional tennis, and modeling—are far removed from the lives of ordinary people. This may suggest that they are irrelevant. My contention, however, is that they illustrate principles that apply equally well to businesses that are far less glamorous.

In the first instance, actresses on both sides of the Atlantic have complained in recent years about the disparities between the salaries given to male and female performers. Meryl Streep, for one, has pointed out the unfairness of playing a leading role opposite a male star who she knows is being paid two or even three times as much as she is.

When Sigourney Weaver was signed to recap her role as Ripley in the third installment of the *Alien* film series, she was promised a reported $4 million, plus a percentage of the box-office take. At the time this was the highest fee ever negotiated by a female star. Yet it was a third, or less, of what a male superstar such as Arnold Schwarzenegger might expect to receive for an action role. And no actress has ever come close to the sort of deal that enabled Jack Nicholson to pull in an estimated $50 million from *Batman* and all its associated merchandising.

In Britain, the actors' union Equity published a report by Dr. Helen Thomas of Goldsmith's College at the University of London on the disparity between male and female pay within the acting profession. An average TV actress in Britain earns around $23,000 a year, whereas her male equivalent can expect to take home about twice as much. Within TV commercials, women earn an average $7,500, whereas men receive $31,500.

The gulf is undeniable, and there's no denying that straightforward sexism is one of the reasons for its existence. Yet it can also be explained in ways that have little to do with gender per se, and everything to do with the marketplace within which the acting profession operates. For example, in Hollywood the key determinant of a film star's value is the ability to "open" a picture: that is to say, to draw in enough people to its opening weekend to create box-office momentum.

At the time of writing, there is a small group of male stars who have this proven ability, including Arnold Schwarzenegger, Kevin Costner, and Mel Gibson. The only contemporary actress who has demonstrated anything close to comparable ability is Julia Roberts. Sigourney Weaver can open a film only so long as it has the word *Alien* in the title (just as Sylvester Stallone can open anything called *Rambo* or *Rocky*, but nothing else). Meryl Streep, meanwhile, is a splendid actress. If payment were allocated on the basis of quality, she would be as rich as Croesus. She does not, however, set the box office on fire very often. And in Hollywood, that is the only talent that counts.

In Britain there is no significant movie business, so the market works in a different way. The membership of Equity is more or less evenly divided between men and women. Yet women have only half the roles on television that men do. It is, therefore, a buyer's market: There is always an oversupply of actresses, so TV companies can afford to pay women less.

Why, then, is there such an imbalance in roles for women? Well, no one can doubt the degree to which both the American movie business and British television are dominated by men. Of the one hundred most powerful people in Hollywood, as listed by *Premiere* magazine in May 1993, only nine were women. In Britain, the BBC may be making special efforts to promote women into senior management posts, but the vast majority of decision-making executives in both public and commercial broadcasting are men. Similarly, it is reckoned that some 90 percent of all commercials are written by men (even though 80 percent of them are aimed at female consumers). The argument seems overwhelming: Male control means female deprivation.

Except that it isn't quite so simple as that, either. The people who make films into blockbuster hits are, roughly speaking, young men. If you want to make $150 million, lots of young men have got to see your film lots of times each. And, just to make sure of boffo box office, they need to take a young woman along with them on as many occasions as possible.

Young women, either because they are naturally keen to please, or because they get off on seeing Arnie blow people up just as much as their boyfriends do, are happy to go to action adventures aimed at a male audience. Young men, however, would rather pull their own entrails out with a blunt fork than be seen going to the gentle, relationship-based stories that are traditionally defined as women's pictures. They will go and see Sigourney slug space monsters. And they'll just about tolerate slush like *Dying Young* in the hope of seeing Julia Roberts without any clothes on. But otherwise, forget it. Once again, the marketplace has spoken.

Fine, you might say, so change the marketplace. Since anything that makes young men feel free to express their emotions is greatly to be applauded, I'd be tempted to agree. But before you do, check to see that it's okay with Madonna. In the music business, she has exerted a hold on the public (or had, at least, until recently) that has given her a worldwide sales power, in terms of both recordings and live appearances, that is the equal of any of her male peers.

The music industry needs no lessons from Hollywood in the arts of corporate sexism. But record company executives can read a balance sheet just as well as anyone else. If Madonna, or Janet Jackson, or Whitney Houston shift units and keep record companies in business, they get paid accordingly and their whims are happily indulged—hence Madonna's personal record label, Maverick, which was set up for her by her parent corporation Time-Warner, or her new $5-million-per-album record deal, or the ludicrous hoopla surrounding her book *Sex*. Women like Madonna make money for stockholders. If their sales start to slip, so will their money. Gender doesn't come into it.

On the other hand, an obsession with achieving equality can sometimes lead to situations in which the desire to give women equality completely obscures, or even helps to create, an equal unfairness toward men. For many years, for example, women tennis players earned much less than men. It was hard for any but the very top women to make a decent living on the pro circuit. So they campaigned to achieve parity of prize money with their male counterparts. As a result, women's prize money at the U.S. Open is identical with men's and at Wimbledon is only 10 percent less. This near-equality has been widely applauded, although some players, such as the 1992 world number one, Monica Seles, have stated that they will not be satisfied until full parity has been achieved.

Few men have dared make any public complaint about the way in which things are moving, although one who did was the Australian Pat Cash. Some years ago, he incurred the odium and contempt of many a female critic by stating that it was absurd to pay women the same as men since they were neither as good as men, nor spent as long on the court. Shortly before the 1992 Wimbledon tournament, a Dutch tennis player named Richard Krajicek went even further when he told a radio interviewer that, in his opinion, 80 percent of women players were nothing more than unfit, overweight pigs.

Mr. Krajicek soon found himself in trouble, not least because the formidable Martina Navratilova threatened to give him a personal demonstration of her fitness, strength, and low body-fat ratio. This was little more than he deserved, if only on the grounds that there is no excuse for bad manners. But however offensive Krajicek may have been, there are scarcely any rational grounds for disagreeing with a word of what Pat Cash said. And what's more, a very strong case can be made to support the proposition that current prize-money policy actively discriminates against men.

Starting with the question of ability, the sheer physical power of the top male players is such that no woman, not even one with the enormous talent of a Monica Seles or Steffi Graf, could hope to take anything more than a game or two per set off any one of the top one hundred men. At forty, Jimmy Connors, who was no longer close to the men's top ten and had to play in an extended court area, was able comfortably to beat Martina Navratilova, who was both five years younger than he and far higher up her respective rankings.

Within the two sexes, there is also a disparity. There is little depth of talent in women's tennis. At any one time, the top half-dozen women tend to be so dominant that there is little chance of any of their being beaten by anyone outside the top ten. And even if the female players should not be described as fat pigs, the BBC's American radio commentator Barbara Potter—a former professional tennis player in her own right—has estimated that no more than 50 percent of the women on the circuit could be described as fully fit. The men tend to be in much better shape, and for a very good reason: They cannot afford not to be. After all, they face far tougher competition and are always liable to be humbled by a supposedly lesser player.

As a consequence of this, the route to the final of a tournament is likely to be much more arduous for a man than a woman. This will especially be the case in those tournaments—most notably the ones comprising the Grand Slam—that require the best of five sets for men's matches.

The 1991 Wimbledon Championships perfectly illustrated this point. The winner of the men's title was a relatively unknown German, Michael Stich. His triumph was as hard-earned as it was well deserved. In the course of his seven matches, Stich played 257 games, spread over 26 sets.

The women's title was won by Stich's compatriot, Steffi Graf. Returning to her most imperious form, Ms. Graf proceeded to play all but one of her matches, the final, without losing a single set. All but one of those sets was won to three games or less. As a result, she played a total of 128 games, almost exactly half the number played by Michael Stich. To emphasize the different demands placed upon men and women, Andre Agassi—who went on to win the 1992 title—was defeated in the fourth round, having played a total of 166 games, 38 more than Graf required for the entire tournament.

How, then, were these three athletes rewarded for their endeavors? Well, their winnings were as follows:

Stich	£240,000 ($420,000)
Graf	£216,000 ($378,000)
Agassi	£16,800 ($29,400)

Let us, as a rough measurement, take each game played to represent one unit of work, comparable, for example, to an hourly rate in an office or factory. If we divide the total amount earned by the amount of units required to earn it, we find that our trio were being rewarded on the following sporting piece-rate:

Stich	$1,634.24 per game
Graf	$2,171.88 per game
Agassi	$177.11 per game

Agassi's figure represents the low value placed on a loser, rather than any gender-based calculation, but even restricting ourselves to the winners, it is clear that a much higher value is placed upon Graf's work than Stich's. This would be further emphasized if any note was taken of the length or closeness of games. Given her domination of her opponents, it is reasonable to assume that Graf spent little time fighting over deuces. Stich, on the other hand, was taken to eight tie-breaks, each of which is only counted as a single game for the purposes of our calculation, but must have lasted at least 50 percent longer than a regular game.

It would further be reasonable to suggest that the closeness of Stich's games—the semifinal, for example, was decided by three consecutive tie-breaks—provided a greater degree of excitement for the spectators than the smooth progress of Ms. Graf, however impressive that might have been. So what we have here, in essence, is a man playing much more tennis, to a much higher standard, in a more entertaining context than his female equivalent. And he's paid a sum that is only 10 percent higher in absolute terms and at least 40 percent lower when measured against the amount of effort required to earn it. A clear case of sexual discrimination, wouldn't you agree?

But wait. Perhaps there is some hidden market mechanism that I have overlooked. After all, I have been unshakable in my insistence that quality is of no importance if allied to a product or person in whom the public has no interest. Michael Stich could play a thousand tie-breaks. But if the fans don't want to watch him do it, he doesn't deserve to be paid a bean.

Except that they do. The BBC-TV ratings for the 1991 Wimbledon finals were as follows:

Men's final	8.1 million viewers
Women's final	7.0 million viewers

So much for armchair fans; what of the paying public? Wimbledon Centre Court tickets are, almost by definition, sold out. So the way in which one judges public appeal is not by the quantity of tickets sold, but the amount one has to pay to obtain one on the black market. A survey of ticket touts (or scalpers) conducted in June 1991 for *Punch* magazine revealed the following range of prices for a single seat at that year's finals:

Men's final	$1,150–1,575
Women's final	$525–700

There is, in other words, no qualitative or quantitative reason why Wimbledon's women, or those at the U.S., Australian, or French Opens should be paid as much as the men. The only reasons that they are lie in the willingness of women to make demands and the unwillingness of men to oppose them. Stefan Edberg, who won the 1992 U.S. Open by playing exactly twice as many games as Monica Seles, who won the women's title, might bear that in mind the next time he listens to Ms. Seles go on about the rights of women players. Perhaps he'll decide that Pat Cash wasn't so crazy, after all.

Men seem equally unable to stand up for themselves when the tables are turned: that is to say when they are operating in a female-oriented environment. In the modeling business, social conditioning acts to women's huge advantage. We have all been told about the ways in which the flood of visual images of perfect female bodies places intolerable pressure on normal women. The reduction of women to the status of sex objects is one of the oldest complaints in the feminist book. But there is another way of looking at our society's mania for the photographic depiction of women.

Walking past a magazine-stall shelf, the most obvious conclusion to be drawn is not that we despise the female form, but that we worship it. Stalin, Saddam, and Kim Il-Sung may have littered their nations with memorials to themselves, but none of them was as regularly glorified as any one of the supermodels who are the paragons of female glamor today. These women are as powerful in their field as any Hollywood stud. If you want to sell large numbers of women's magazines, bottles of perfume, tubes of makeup, or pairs of jeans, the best way to do it is to advertise them with a picture of a world-famous model.

As a consequence, those women who are, by a freakish coincidence of genetics, diet, and exercise, at the very top of the modeling tree can charge enormous sums of money for the use of their face. At twenty-three years of age, Christy Turlington signed a four-year, $5-million-plus deal with the American cosmetics company Maybelline. The company felt that Ms. Turlington embodied "the heart and soul of the Maybelline woman— savvy, self-assured and surprising." For someone with so many marketable qualities, a deal that worked out at some $100,000 for every day of actual modeling seemed eminently reasonable.

According to *Time* magazine, deals such as Turlington's, or Paulina Porizkova's reputed $6 million contract with Estée Lauder, ensure that, when runway, editorial, and other advertising fees are taken into account, the very top half-dozen models can earn around $2.5 million per annum. Another thirty or so can make around $500,000. And, away from the L.A.–New York–Paris–Milan axis, top models in a city such as Miami can pull in a cool quarter of a million bucks for a job that consists, in many people's opinion, of standing around and saying "cheese." As Porizkova once told me, "You feel exactly like the apple in a still life. They polish you. They set you in the middle of the bowl. They put the things around you. They light you and they shoot you. That's what modeling is to me. It's about as creative as that."

Male models don't even get to be decent apples. Although men need to wear clothes, they consume a fraction of the cosmetics that women do, and they do not need accessories such as tights, handbags, jewelry, and so on. Furthermore, heterosexual men are, by and large, extremely unwilling to admit to any interest in studying pictures of other men in search of tips on how to make themselves more appealing.

So the fees for male models are far less than those paid to women. Typical rates for a male model at the Paris and New York shows are a fraction of the five-figure sums earned by the female superstars. Nor are there male cosmetics contracts comparable to those awarded to Turlington or Porizkova. If a man has made $30,000 from a jeans commercial, he's been doing very well.

There is one faint sign of a male supermodel on the horizon: A 220-pound chiseled Milanese called Fabio was recently given a six-figure "writing" contract by Avon Books after appearing on more than 350 of their book jackets, and his calendars are said to outsell their cheesecake equivalents. But so far Fabio is strictly a one-man band—and there's no multimillion-dollar aftershave deal in sight, either.

There have been few complaints from male academics about the gross inequalities—far greater than any in the acting profession or the game of tennis—that exist in modeling. The men's studies movement has yet to establish itself in the way that women's studies have done. Besides, everyone understands that our culture is not particularly interested in looking at men who aren't actually doing something, or who haven't already established a reputation in another field.

Yet the fact that men do not actually deserve to be paid as much as their female counterparts should in no way inhibit them from demanding that their rates be equalized. If Steffi Graf can pull down 90 percent of what Michael Stich makes for winning Wimbledon, then Fabio should hold out for 90 percent of what Christy Turlington collects from Maybelline. Which, at something in the region of $4.5 million, sounds as if it's well worth holding out for.

AND HOW IT'S SPENT

Earnings are one way of judging relative prosperity. But there is another measurement, which is the access one has to money after it has been earned. If, for example, one class of person does all the work and another does all the spending, you do not have to be Karl Marx to conclude that the second of those two classes is the more privileged. Except that, in real life, it isn't a class, it's a sex.

The economics of a typical household make an interesting subject for examination. To begin with, there are more men at work than women. Men comprise about 48 percent of the population as a whole, but they occupy roughly 58 percent of all jobs. They also get paid more. The median female wage is just 70 percent of the median male wage. There is always the possibility that this disparity may, in part, be due to the many mothers who choose to work part-time in order to give themselves time with their families, or who choose to sacrifice pay and promotion in exchange for reduced responsibilities and greater flexibility. But let us, for the sake of argument, agree for now that the system appears to be working in favor of men.

Once that money reaches the family bank account, however, it's a very different story. In November 1991, a survey in England by the Britannia Building Society revealed the extent to which women controlled the family purse strings. The report's author, Rachel Vining, was quoted as follows: "Women emerge as the primary decision-makers in most areas connected with money. About 75% decide what to buy and how much to spend on the home. They also rule over presents and children's clothes. For holidays and larger items, most women make a joint decision with their partner. Even when it comes to the traditional male preserve of the car, joint decisions are more common than the man deciding alone."

Specifically, 77 percent of domestic purchasing choices are made by women, 70 percent of whom also decide how much to spend. The figures are roughly similar for gifts and children's clothes. But only 35 percent of men decide which car to buy (31 percent determine how much to spend). In other words, they are less than half as powerful in their sphere of influence as women are in theirs.

The survey also showed that in two-thirds of the respondents' households, both partners held checkbooks. However, three times as many women (24 percent) held the only family checkbook as men (8 percent). Whichever way you look at it, this survey suggests that the British family purse strings are firmly clasped in Mummy's hand.

Nor is Britannia the only company to have come to this conclusion. The research organization Mintel also asked women a series of questions relating to decision-making in matters of domestic finance. Mintel asked respondents to express their influence on a percentage basis. If the woman questioned felt that she had sole control of a decision, she should claim 100 percent. If she discussed it with her partner, but then made the final choice, she got 75 percent. If they both discussed and chose together, the figure was 50 percent; if they discussed, then he chose, 25 percent; if he decided unilaterally, 0 percent. Mintel then averaged out all the responses to arrive at a percentage figure which described the typical degree of female influence in any given area.

The results were as follows:

Choice To Be Decided	**Female Influence**
In-store credit card	80%
General credit card	65
Current account	62
Other bank or savings and loan accounts	57
Endowment assurance	51
Whole life insurance	47
Stocks and shares	43
Mortgage	43
Pensions	41
Health insurance	38
Car insurance	36

From this one can see that although men have marginally more influence in six out of the eleven categories, in none of them do they have the dominance enjoyed by women in their most influential areas. The overall average works out at a marginal advantage for the female partner by 51 to 49. But it's worth noting that the two strongest areas for men—car and health insurance—have to be considered in light of the fact that, for British white-collar workers, both may well be included as part of a man's professional remuneration. So the woman's lack of influence here should not be taken to imply male power: It's just that he's abandoned his wife's decision-making in favor of his boss's. Either way, he's the junior partner.

This phenomenon is by no means confined to British society. In fact, it might even be true to say that the more a society appears to be financially biased in favor of men, the more the reverse is actually the case. In Japan, for example, men still hold the vast majority of positions of executive and political power: Feminism has made nothing like the strides there that it has in the West. Japanese wives are seen by their occidental sisters as hapless servants, waiting hand and foot on their male masters, like geisha girls ready to provide everything that their man might require. The truth, however, appears to be rather different.

As a Japanese *salaryman* slaves away at the absurdly long hours that can, as we have already seen, induce premature death, or *karoshi*, his wife is out enjoying the fruits of his labors. A Japanese woman has the same lock on the family finances as her Western counterparts, a privilege that merely adds to the traditional power she enjoys as the matriarchal ruler of the family home. For the purposes of public consumption, she may play the dutiful helpmeet. But in private, she's the boss.

The Japanese name for a domineering, dictatorial wife is *obatalian*. So common is the species that in 1992 Fuji Television launched a series called

Obatalian Watching. In the words of Joanna Pitman, reporting from Tokyo for the London *Times*: "A group of scowling harridans were unwittingly filmed on one of their power-shopping sprees, swarming through sales like locusts, dolling themselves up in Chanel suits and Italian shoes. The cameras then followed them onto a crowded underground train where they were seen doing battle for seats armed with designer handbags and umbrellas. The obatalian gets what she wants.

"The comedy of the series depends on the gap between social pretension and reality. Everyone knows that if the cameras were to arrive at her home, the obatalian would slip into her public role as the simpering wife who selflessly tends to the needs of her husband."

Social attitudes toward the family's supposed patriarch can be guessed from the title of a popular Japanese comic book series (the Japanese, incidentally, consume *manga*, or adult comic books, with a voracity and seriousness unknown in the West). It is called *Stupid Dad*. Its hero—if that is the right word—is eerily reminiscent of the hopelessly inadequate male to be found in so many British and American TV commercials (and Japanese ones at that). After a hard day of ritual humiliation at the workplace, he comes home for more of the same at the hands of his wife and daughters—virulent shrews who would give Regan and Goneril a thoroughly good run for their money. Bossed at work and bullied at home, no wonder the poor old Japanese male spends so much time getting drunk in *karaoke* bars.

Logically, one might imagine that if patriarchy at work led to matriarchy in the home, the reverse would apply as well, so that equality in one arena would necessarily lead to a similar liberation in the other. In fact, contemporary ideology merely reinforces the notion that the woman must be the mistress of her own household—overtly, as well as covertly.

In the summer of 1991, the British advertising agency Lowe Howard-Spink announced the arrival of the Self-Regulating Household. This was defined as one in which the female partner earned at least 60 percent or more of her husband's salary and was thus able to become a Successful Negotiator, who used the bargaining power of her income to whip her once-indolent husband into line.

There's no doubt who wears the trousers in the Self-Regulating Household. Ninety-seven percent of Successful Negotiators (all of whom are female) manage the family finances, while 70 percent initiate sex. Meanwhile the man is busy with the housework: 80 percent do the shopping (although not very well, according to the survey, since they eschew reliable products in favor of "novelty and gadgetry"); 66 percent do the vacuuming and 50 percent do an equal amount of cooking. The result? "Having actively and consciously renegotiated their roles, they are happier and respect each other more."

This is the voice of the new orthodoxy. But is it really telling us anything particularly novel? One might equally well argue that we haven't come very far from the days when a man would come home from a hard week at the factory, hand over his pay-packet to his wife, and then hope she'd dole him out some beer money. Men seem to be dismally willing to bring home the bacon to their families without keeping any for themselves.

Part of this is nothing more than willed incompetence. After a hard day's work, it seems like more trouble than it's worth to sort out the bank accounts and credit cards. But women, accustomed as they are to having to do more about the house in any case, have clearly understood that the effort is justified if it brings with it control.

In the old days there may have been some justification for the male point of view. Mom ran the house and Pop let her boss him about within the confines of their own four walls, secure in the knowledge that once he stepped out into the big wide world, everything was run to his advantage. But now that life at work is not nearly so cozy as it was, it may pay him to reclaim some of the territory he has forfeited back home.

JUST SAY, "NO"

A Martian who landed on earth and observed the behavior of the male sex would note that:

1. Male life expectancy is diminished by work.
2. A man's powers of attraction are largely determined by his job status, which is, in turn, largely dependent on the degree to which he is prepared to devote his life to work.
3. Once married, he can expect to lose control of the majority of his income.

Which might well make our little green friend conclude that the human male is little more than a drone. He's a worker bee, or a soldier ant. He's socialized from an early age to submerge his own personality in order to serve the interests of his community, and he is discarded the moment he has outlived his usefulness.

Amazingly, whatever Mr. Martian might think, that's not how our society sees it. We still persist in imagining that man's burden of work is his greatest privilege.

Every man grows up watching what work has done to his father. In my own case, I was profoundly affected by the knowledge that my father, whom I idolized, went off every day to work at a job that, to my young eyes, he did not appear to enjoy, purely in order to meet the needs of his family. I always swore that I would never be in the same position myself.

And yet, as I lived through my early thirties, I found myself doing exactly what Dad had done: working foolish hours at a job that, though prestigious and intellectually stimulating, often brought nothing but frustration and endless wars of corporate attrition. Nor was money a compensation: The more I earned, the greater my expenses seemed to be, until I finally had a year in which I made more money than I had ever done in my life, but still ended up $35,000 in debt. The greater my debt became, the more I had to earn. I felt trapped on an endless treadmill of perverted aspiration.

It was only when I found myself out of a job, stripped of all the status that senior position brings, but happier than I had been in years, that I fully understood the insanity of the life that I, like millions of middle-class men all over the Western world, had been leading. And the question arose: Why the hell should we bother?

Faced with the loss of their automatic preeminence in the workplace, men today have a golden opportunity to reassess their whole approach to work. After all, for hundreds of years, work was regarded as a burden from which to escape. The middle classes were defined by their freedom from wage-slavery.

The desire to free oneself from work was common to all classes and both sexes. Dr. Joanna Bourke of Birkbeck College, London, has studied the diaries of five thousand women who lived between 1860 and 1930. During that period, the proportion of women in paid employment dropped from 75 percent to 10 percent. This was regarded as a huge step forward for womankind, an opinion that was certainly shared by the women whose writings Dr. Bourke researched. Freed from the mills and factories, they created a new power base for themselves at home. This was, claims Dr. Bourke, "a deliberate choice . . . and a choice that gave great pleasure."

In recent years we have reversed the beliefs of centuries. Throughout the eighties, achievement was judged by the number of hours one worked. Friends and family were relegated to a few moments here and there of "quality time," that most bogus of all fashionable ideas, while our lives were willingly sacrificed to the great god of labor. We must have been crazy. Maybe we still are. For most office work—which is to say, most work these days—is tedious, stressful, and burdened with pointless corporate politics.

Few men have the huge privilege afforded to writers, which is to earn one's money doing the thing that affords the greatest creative satisfaction. The vast majority began their working lives knowing that they are placing themselves upon a treadmill from which there is no release until they reach death or retirement, save that which is forced upon them by the indignity of unemployment. No wonder that they care about the size of their desks or the quality of their company cars—what else is there to care about?

We have now reached the ultimate absurdity, in which people would rather die than be without work. As the recession deepens, newspapers are filled with stories about senior executives who have killed themselves after losing their high-powered jobs. Stripped of their office, they have nothing left to live for. It is as if they no longer exist once their job is gone. As individual human beings, they have simply disappeared.

These suicides in suits are the victims of social expectations. If they are to be successful in the terms laid down by Western society, men must work hours that can cause them to become alienated from families whom they scarcely ever see. Even if they don't sit in a fume-filled car or walk off a seaside cliff, they may well drop dead long before they reap the full benefit of all the work they have put in. That, as the history of Florida and the growth in the cruise industry so forcefully demonstrate, is a privilege left to their widows.

The vast majority of men, of course, are no more likely to reach positions of power than are women. U.S. government statistics show that more than 70 percent of all families have a total income—even when both partners are in paid employment—of less than $50,000. But even should they finally reach the top, they will discover that their position is just as precarious as it ever was at the bottom. The great tycoons of the eighties are often the bankrupts and jailbirds of the nineties.

Those entrepreneurs and executives who survive do so at the mercy of stockholders, fellow directors, and predatory rivals. In general, corporate success teaches one that the greater rewards given to those at, or near, the top are almost always matched by the greater intensity of the crap they have to face when they get there.

We glorify work for its own sake. We worship all things material: new cars, designer labels, fancy gadgets, and so on. Yet here we all are, killing ourselves with stress, killing our own planet with the effluent side effects of our lust for more possessions, and seemingly quite unable to free ourselves from our addictions.

Of course it is nice to wear well-made clothes and drive elegant cars. Of course it is rewarding to dine in fancy restaurants and stay at luxurious hotels. But are these fleeting pleasures worth the price of admission? My strong belief is that men can do the world a great service by kicking the drug of work. Do as much as you have to in order to provide the basic necessities of your life, to keep your mind or body in shape and to fulfill your need to feel involved. Then stop.

You might make a bit less money, but just think of the benefits that can be derived from all that extra time—all those things you had always wanted to do, but had never quite got around to. It is perfectly possible for a man to redefine himself in a way that involves more than work. He just has to give himself the chance to do so.

Tragically, the understandable desire to achieve financial equality and independence has driven women onto the same treadmill as that upon which men have long been toiling. But if women are crazy enough to take over the burden of corporate life, terrific—they're welcome to it. They certainly can't do a *worse* job than male managers, politicians, and generals have done. Meanwhile, if men can lead the way out of the mess we find ourselves in, that might prove a service to us all. It would certainly be a more constructive reappraisal of the male stereotype than some of the images of men that have been foisted upon society of late, images to which I now turn.

CHAPTER 3
Macho, Macho Man, Who Wants to Be a Macho Man?

"So who cares about getting big, healthy-looking, good-looking muscles? Only a pencilneck would ask such a dumb question! Who indeed! Everyone! That is, if you have the guts to try and if you have the right information."

The words come from an advertisement for ICOPRO, a "professional bodybuilding program" created by TitanSports and published in *WWF Magazine,* the magazine of the World Wrestling Federation. The advertisement, whose copy is, apparently, written by one Frederick C. Hatfield, Ph.D., of Stamford, Connecticut, promises "an integrated conditioning program" through which the would-be bodybuilder can achieve "a level of muscle mass that few dare dream about, let alone achieve. If you can visualize yourself growing massive beyond mere convention, that is where you must go!"

But there's a price. You've got to want it badly enough to do what it takes. You've got to use ICOPRO, which is, Dr. Hatfield explains, "Something so profoundly superior to its relatively paltry predecessors, so utterly complete and powerful in its unique assemblage of both man-made and natural forces that nothing could possibly surpass it." Which is just as well, if you're about to enter "a state of being where only the strong survive," where, my friend, "You will have to do battle with men infinitely wiser than the greats of yesterday ever encountered."

The ad is illustrated with a picture of a man pumping iron. We know he's a man because he has a man's chest, a man's vein-knotted biceps, a man's neck, and a man's face, contorted by a rictus of agony (You've gotta want it!). But here's the weird thing . . . he has a girl's haircut.

Welcome to the world of pro wrestling, the cultural nexus for all the gender obsessions and confusions of our age—a so-called sport that could, without undue exaggeration, be thought of as the single most highly evolved fictional enterprise of our time. In WWF wrestling, men who have never been near an acting class stay in character in a way that would put DeNiro to shame. They become someone else for the purposes of marketing. Everyone is acting: the fighters, the TV commentators, the journalists—everyone.

For example, the same issue of *WWF Magazine* features a controversy that has been dogging the wrestling world, to wit: Did a wrestler called Ric Flair, pictured for *WWF Magazine* in a pink, marabou-trimmed sequined housecoat, really play by the poolside with a woman known as Miss Elizabeth before she got together with another wrestler, Macho Man Randy Savage . . . or were the pictures faked? In huge, EZ-read type, the kind that's normally reserved for half-blind oldsters or the under-fives, Flair and Savage battle it out. Flair claims to have had Miss Elizabeth before she became Savage's wife (for which, subtext fans, read "property"). Backing Flair is his Executive Consultant Mr. Perfect, whose thick neck, pink skin, squishy features, and defiantly baffled expression put me unavoidably in mind of Link Hogthrob, the porcine starship commander from the old Muppets sketch "Pigs in Space."

Meanwhile Savage wants to make the world eat its words. He's after Flair. He's after Bobby "The Brain" Heenan, the florid, thickset reporter employed by WWF to spice up its TV coverage, who's photographed loosening his collar as he swears that he was just doing his duty as "a good broadcast journalist." He's even after *WWF Magazine* itself . . . help!

All sports reporting is overladen with myth and fueled by bullshit. But this is worth a Pulitzer Prize for fiction. Remember, these people don't really exist. Their feuds are phony. Even their names are not their own, being, as it happens, the property of TitanSports, as is ICOPRO, as are such valuable properties as Super Wrestlemania, WWF, and, indeed, "all other distinctive titles, names and characters" mentioned in *WWF Magazine,* which is itself, of course, a division of TitanSports.

Anyone who still believes in the New Man should check out the WWF. Everything about it screams testosterone fever. Managers make outrageous claims about their clients' destructive powers. Wrestlers threaten to smash one another to bits. Just look at the names: Psychotic Sid Justice, Ultimate Warrior, The Boss Man, Sgt. Slaughter, The Undertaker, and British Bulldog.

This is all patent nonsense. And yet, at the same time, it is also, like all successful mass culture, a genuine reflection of desires and appetites that really exist—out there, in the real world.

THE ALAN ALDA DOLL

In an appendix to his book about masculinity, *Fire in the Belly,* Sam Keen prints the results of a survey printed in *Psychology Today* in March 1989. Six thousand respondents gave their views on "What makes an ideal man?" One question asked them to name "The Man of Our Dreams." Among women, the top three dreamboats were Jesus, Gandhi, and . . . Alan Alda. Men named Jesus, Gandhi, and John F. Kennedy. Both sexes listed the three most important male qualities as being caring, loving, and intelligent and moral/honest. When asked to name good men, the women came up with George Bush, Ronald Reagan, and yes, Alan Alda (please, no laughing at the back). The men named Jimmy Carter, JFK, and, believe it or not, George Bush.

Fine. Let's leave Jesus out of this, on the assumption that He is the Son of God and thus exempt from criteria we might apply to mortals. And let's do our best to ignore Kennedy's obsessive promiscuity and documented links with the Mafia. Let us also turn a blind eye to the judgment American voters made on Jimmy Carter when they had a chance to vote in 1980. After all, he's had a pretty clean record since then. Let us allow a little leeway on Iran-Contra, the hundreds of indicted Reagan/Bush officials, Dan Quayle, Nancy Reagan, the botched conclusion to the Gulf War, and the 1992 election. Let us simply ask this question: When did you last see an Alan Alda doll?

Does the one-time star of *M*A*S*H* and *California Suite* sell movie tickets like Arnold Schwarzenegger?

Does he fill stadiums like Ric Flair and Randy Savage?

Has Nintendo created a whole range of games dedicated to his adventures? Yes, you too can play *Bourgeois Angst,* the ultimate on-screen challenge!

Can you find his face on souvenir backpacks, cameras, bandanas, T-shirts, posters, painter's caps, and wrestling buddies? Because you can find Hulk Hogan's there . . . and Savage's . . . and the Legion of Doom's.

When *WWF Magazine* was launched in Britain, with minimal promotion in the traditional media, it rocketed to sales in excess of two hundred thousand a month. That is more than the combined monthly sales of the three major U.K. men's glossies—*GQ, Arena,* and *Esquire.* All those middle-class pencilnecks can go on all they like about their suits and cars and hidden sensitivities, but what Joe Public really wants is guys with gorilla muscles and skintight Lycra panties beating the shit out of one another. When Wrestlemania came to London, they had to hire Wembley Stadium so that eighty thousand fans could get to see their hulking heroes.

The motor that drives the WWF machine is television. The broadcasts are conducted in the same hysterical tones that echo through all the

WWF's various outlets. I switched on to one wrestling show just a few days before writing this chapter. Kamala, an enormous black wrestler, dressed as an African witch doctor, was climbing into the ring. Two commentators were analyzing his chances. This is what they said, word-for-word:

FIRST COMMENTATOR: He's a savage!

SECOND COMMENTATOR: Of course he's a savage! He comes from Uganda, from the dark jungles. That's where savages come from.

FIRST COMMENTATOR: Not everyone from Uganda is a savage, surely?

SECOND COMMENTATOR: How would you know?

Answer: You wouldn't. Not unless you were some weenie, pointy-headed, pinko, intellectual *pencilneck* . . . right?

BOYS WILL BE . . . WHAT?

To authors such as Myriam Medzian, wrestling is just one element in a package of media manipulation that condemns Western boys to a life trapped within a destructive and all too often self-destructive stereotype of insensitive machismo. In her book *Boys Will Be Boys: Breaking the Link Between Masculinity and Violence,* she points out that children's weekend daytime TV programs average 15.5 violent incidents an hour. The popular cartoon series *Transformers,* which was created to peddle a mid-eighties toy craze, averaged a staggering 83 acts of violence per hour.

WWF has special programming aimed at kids, who then flock to see their heroes in the flesh at gigantic arena shows. "Some of them are only two or three years old, although most of them seem to be in the six to twelve range," comments Medzian, who notes that when she attended a wrestling exhibition at New York's Madison Square Garden, about one-third of the audience for this school-night show was made up of children.

She further points out that whereas adults know that the whole performance is little more than playacting, the children mostly believe that the violence is real. She says, "The reality of the punches, the groans, the bodies falling to the ground is amplified through the loudspeakers hidden under the wrestling ring. In spite of this heightened reality no one ever gets hurt. There are no concussions, no broken legs, almost no blood. Children are being completely misled as to the effects of physically attacking others."

Having gone to the 1992 Summerslam at Wembley Stadium and seen thousands of kids cheering and screaming as grown men pretended to pound one another into pulp, and having spoken to cousins and nephews of mine who watch WWF wrestling on TV and also have gone to Wrestlemania shows, I would disagree with Medzian in one respect. I think that they do know that there is an element of playacting in a WWF show. But that only underlines Medzian's central point about the trivialization of violence. Wrestling teaches kids to regard brutality as harmless fun. Compromise, debate, and broad-mindedness are notions that have no place in the world of snarling musclemen, who magnify trivial (and fictional) slights into causes of war, and boast about the physical damage they intend to inflict upon their latest enemies.

Wrestling plays upon the basest elements of human nature. As the Nuremberg rallies demonstrated, rational human beings can, when taken as a mass, turn into a howling mob willing to do anything in the service of perverted values. The WWF is not, by any means, a Nazi organization. But it depends upon the same manipulation of our worst characteristics. And its target audience is still too young to have any kind of understanding about the process to which it is being subjected.

I interviewed Ms. Medzian on her visit to London in 1992. Confronted with the view that it's all just entertainment and that none of it actually affects young minds, she told this story about a meeting with the Terminator himself:

"I had a personal meeting with Arnold Schwarzenegger. It was eyeball to eyeball. I was up in Vermont giving some lectures, just before my book came out, and there were some demonstrations against him because he had been chosen by President Bush as the head of the council on physical recreation and sport and it was an extraordinary choice. Some of the people that had invited me to lecture asked me if I'd like to join one of the protests, and I said, sure.

"Afterwards there was a press conference at an elementary school, where he was talking to the kiddies about health. I already had my book, even though it hadn't come out yet, so after they had finished taking photographs, I stepped out, holding my book, and said, 'Mr. Schwarzenegger, I'm the author of this book and my research reveals that there have been over 235 studies done on the effects of viewing violence on the screen, and they show overwhelmingly that viewing violence on the screen encourages violent behavior. Violent behavior is bad for your physical fitness. It seems to me, therefore, that you are an unfit spokesman for this cause.'

"He gave me a look that could have terminated me. He said, 'It's irrelevant to my being here. When I'm here to promote my films we'll discuss this.' But then, in answering someone else, he boasted about how he had inserted seven minutes of physical fitness scenes into *Kindergarten Cop* because he knows how much films influence children.

"He went on to say that when John Travolta did *Saturday Night Fever* people around the world were disco dancing. So he's admitting the enormous impact of these films, but somehow he can make films with endless, endless violence and they have no impact and it's irrelevant to his being a spokesperson to children.

"I don't think he's stupid. I just think he has a complete denial of the effect of what he's doing."

REAL MEN

Before we rush to condemn WWF, the Terminator, and the makers of children's TV cartoons, it's worth remembering that the big lesson of WWF is: *People want this*. Whatever they may say about wanting men to be gentle and kind, junior Gandhis for the New Age, that's not what the customers choose when the time comes to open up their wallets.

The same applies to real-life relationships. When speaking to counselors at London Marriage Guidance, I was told that one of the most common complaints they receive is from women who are dissatisfied with their husband. They have been pestering him to participate in housework—to clean and cook and wash just as much as they do—but when he complies with their demands they discover that they start to find him unattractive. By doing "women's work" he has forfeited his masculinity. Suddenly, they are filled with an overwhelming desire to run away with the utterly unreconstructed garage mechanic down the road.

I remember once doing some research for a magazine feature about the way in which the traditional male habit of dividing women into virgins and whores was echoed by a female propensity to split men into two camps, wimps and bastards. (In the end, incidentally, the editor of the magazine had to copy-edit, check, and proof the story herself, since her staff refused to work on a piece that was based on such a grossly sexist concept, even if it happened to be true). Anyway, I talked to a friend who had just ditched her latest lover. The reason she gave for this was that she had rung him up one Saturday afternoon and asked him to come over and help her decorate her flat. So he did. This willingness to drop everything at her beck and call, she decided, was so pathetic that she could no longer respect him, and she dropped him immediately.

"But," I said, "he was probably just trying to be nice."

"Exactly," she replied.

More recently I've heard it said by commentators such as Joan Smith, the critic and author whose book *Misogynies* is such a fascinating read, that society is tending toward androgyny. One can quite understand why she should feel this. The eighties, for example, were the years in which Mrs. Thatcher ruled Britain while Boy George put ribbons in his hair. And yet, when you cruise around our TV channels and feel the beat of popular culture, it's impossible to ignore the unquenchable desire for differentiation.

Look at the TV show *Studs*, for example. Check out those giggling girls in high heels and low dresses and those beefcake hunks with neck measurements bigger than their IQs. Then listen to the things they talk about. The young women want their men to be kind and considerate, but they also want them to be real men. They want a cute butt in tight jeans. The young men want big laughs, a hot bod, and great sex. They both, in their own sweet ways, want each other—*nothing's changed.*

Of course one can claim that this is just an example of the way in which media moguls manipulate our sensibilities. We could all be the victims of some vast male plot, designed to trap us in outmoded sex roles for the benefit of the patriarchy. But it just doesn't work like that. What gets on the air is, by and large, what sells.

Personally, I see no problem in any of this. Or I wouldn't, were it not for the fact that there is something so obviously problematic about the sex-role caricatures for which we have all so happily fallen. I will leave it to others to reiterate—again—women's difficulties. For now let's concentrate on men. More specifically, let's look at the archetypal masculine hero as he's developed in Hollywood movies over the past few decades.

In particular, I want to focus on three figures: John Wayne, Clint Eastwood, and Arnold Schwarzenegger. Sure, there have been many, many others. Just among the tough guys you could include Mitchum, Douglas, McQueen, Bronson, Stallone, and all those new-wave European bodybuilding types, like Lundgren and Van Damme. Then there are the all-American decent men, from Gary Cooper to Kevin Costner. And somewhere in there you've got Bogart and even the hero-as-schlemiel, Woody Allen. But since the subject here is machismo, let's keep the focus tight.

THE DUKE

John Wayne, the all-American cowboy, was shown fighting battles for clearly defined moral causes (always assuming, of course, that one regards the slaughtering of Japs and Apaches as morally worthwhile). He was clearly on the side of truth, justice, and the American way. His violence was administered in two basic forms. The first was a manly punch to the jaw, usually of another white man. This was often seen as an act of bonding, after which both parties would recognize one another's mas-culinity and join forces against some mutually agreed foreign foe. In *The Alamo*, for example, John Wayne spends several minutes exchanging punches with Richard Widmark before going off to die heroically by his side in the service of Texas. Wayne directed this film, which, along with *The Green Berets*, a trenchant defense of America's involvement in Vietnam, pretty much marks his ideological card.

Wayne's second weapon, of course, was a bullet from a gun. The true effects of this bullet were never shown; bad guys or injuns dropped dead—give or take the odd famous last word—and such extraneous details as blood, guts, and agonized screams were kept to a bare minimum.

Having done what a man had to do in the big wide world, Wayne then turned back to hearth, home, and the little woman who waited for him there. In the superconventional forties and fifties, the public was suitably reassured when Wayne took Maureen O'Hara in his arms, paused a while as she beat her delicate female fists against the broad expanse of his chest, accepted her eventual submission, and went off to raise a family (unspoken postscript: She became the Great American Matriarch and was left in charge of her man's life from there on out).

The effect of Wayne's work was most marked on American servicemen. Myriam Medzian reports on the way in which the fantasy of glorious, righteous conflict embodied by Wayne was a major factor in the minds of men enlisting for the Vietnam War. When they discovered the enormous gulf between the portrayal of battle on the big screen and the horrors of the real thing—a horror exacerbated by the absence of any justifiable sense of moral purpose from the Vietnam campaign—their disillusion-ment and anger were profound.

Nor was this a new phenomenon. As William Manchester recalled in a 1987 *New York Times Magazine* article (cited by Medzian), World War II soldiers felt equally repelled by the gulf between truth and fiction. When in 1945 Wayne made a supposedly morale-boosting appearance at a naval hospital in Hawaii after the battle for Okinawa, he walked on stage, dressed in cowboy hat, bandana, pistols, chaps, and spurs, only to be greeted by a chorus of boos. In Manchester's words, "This man was an example of the fake machismo we had come to hate, and we weren't going to listen to him."

CLINT

If John Wayne was a phony, and everything he stood for was equally rotten, what was left for men? Clint Eastwood, whose first major film, *A Fistful of Dollars*, was made in 1964, halfway between the existentialist movement and the first burned bra, portrayed a man whose morality was generated, not by social or patriotic obligation, but by his own, internal code of conduct.

As the Man with No Name he appeared, resolved a conflict, and then disappeared. Barring the occasional use of a Gatling gun or two, the fights may have lacked the scenes of mass slaughter common to Wayne's westerns and war films, but when it came to one-on-one gunslinging, Eastwood was a far more efficient executioner than his predecessor.

Forget the love-interest. Although he was involved with women, they seldom appeared to establish any permanent hold on his emotions: Despite the greater sexual freedom available to filmmakers, Sergio Leone, director of the classic spaghetti westerns, scarcely ever gave his hero a significant love scene. It is as though relationships with women were becoming too problematic to be dealt with in the confines of a male-oriented action film.

As Dirty Harry, or to give him his full name and rank, Police Inspector Harry Callahan, Eastwood's belief that his first duty was to rid the city of San Francisco of wrongdoers—or, as he would put it, "punks"—was contrasted with the liberal (and, by implication, effeminate?) attitude of politicians and senior officers who seemed more concerned with the perpetrators' civil rights. By now, the dose of violence required to achieve an audience's arousal was beginning to rise considerably. The first, eponymous Dirty Harry film makes do with four slaughtered punks and one dead psycho. In *Magnum Force*, Harry offs two hijackers, a couple of hoods, a pair of punks, and five corrupt policemen. Having paused for breath in *The Enforcer*, whose body count drops to nine, Harry peaks in 1983's *Sudden Impact*, in which his score includes three black punks, three white hoods, one gangland boss, three white punks in a car, one further hood, a brace of punks on foot, and a solitary token psycho to boot.

By the time of 1988's *The Dead Pool*, Harry was past his prime. Eight bad guys meet their maker, courtesy of his Magnum, within the first half-hour or so. From then on, however, both Harry and the film decline. Not even a token harpooning in the final reel can save a concept that is clearly over the hill.

In his heyday, Clint was the absolute epitome of masculine cool. But he represented a fantasy figure for men in an age beset by insecurity. His fans would never be inspired to sign up to fight for their country as a result of seeing his films. Instead, they dreamed that the next time the boss gave them hell, or they got jostled on the street or ripped off by a garage mechanic, they would not simply mutter some feeble excuse and run away, but clench their jaw, give an ominous twitch to their narrowed eyes, pull out their great big Magnum and say, "Go ahead. Make my day."

Their identification was reinforced by the fact that Eastwood was still, like Wayne, a good, all-American hero. While much of the certainty about both man's and America's place in the world had been eroded, enough confidence still remained for Eastwood to be recognized as the embodiment of masculinity. That he appeared to have a certain real-life sense of style and was prepared to make films like *Every Which Way But Loose*, which satirized his popular image, only added to his appeal.

But what of women? For Wayne, they were one of the two reasons—the flag being the other—that a man did what he does. They needed protecting. They were, with the occasional feisty but tameable exception, gentle and loving and could be relied upon when a guy had just taken a bullet in the gut and could do with a cold compress across his fevered brow. Women were patently inferior to men but they were, nevertheless, very much a good thing.

For Dirty Harry, however, the whole situation was much more complicated. He had girlfriends, but, like so many movie characters of the past two decades, he was divorced. So we knew that there had been a fundamental breakdown in his dealings with the opposite sex. Work, too, got in the way. Whereas Wayne could count on his girl's understanding, Eastwood operated in a world in which women competed with his duties for his attention. They refused to take second place.

In his own, self-directed films, such as *The Gauntlet* or *The Outlaw Josey Wales*, Eastwood tended to be more tolerant of emotional entanglement. In fact, *Josey Wales* ends on an almost pastoral note as the hero finds peace and tranquillity. The drawback for Eastwood aficionados, however, was that the woman with whom he settled down, in real life as on screen, was Sondra Locke—Clint's answer to Linda McCartney. In any case, by the time their ardor had cooled, on both sides of the camera, the man himself had fallen from his perch at the top of the box-office charts.

His decline was due to two mutually reinforcing concepts. The first and most brutal was time: When a man approaches pensionable age (Eastwood was born on May 31, 1930) he may, as Sean Connery has discovered, carve out a new career as a cinematic father figure, but his days as an action-movie lead are numbered. To add to his box-office woes, Eastwood as a man discovered that his interests were more varied and more subtle than his screen persona would allow. As an actor and/or director of films like *Bird* or *White Hunter, Black Heart*, he has revealed himself to be a mature, intelligent filmmaker of the highest quality. It's just a shame that the movie audience is predominantly adolescent and brain-dead.

In the end, Eastwood was able to recreate his box-office appeal with his role as the grizzled old gunfighter in his Oscar-winning triumph *Unforgiven*, a film whose message is that violence is profoundly serious, profoundly damaging, and always has consequences. This was, as Eastwood himself admitted, almost an act of atonement for his earlier work. But it was also a strong warning to those who had followed him. For his position as Hollywood's leading man had—following a brief interregnum involving such major, but myth-free stars as Harrison Ford, Mel Gibson, and Tom Cruise (the latter two of whom are far too pretty to be seen as true male archetypes)—been taken by the one and only Arnold Schwarzenegger.

ARNIE

As this book was nearing completion, Arnold Schwarzenegger was preparing to mount the publicity bandwagon for his latest film, *The Last Action Hero*. In response to the media furor over violence in the movies, this latest blockbuster had, it was said, cut back on the Teutonic brutality that has long been his stock-in-trade. *Pace* his occasional attempts at lighthearted comedy, such as *Kindergarten Cop*, Schwarzenegger's work has generally been notable for the ruthless eradication of all the redeeming features used to justify violent action by earlier Hollywood stars. For Schwarzenegger, brute force is his own justification. Why does he kill someone? Because he's there. Schwarzenegger is a new phenomenon, the superstar as bully.

This is not to deny his visceral appeal. When, halfway through the first *Terminator*, Schwarzenegger chops his hair and puts on a pair of impenetrable shades, the result is an icon of macho grace fit to rank alongside Brando. When, in *Terminator 2*, he equips himself with leathers, shades, and a pump-action shotgun, before sitting astride a Harley-Davidson bike, he achieves a level of high-tech cool that equals Eastwood. To see these scenes in a cinema and feel the twin forces of female excitement and male identification is to realize that, whatever our politics may say, our hormones have their own agenda.

In keeping with the supposedly more benevolent nineties ethos, however, *T2* sees Arnie adopting the persona of a benevolently destructive robot, reprogrammed to avoid unnecessary death. But this is as unconvincing as decaffeinated coffee. If you want to know what Schwarzenegger is really all about, take a look at *Total Recall*.

This film, which may have cost as much as $70 million and will end up grossing many times that amount, once foreign, video, and TV sales are taken into account, is a happy hunting ground for gender deconstruction. In the first place, Arnie is very big and tough and strong . . . but he doesn't know who he is. His mind, his role, and his very identity are all fake. His real self has been taken away. His new self is an invention. The metaphor for the male condition may well be unintentional—Arnie's public image is that of the last entirely unconfused male—but it could not be more apparent.

Among the many betrayals he faces during the film, the most telling is committed by his wife. She is willing to have sex whenever he wants, but she really belongs to another man, the spymaster who is out to kill him. Given half a chance she attempts to kill him herself, thereby forcing him to beat her up. On Mars, Arnie meets another woman, who was—though we have little reason to believe this—his lover in the days when he was someone else. He joins up with her to defeat their mutual enemies and they end the film standing together on the newly oxygenated surface of the Red Planet.

They will, we assume, stay together, although no justification has been given for any emotional closeness, save the fact that they may have been together when he possessed his original identity. Except, as we also dis-cover, his original self was a double agent who was working for the baddies, so . . . oh, what the heck, who ever said that a movie had to be consistent?

During the course of the film, Arnie kills innumerable enemies. He breaks their necks. He shoots them. He runs them through with pneumatic drills. He rips their arms off while they're hanging from an elevator. Really, he's very inventive.

I'm not particularly squeamish and I love a good thriller, but I was genuinely disgusted by my first viewing of *Total Recall*. The violence was so frequent and so relentless that it allowed for no real tension to develop. It was just a series of cheap thrills, based—as the English journalist Toby Young has observed—on the nonstop action of a Nintendo game (a toy possessed by a vast proportion of the movie's target market), rather than any more traditional, dramatic pattern. To make matters worse, the au-dience reacted with glee and hilarity to this display of pointless and graph-ically depicted bloodshed. Men and women, boys and girls, they hooted with delight at each fresh atrocity.

Yet here was a film that displayed the insecurities of its parent culture with terrifying clarity. Look how frightened men are. They're surrounded by enemies. They can't trust their workmates (Arnie's best pal turns out to have been a spy, hired to keep an eye on him), they can't trust their womenfolk, they can't trust themselves. In desperation, they retreat to the last bastion of masculinity: They pump up their muscles and get out their guns. They become killing machines.

PUMP IT UP

Is it any coincidence that America should be pouring out such a stream of bilious violence at the very time when its own identity and power is under challenge, from outside and from within? After seventy years of unchallenged prosperity and power, the United States is threatened by the economic resurgence of Europe and the Far East. The Japanese can't be killed in movies anymore. They own Hollywood. And the cultural assumptions of the white heterosexual male—the breed epitomized by Schwarzenegger—are lying in tatters under the force of racial and sexual criticism.

Total Recall demonstrates that wanton violence is not a function of masculinity, but a dysfunction. It's what man resorts to when all else has failed. Violence on this scale—both in the movies and in such real-life incidents as the L.A. riots of 1992—is a destructive cry of despair from individuals, from a society and from a gender that are all profoundly messed up. Guns and muscles are not a demonstration of power, but a last line of defense.

So bulking up has become Mr. America's final resort. During the 1980s, rock stars abandoned the old, drug-induced, emaciated figure epitomized by Keith Richards or David Bowie in favor of the kind of power pectorals that would allow them to strip off their shirts on MTV. Bruce Springsteen, for example, began his career in the early seventies looking like a skinny street urchin and playing music of lyrical, freewheeling romanticism. By 1985, and the second leg of his "Born in the USA" world tour, he was a pumped-up hunk, pounding out beefcake rock 'n' roll to stadiums filled with young Republicans.

Springsteen pared himself down, both physically and musically, once the mid-eighties madness had passed. But what of the children of America? What was their response to the hard bodies paraded before them on their TV screens? In December 1988 the *Journal of the American Medical Association* revealed that as many as 6.6 percent of all high school seniors, and perhaps five hundred thousand teenagers in total, had taken anabolic steroids in pursuit of the perfect physique. This was the flip side of the beauty myth that had been producing countless thousands of anorexic girls (although it should be noted that the number of anorexic boys is rising dramatically, too). And, just as starvation has drastic effects upon the development of the female form—which, after all, is partly the point of it—so steroid abuse produces a catalogue of physically and socially abusive side effects.

In the words of *Time* magazine, "Steroids can cause temporary acne and balding, upset hormone production and damage the heart and kidneys. Doctors suspect they may contribute to liver cancer and athero-

sclerosis. . . . The drugs can stunt growth by accelerating bone matura-
tion. . . . Steroid abusers have experienced a shrinking of the testicles and
impotence.''

Not bad, eh? But there's more. Because as well as leaving you spotty,
bald, and shrunken, steroids also provoke bouts of depression, irritability,
and rage, even leading to outbursts of violence. All this for the sake of
looking butch.

There are other ways of achieving physical perfection. You can work
out in a gym. If you really want to take it seriously, you can go to the
granddaddy of them all, Gold's Gym in Venice, California, just a couple
of blocks off the beach. There you can parade the muscle tone you acquired
by strapping yourself to the bright yellow torture machines that stand in
long, implacable rows, like the tools on some perverted assembly line,
where the finished product is pain and muscle fiber.

You can help the machines achieve the desired effect by eating Gold's
vanilla nut flavor Metabolic Optimizer, the great-tasting, high-energy performance bar from Gold's Nutritional Products Division. Unlike other
candy bars, it doesn't try to sell you on chocolate or toffee. Instead its
wrapper tells you about the contents that count when it's body bulk you're
after: amino acids, medium chain triglycerides, and, best of all, chromium.
Yum, yum!

Still, if that doesn't work, and the TitanSports ICOPRO doesn't leave
you feeling fit enough to fight against the masters, there is another way
of getting the body beautiful. You can buy it from a surgeon.

Cosmetic surgery has traditionally been thought of as a means of making
money out of female vanity. But then again, one of the weirder ironies
of these postfeminist years is that, rather than women being freed from
the cruel rules of appearance imposed by the patriarchy, etc., etc., what
has actually happened is that *both* sexes have become imprisoned. The
increased competition for jobs brought on by the recession, coupled with
our society's deeply ingrained belief that young executives will work
harder and better than older ones, has led to a boom in plastic surgery
for middle-aged men.

According to America's Society of Plastic and Reconstructive Surgeons,
44,000 American men anually undergo eyelid surgery, 38,000 opt for
liposuction, 14,000 have facelifts, and some 14,500 are injected with
collagen. There's no shame involved. When *The Star* claimed that singer
Kenny Rogers had undergone liposuction to remove some unwanted
avoirdupois, he immediately wrote to the paper.

He didn't want to complain. After all, as he said, ''Cosmetic surgery . . .
has made a major improvement in my life.'' No, Kenny just wanted to
get the details right: ''Dr. Martin, whom you quoted, did my first liposuction some three years ago, when he removed 3 to 4 lbs of excess fat.

My latest surgery was performed by Dr. George Semel of Los Angeles, who has developed a new procedure which allowed him to take 4,500cc (approximately 11 lbs) of additional fat from my stomach. I'm so impressed with the results I wanted to make sure he got the credit."

That's real neighborly, for sure. But what happens if you don't want to take anything off, but you do want to put a bit on? If you're looking for those macho calves, buttocks, or pecs that the gym just can't provide, I know just the man. . . .

In a medical center on Beverly Boulevard, Los Angeles, I met Dr. Brian Novack (he's since moved across town to a suite on Wilshire, if you want to get in touch). Floppy-haired and mustachioed, this then-thirty-eight-year-old flesh-carver looked like a seventies singer-songwriter: James Taylor's kid brother, maybe. As he talked, he toyed with a translucent sac, which sagged and flopped between his hands. "It's a fun thing to play with," he said. It was a female breast implant.

The men's ones don't behave like that. They're made of silicone, but they're solid, hard to the touch, with a slightly sticky surface. They look and feel like those giant novelty erasers kids used to have at school. Dr. Novack carves this stuff. On the night before an operation, he whittles away at it, like a surgical Rodin, aiming for the shape that will give his patient total satisfaction.

He know's what's wanted because he's already had a long consultation with his patient. "They'll bring in photos of a model or someone they saw in some surfing magazine and they'll talk about what they want. And if they don't know, then I'll make them know. I tell them to go away and look at some pictures and come back. Because I want them to be happy."

Not that Dr. N. is a slave to his customers' desires. "I won't do anything that's against my artistic judgment or taste, because I don't want to have a bad product out there."

Absolutely not. For the best part of ten thousand bucks, you don't expect anything but the best. And you get bespoke treatment on the big day, too. Once he has his patient anaesthetized and in the operating theater, Dr. Novack arranges him in the shape of a cross, with the arms at 90 degrees to the body. He then cuts a tiny incision, one and a half inches long, and slices open a pocket underneath the existing pectoral muscle. Into this he inserts his hand-tooled implant.

As he explained, "The implant goes in and out, back and forth, and I'll say, 'Gee, it's a little high here, or low there. I want to build it up a little bit here, or take it down a little bit there.' " No matter how much work you do beforehand, it still takes a little sculpting on the day.

"That takes a few hours and once it's done I make pretty close to a mirror image on the other side and make the final touch-ups. Then I close the incisions with special plastic surgery techniques. I don't have any stitches going through the skin. The patient can basically take a shower the next morning."

Dr. Novack has no ethical worries about putting lumps of plastic in people when he could be curing cancer or tending to sick refugees. In fact, he has a message for any would-be critics, which is, "Let them eat cake. I could show you books of cards that people send me when I've done their surgery and they just feel fabulous. They can go through years of psychotherapy and they don't feel as well. People get in a bad mood, so they go to a store and blow a couple of thousand bucks on clothes. Here I'm giving them a lifetime product. They're buying a sculpture that they can wear and enjoy."

They certainly seem to. I spoke with two of Dr. Novack's patients and they were both delighted. "I'd always been very flat-chested. I felt like the perennial ninety-eight-pound weakling," said Cloy Morton, a scientist at the University of Southern California. "This was the answer to my dream. It really made me happier and it was well worth the money for the change in the way it made me feel about my body.

"I have some friends and I was over at their pool not long after it was done. I just walked in and they said, 'My God, you have been going to the gym lately, haven't you?' "

Right now, the majority of men approaching Dr. Novack for chest implants are gay. This should come as no surprise. Homosexuals are pioneers for the male sex. They experiment with attitudes and lifestyles that may take decades to reach the straight community. Gays are to straights as California is to Arkansas.

Still, it is one of the many paradoxes about extreme masculinity that it carries with it such a pungent air of camp. When Arnold Schwarzenegger wanted to break out of the bodybuilding scene into general celebrity status in the early 1970s, it was the gay magazines that first were prepared to put him on their covers, or show him, naked, on their inside pages. The WWF wrestlers, with their permed, peroxide hair and their outrageous clothes, share with heavy metal music—which is, no surprise, the sound-track of choice for their adventures—a bizarre effeminacy.

Metal musicians, who pride themselves on their machismo and sing songs about devil-worship, suicide, and slaughter, will primp themselves up with leotards, mascara, and those blond, shaggy-dog hairdos more associated with the stiletto-wearing bimbos of the world's shopping malls. Then they shave their chests and limbs, disposing of the body hair that is one of the male's most distinctive secondary sexual characteristics, in order to achieve a perfect smoothness that is usually considered an ultrafeminine prerogative.

Ultramasculinity seems to be so self-conscious that it ceases to be truly masculine. It's as if the muscles are really just a disguise. Maybe Joan Smith is right about our move toward androgyny. Maybe all these guys are pumping themselves up to look just like Rick Savage, when all along they'd much rather be Miss Elizabeth. There is, however, a more direct route to achieving that effect.

FROCKS AWAY

If you're a man and you ever get invited to dinner at Mick Jagger's house, here's a tip: Pack a dress. They say there's nothing the old Stone enjoys more, when hosting a weekend at his French château, than a spot of Saturday night drag. Ray Davies of the Kinks once sang that "Girls will be boys and boys will be girls," and chez Jagger much the same applies to the middle-aged.

Speaking of whom, if you're a fiftysomething billionaire, or an aging political heavyweight, you may find yourself making a visit to Bohemian Grove, the all-male, members-only (pun unintended) summer camp in Sonoma County, California. Once inside the four-and-a-quarter-square-mile compound, you may feel the need to participate in one of the many entertainment events, like the annual Low Jinks revue. And since women are not allowed inside the camp, you may well be called upon to be a good sport and put on a pretty frock for the purposes of the performance. After all, what's the point of a show without chorus girls?

Don't worry, though. No one's going to call you a sissy just because you're wearing a skirt. Hell, they don't say that to the guys at Harvard's Hasty Pudding Club, do they? And when some of New York's toniest gentlemen's clubs were revealed to be hotbeds of preppy cross-dressing, we all knew that was just a case of busy, overworked guys trying to let off a little steam . . . didn't we?

Downtown, the scene is remarkably similar, even if the clientele is different. Men dressed as women pullulate through the nightclubs of New York. Films such as *Paris Is Burning* have been made about Manhattan's vogueing she-males. Fashion magazines have run spreads of boys in mini-skirts and feather boas. Gorgeous drag queens have even paraded upon the Paris runways. Ru-Paul Charles, a dazzling male Grace Jones, who stands six feet seven in his/her thigh-high stiletto boots, has signed a record deal with the Tommy-Boy label.

Vanity Fair's November 1992 edition put the seal of approval on the drag explosion, as it printed a picture of Lypsinka (alias John Epperson), the prettily painted star of both a Gap ad and a George Michael video, who could also be found modeling women's evening gowns over several pages in *Esquire*. Commented *VF* excitedly, "This year's Wigstock, the eighth annual Labor Day celebration of outrageous coifs, too much eyeliner and too high heels, drew television cameras and larger-than-ever crowds to New York's Tompkins Square Park. Drag isn't just socially acceptable now; it's the baton twirler at the head of the parade."

Maybe that's how they see it in Tompkins Square. But things are very different in the average suburban bedroom. In December 1990, the British edition of *Cosmopolitan* ran the results of a massive reader survey on attitudes toward sex. More than fifteen thousand women replied, and they revealed themselves to be a lively, broad-minded bunch. To the question, "How often do you have sex?" the most common answer (34 percent) was three to five times a week. On the other hand, when asked, "How many partners have you had?" the largest single group, 36 percent, answered two to five. So you might conclude that they were energetic but faithful—a laudable combination, to be sure.

Respondents were also asked which of a number of sexual activities they had participated in, and whether they enjoyed them (the latter figure included those women who thought they would enjoy the activity if given the opportunity). The table below reproduces their answers:

	% participate	**% enjoy**
Cunnilingus	59	84
Fellatio	77	59
Wearing sexy underwear	53	67
Being held down	20	32
Pretending to fight	16	22
Pinching, biting, slapping partner	15	17
Being pinched, bitten, or slapped by partner	14	18
Performing striptease	12	15
Anal sex	12	8
Role-playing with partner	8	9
Cross-dressing	2	1

Some of these responses come as no surprise. Are we, for example, overly amazed that women give more head than they'd really like to, but they get less than they deserve in return? I don't think so.

Others, on the other hand, are rather more unexpected. I dare say that most men would be delighted to discover that women want to wear more sexy underwear and perform more stripteases than is currently the case. And the proportion of women who think that sex would be improved by a bit of good-natured rough-and-tumble, complete with slaps, bites, and restraint also suggests that bedrooms could soon become a lot livelier, even if those same slaps may seen a lot less amusing once we have considered the subject of domestic violence.

One women in twelve even enjoys anal sex (although one in eight has to put up with it anyway). Only one activity, it would appear, is rejected by 99 percent of all known women: cross-dressing. Whatever Mick Jagger may think, the moment a man puts on a dress, he can forget about having a happy wife or girlfriend. The overwhelming odds are that she'll hate it.

To psychologists, transvestism can be seen in a number of different ways. Some liberal analysts, proceeding from the observation that the vast majority of transvestites (as opposed to showbiz drag queens) are heterosexual, interpret their behavior as an act of love. They wish to identify themselves with the object of their adoration, which is women. To others, the phenomenon is a typical example of the distressing way in which men display forms of sexual perversity that are alien to women.

Male cross-dressing is, they would say, maladaptive, perverse, and fetishistic. Given the observations already made by Liam Hudson, it is an understandable consequence of the distortions that can be caused by a malformation or malfunction of the Male Wound. Men tend, as we have already seen, to invest inanimate objects with animate emotions. If a boy failed to make a successful transition from his mother to his father, but stayed too long on the mother's side of the fence, one might not be surprised if he were to end up having an overintimate relationship first with her clothing and then with female clothing in general.

To some feminists, the transvestite is insulting and mocking women; they see this as a profoundly misogynist act. But, more recently, academics such as Marjorie Garber, author of *Vested Interests: Cross-dressing and Cultural Anxiety*, have seen the cross dresser (among whom she appears to include figures as diverse as Peter Pan and Elvis Presley) as a sexual radical who wages war on culturally predetermined notions of masculinity and femininity. The drag queen deconstructs the whole notion of gender, ending up—in Joan Smith's words—as "an erotic rebel, a disruptive third force in the false dualism of conventional gender politics": a guerrilla in a girdle, as it were.

On the other hand, there is the view put forward by the rock singer Bono Vox. Standing backstage at the Minneapolis Target Center, following yet another triumphant show by U2, he allowed himself to be photographed wearing a diaphanous floral dress before pronouncing, wistfully, "Women get to wear all the good clothes."

The most significant word in Bono's remark is *all*. Women can, indeed, wear whatever they like. Women don't indulge in the "perversion" of cross-dressing, because it's not a perversion for them. Flick through the pages of any fashion magazine and alongside the dresses you will see models in mannish suits or leather jackets, lumberjack shirts and heavy boots.

In his April 1992 show, displaying the year's fall collection, Ralph Lauren was inspired—or so that month's fashion pages informed me—by turn-of-the-century men's tailoring. His women wore pinstripe pantsuits, shirts, ties, bowler hats, and pocket handkerchiefs. They even carried walking sticks. They looked great. But imagine what would happen if Mr. Lauren sent his male models down the runway in turn-of-the-century women's tailoring, looking like the chorus line from *My Fair Lady*, complete with bustles, floor-length skirts, and huge, diaphanous hats.

A woman has to retain only one or two visible elements of femininity in order to keep her gender identity intact. In front of me as I write these words is an advertisement for the Jaeger chain of clothing stores, published in the September 1992 edition of *Vanity Fair*. It is a three-quarter-length portrait of a woman wearing a man's charcoal-gray, double-breasted suit, together with a striped shirt and woven silk tie. She is, to put it crudely, in drag. But her flowing hair and delicately made-up face reassure us that she is still unequivocally female.

For men, the opposite is true. It takes only one or two nonmasculine elements to intrude upon a man's appearance for his whole identity to fall apart. He may be six feet six, bearded, and wearing combat boots on his feet, but if he's got a skirt around his waist, he's no longer a man in the eyes of the world. Once again one should note the extreme fragility of masculinity in the face of any threat to its conventions.

Women can become irate if their right to cross-dress is impeded. When the authorities at Birmingham University, England, decreed that female students should arrive at their graduation ceremony wearing dark skirts, white blouses, and dark shoes, the response was instantaneous. More than a thousand undergraduates signed a petition demanding that the university's vice-chancellor, Professor Sir Michael Thompson, should reverse the order.

One history student, Emma Thompson (no relation), huffed, "We feel it is a sexist attitude to enforce this dress requirement. Many women feel in this day and age that they should be able to wear trousers."

Now I don't give a damn whether Birmingham's female graduates wear skirts, pants, pajamas, or bikinis to their graduation. I merely note that educated young women in their early twenties, just like them, form the core target market for *Cosmopolitan*, a magazine in which 99 percent of their peer group announced that they would not wish to associate with a man in a skirt. In other words, they denied their menfolk an option they would fight to preserve for themselves.

Transvestism is an unlikely mast upon which to fly the banner of men's liberation. The right to put on a dress is not one for which most of us

would man the barricades. But it illustrates two typical processes in society's treatment of men. The first is that we drastically limit male freedom
of action by drawing rigidly defined boundaries around the perimeters of
acceptably masculine behavior. The second is that we then classify any
action outside these boundaries as either criminal or, in this case, perverse.
Neither of those processes applies to women, whose femininity is in no
way compromised by the clothes they choose to wear, any more than it
is by the job in which they choose to be employed.

The consequence of this is that those men who do not wish or feel able
to conform to society's expectations are pushed into a cycle of denial,
suppression, and fear. The irony is that their initial impulse may not be
nearly as kinky as is always assumed. After all, women choose between
pants and skirts on any particular day not because of any weird fetishism,
but simply on the basis of how they feel. Maybe it's hot, so they wear a
skirt. Maybe it's cold and they can't be bothered with finding matching
tights, so they wear pants. Maybe it just feels like a pants day, or a long
skirt day, or a short skirt day—who cares? When women put on their
clothes, they automatically express themselves as the person they want
to be. And if, a few hours or a few days later, they feel like someone else,
then they just express her, too.

Men, by contrast, cannot satisfy their needs within an innocent context,
so they are forced to do so in one that is considered perverse. What may
start out as an innocent desire is forced into a cul-de-sac of fetishism and
warped sexuality. Unable, thanks to the male code of silence, to talk to
friends lest they be exposed or ridiculed, these men carry their guilty secret
like a festering wound. They long for sympathy and understanding. They
know that they are unlikely to find it.

As a social spectacle, cross-dressing is gruesomely intriguing. Why, one
might wonder, is it so disturbing? Why are inappropriate clothes such a
threat to male self-image? Perhaps our response is a sort of metaphor for
the limitations that are placed upon male behavior as a whole. In the
reasons why transvestism should be feared by the many, and desired by
the few, lie many of masculinity's most delicate hidden secrets—secrets
that relate to all men, even if they've never, in their wildest nightmares,
dreamed of wearing a dress.

SAMANTHA'S CHANGEAWAY

Some drag queens can look amazing. And women who spent the first
decades of their lives as men have posed for *Playboy*. But the sight of an
average man dressed as a backstreet slut is not, it must be said, a particularly appealing one. "Samantha" was the femme name used by a twenty-

nine-year-old sales manager from Manchester, in the northwest of England. We met in an unprepossessing lounge in the flat above a shop called Transformations in Prestwich, a Manchester suburb. Here men can come to buy transvestite clothes and accessories—false breasts, man-size women's shoes, makeup, and so forth—and, if they so choose, to spend a few hours as a Changeaway.

For around $110 they are given a makeover, a wig, and the run of the Transformations wardrobe. Then, decked up in all their finery, they retreat to the lounge where they sit and talk and watch television and gaze longingly at the world outside, wishing they too could go tip-tapping down the street, just like a real woman.

Samantha arrived as a man wearing jeans and a purple T-shirt. He had brown hair, looked about five-seven, light build. One transformation later, she (strictly speaking, transvestite etiquette demands that a fully dressed trannie should always be referred to as "she") was bedecked in a blond wig and, inevitably, the TV uniform of black microskirt, seamed stockings, and patent-leather black stilettos. Despite the copious quantities of thick Dermablend makeup that had been lavished upon her face, her stubble was still clearly visible on her chin and her skin—this being a stuffy room and a hot September afternoon—was coated in a thin film of sweat. She looked a proper sight.

Her transformation had been accomplished thanks to the tender ministrations of Judy, one of Transformations' beauticians. She seemed remarkably tolerant of her unusual clientele. "They're all sorts, just everyday men. They come from all walks of life. But when they get changed they become a different person. As soon as they get the clothes on, they become a she. You talk to them as if they were just another woman. They're more gentle than most blokes. They're softer."

Did she, I wondered, think any less of them for their habit?

"No, not at all."

What if her husband did it?

"That's a very difficult question to answer. I'd probably be concerned, but I just don't know how I'd cope with it."

Samantha was displaying little evidence of increased gentleness or sensitivity. "I'd like to bonk. I just feel horny wearing this gear," she said. "I'm relaxed. And the more I do it, the more relaxed I become."

Samantha, who was married, had been dressing up for a decade or more. She didn't think much of Transformations' wardrobe—which was, it has to be said, a blizzard of man-made fibers—but she was pleased, nonetheless, with her overall look. "I wanted to be a bit of a tart. The girls downstairs said I looked good, but they probably say that to everyone. As soon as the wig goes on it makes all the difference. I felt embarrassed walking through the shop without my wig, but as soon as I had it on I was a right little flirt." A pause; then: "You know I envy women to some degree. They look great."

Transformations is owned and managed by Stephanie-Anne Lloyd. This might come as a shock to the executives at Disney, but she believes that she is in the same business as they are. "I've always said that our nearest competitor is Disneyland, because it's sheer escapism—the thing of leaving that body with all its responsibilities and pressures and escape for a few hours until they go back."

Both places, too, deal with cartoon stereotypes. Samantha wanted to be "a bit of a tart" because, in his/her eyes, that was the most female she could be. She didn't want to be an ordinary woman, walking around in a pair of jeans, or a cotton dress from Laura Ashley. She wanted the thrill of going to the extreme.

Of course, there are some differences between Walt's Magic Kingdom and Stephanie-Anne Lloyd's. At Transformations, it is the guests, rather than the staff, who dress up in funny costumes. "Some want to be French maids, some want to be schoolgirls, some want to be princesses, and we even have bridal wear for the ones that want to be brides," she says. Also, few of us think of a desire to visit Disneyland as a guilty secret that has to be kept from the world at large.

For Ms. Lloyd's customers, things could not be more different: "I've had guys cry, absolutely break down and cry and say, 'I've kept this secret for forty years, I've never told anyone' . . . I feel sorry for them because they've bottled it up for so many years. But I don't feel sorry [about their cross-dressing] because it's a good outlet. I think that on the scale of things that they can do . . . it's escapism, it's harmless, it's safe, you don't transmit any sexual diseases, it doesn't require emotional involvement with another person . . . I think it's healthy. It gives them a much-needed release."

WHAT'S THE PROBLEM?

When one thinks of "Samantha" with her hairy legs peeking out over the top of her sheer stockings, or the full-frontal nude photographs of Stephanie that were on sale in her shop on the day of my visit, along with an assortment of explicit "she-male" transvestite videos, it's hard to think of cross-dressing as being entirely healthy. But is it any worse than the pastimes that are considered acceptably masculine? Is it any more deviant to wish to put on a dress than it is to wish to buy a twenty-four-shot repeater shotgun and go into the forest to slaughter deer? Or people, come to that? Is it more dysfunctional to put on mascara than it is to pump oneself full of steroids, cortisone, and painkillers in order to get through a professional football game? Is it really that much more weird than bodybuilding?

Perhaps the way to look at cross-dressing is to see it as a reasonable response to an unreasonable situation. The real perversion, one might say, is the definition of masculinity we insist upon for "regular" guys. What is it about being male that forces people to act in this way? If men were kept on a looser rein, would they need to go to such extreme lengths in order to express every aspect of their personality—a form of self-expression that women increasingly take for granted?

Whatever its root causes, the fact remains that this is a pan-global activity. Transformations has expansion plans for European branches and there are transvestite groups the whole world over. Sydney, Australia, has a flourishing transvestite and transsexual community (the two phenomena are linked, but quite distinctive). In Japan, where *onnagata*—actors who train all their lives to play female parts, not as impersonators, but as women—are superstars, the Elizabeth Club caters to Tokyo's cross-dressing businessmen. According to an August 1991 feature in *New York Woman* magazine, somewhere between three and five percent of American males are thought to cross-dress, and they are supported by more than three hundred self-help groups across the nation. In Kansas City, local TVs attend the annual Harvest Moon Ball, while every October Provincetown, Massachusetts plays host to the Fantasia Fair, an annual cross-dressing convention.

To judge by the *New York Woman* report, there are few differences between cross-dressers in America and those on the other side of the Atlantic. Many had repressed their needs for years, following the pattern of compensation via displays of overt masculinity. Once dressed, they softened, becoming more gentle, relaxed, and emotionally expressive: They displayed the qualities of empathy and communication more normally thought of as feminine.

Some could pass as women in the outside world without being "read" as transvestites: They were party girls who went to clubs in tight leather skirts. But, by and large, the more they were allowed to cross-dress, the less they used it as a source of sexual frisson, preferring instead to relax and explore previously hidden sides of their personalities. As one of their girlfriends said, "Some guys shoot pool to unwind. These fellows put on dresses."

Other women, however, found their men's proclivities more threatening. In the words of Dr. Richard Docter, a clinical psychiatrist and the author of *Transvestites and Transsexuals: Toward a Theory of Cross-Gender Behaviour*, "Not only do the wives live under the cloud of potential social rejection if the cross-dresser is found out, but they also become aware that the husband has a girlfriend on the side—himself."

One can quite see how this might imperil a relationship. But why should society as a whole be so threatened by male cross-dressing? The most obvious answer is that it is a blatant challenge to the patriarchy. Men who put on women's clothing are letting their side down, forfeiting their power for the pleasures of the supposedly inferior sex. More than that, they are issuing a challenge to the very structure of masculinity.

Society has traditionally been constructed in such a way that all men make a form of Faustian pact. They sign away their emotional and sensual freedom of action and constrict the range of their personalities in exchange for the promise of power. The cross-dresser is refusing the terms of that contract and insisting on his/her right to be whoever he/she wants.

This may be an entirely logical move, given that the Devil can no longer deliver on his half of the deal. Men are losing their monopoly on power. Why, then, should women have the monopoly on gentleness and sensuality? And here we come to an important issue. Women dislike the notion of cross-dressing for two distinct reasons. In the first place, however much they may maintain that they want men who display more feminine characteristics, the truth is that they do not: They want their men to be men.

To be fair, heterosexual men feel the same way about women. However much a man may say that he wants his partner to possess such traditionally male virtues as financial independence, that desire ceases the moment that her success intrudes upon what he perceives to be her role as the woman in his life. The difference lies in the degree of tolerance. One woman, reading an early draft of this chapter, commented, "I want a man with feminine characteristics. I just don't want a man in a dress." Few women would disagree with her and most men (myself included) would understand her point of view. But I have to point out that when she made the remark, she was wearing pants.

Deep down inside, the average woman is as conservative as the average man when it comes to defining sex-role stereotypes. In the words of Stephanie-Anne Lloyd, "Women have a desire for someone strong to lean on. It allows them to show frailty and weakness because then they've got an anchor. So it passes the responsibility from them onto the man. If he becomes a New Man—I hate that phrase—the wife is liable to go off with someone she regards as being manly. And the guy's stood there with his feather duster thinking, 'My God, what went wrong?' "

Second, the man who puts on a dress not only betrays his manhood, but he enters into the woman's sphere of influence. Those young women from Cambridge—who went on in later years to become bankers, lawyers, doctors, and media stars—had no desire to be parted from their sartorial weaponry. Women often say that they don't want their men to be too good-looking or to take too much trouble over their appearance. Not only might that seem effeminate, but it might also distract attention from them, and, as any traditional black-tie ball demonstrates, men are supposed to be the somber backdrop against which women are displayed in all their glory.

No wonder, then, that men like Samantha envy real women so. But before "she" becomes too caught up in her desires, she might like to consider the words of Stephanie-Anne Lloyd, the doyenne of Transformations: "Our customers only want one percent of femininity. They don't want the other ninety-nine percent. They don't want to be real women with responsibilities or kids. They don't want to have periods. They don't want to do the housework. They want the one percent of glamour that a woman has in her life when she gets dressed up to go to a dinner party. That's the only bit they want because it's the ultrafeminine bit. It's the escapism, the pampering. It defines a man's idea of what a woman should be. But their idea of femininity is slightly different from reality." Maybe. But as I am about, I hope, to demonstrate, our ideas about masculinity are a long way from being reasonable or accurate, either.

CHAPTER 4
Being the Bad Guy

When I started work on this book, one of the issues by which I was most deeply troubled was the sheer amount of evil that men appeared to do. Wherever one looked, from the pictures on the TV screen to the words on a vast array of newspapers, books, and magazines, one was confronted by the violence and abuse wreaked by men upon defenseless women and children. Men harassed, and raped. They punched and abused. They butt-fucked little children, for God's sake. (I apologize for the crudity of the language, but it's only when you strip accusations of their jargon and technicalities that their horrors become apparent.) There seemed no end to men's depravity.

I had never done any of these things, nor even wished to. Nor had I ever witnessed any of them. It sounds like the height of naïveté to say this, but in more than a dozen years as a journalist, including several spent as a senior executive on a number of different publications, I am not aware that any of my female colleagues has ever been sexually harassed by me or anyone else. Naturally, I have heard plenty of gossip about goings-on in the business as a whole, but have I ever witnessed an act of harassment? I don't think so. Nor do I for one moment believe that any of my close friends has ever beaten up his wife or sexually abused his little children. Nor does my wife recall that any of the women she knows has ever made the slightest reference to any such acts. We simply cannot afford to believe such things. Because if we did, we would lose whatever faith we have in the power of love or friendship, or indeed, any of the values that make life remotely tolerable.

And yet, if the reports I read were to be credited—and many of them came from apparently unimpeachable, nay, official sources—the Western world was steadily being overrun by a plague of abusive behavior. One in three children had experienced some form of sexual abuse. One in five women had been the victim of an attempted rape, or was it 44 percent, or even, as some researchers claimed, one in two? One in seven university students actually had been raped. According to a respected academic authority, between 21 and 35 percent of all women had suffered some form of domestic violence. And, in every case, the perpetrators of the terrible acts were men.

Try as one might to deny the claim that all men were rapists, or abusers, or wife-beaters, it was impossible not to feel overwhelmed by a sense of guilt. Trying to be a good man was like trying to be a good German— you could always feel the Nazis (or, in this case, the perverts) in the background. Just as those Germans who were not involved in the Holocaust had to explain, both to the world, and perhaps more important, to themselves, how they could possibly have allowed it to happen, and then had to find some means of atoning for it, so I struggled to resolve my feelings of complicity in the crimes that man was apparently wreaking upon the rest of humanity.

Much of the work done by the men's movement has proceeded from a position of culpability. It is accepted that there is something wrong with men. The only questions remaining are, what, exactly, is the root of the problem, and what should be done to eradicate it? I must confess to having accepted this basic premise when I started work on this book. My early interviews—conversations with psychologists, scientists, therapists, counselors, and even the odd advice columnist—were all directed to discovering why men behaved so badly. Was it something that was unavoidable, a malevolence buried deep within the genes? Or was it a matter of conditioning, an anomaly that might, who knows, be "cured" by changing the way in which we educated and conditioned little boys?

Some of these questions have been examined elsewhere in this book. They remain, I hope, central to any consideration of men today. But there's something else. The more I looked at the subject of male dysfunction, the more it seemed that the view society was taking had become seriously distorted. This distortion took two main forms: In the first place, the accusations made against men had been inflated far beyond anything that was justified by the actual—as opposed to the claimed—evidence. And second, the ways in which women hurt their fellow human beings had been virtually ignored. Men, in other words, were being forced to take the rap for problems that were common to both sexes.

Just consider what happens if one takes all the claims about male malevolence at face value. Take all the estimated figures for female victimization that I have mentioned above and add up the percentages. They come to more than 100 percent. Now, it could be that some women suffer disproportionately, but the same campaigners who come up with these figures also insist that the problems they described are spread evenly throughout society. So, by their criteria, every single woman in the Western world has either been abused as a child, or raped, or attacked by a male partner.

Who's been doing it? Well, it could be that a few men commit many crimes each. That would be the commonsense view. But we're not dealing with common sense; we're dealing with political correctness, which insists that perpetrators are as evenly spread as their victims. So, if we believe their propaganda, we have to conclude that every single man in the Western world has committed at least one of these acts.

Can this be possible? Do you believe that every single man you know, without exception, has actually committed some form of sexual or physical assault on a woman or child? Look around the dinner table at your friends—are they all sex criminals? Think of your father, brother, husband, boyfriend, son, and workmates. Think of the firemen, ambulance drivers, air-sea rescue pilots, doctors, and teachers you've come across or seen on the TV news. Think of the newscaster, come to that, and the weatherman, and the guy behind the camera. If you believe the propaganda, you've got to believe that every single one of them deserves to be locked up.

Let's get specific and name names. How about General H. Norman Schwarzkopf? His leadership of the allied forces in the war against Iraq made him a hero all over the globe. He has devoted his life to the service of his country. He is a devoted husband and father (he has said that his greatest regret about the Gulf War was that it took him away from home just as his teenage son was changing from a boy into a young man). And he even has hidden liberal tendencies: On the BBC radio program *Desert Island Discs,* he picked Bob Dylan's *The Times They Are A'Changing* as one of the eight records he would take with him if marooned on a desert island.

So, think about this paragon of manly virtue, and figure out his perversion of choice. Does he beat his wife? Does he harass junior staff? Does he abuse his kids? Has he raped anyone? If we believe the figures, he must have been doing something. What with him being a man, and all.

Now, the last paragraph may have made many readers feel nauseous and disgusted. That's precisely the point. Because every man has, implicitly, been put in the position into which I have just put General Schwarzkopf. And the choice before us is either to believe the statistics that supposedly condemn these men, along with every other man in the land, or to consider that the people who compiled them are either (a) misguided, (b) malevolent, or (c) plain nuts.

I think I know where my vote is going.

Before we go any further, let me get one thing straight. I have no desire whatsoever to try and put the boot on the other foot. I do not believe in some grotesque misogynist fantasy that men are the helpless victims of a vast gang of scheming, manipulative, violent bitches from hell. I just want to say that men do rather less harm than is currently believed and women do rather more. Not all of this harm takes the same form. Not all of it is looked at in the same way by our legal system: By and large, the harm that men do is illegal; by and large, the harm that women do is not. Some of it, perhaps, ought to be. But, in the end, we are all mortal, fallible human beings. And we all work out about equal.

That is not, however, the way that everyone sees it.

NEW LEFT, OLD NEWS

The process by which academia, government, and the media came to be persuaded that men—particularly white, middle-class, heterosexual men—were, by definition, an oppressive, possibly violent group unlike any other is a fascinating one, and it deserves more study than I can give it here. In years to come, historians may wonder why Americans, who were so resistant to conventional Marxism, were so willing to be taken in by the theories of the New Left.

After all, the United States has never wavered from its belief in the profit motive and private enterprise. It has never been possible to persuade the majority of Americans that capitalism is evil, principally because— until recently, at least—it was so clearly delivering improved living standards across the whole range of society in a way that no state-run economy has ever achieved.

Proponents of radical change in America have had to deal with the fact that its citizens have, on the whole, been richer, healthier, and less politically or religiously oppressed than any people in the known history of the world. In an article in the July 1976 edition of *Harper's Magazine,* entitled "The Intelligent Co-Ed's Guide to America," Tom Wolfe described the attempts of American intellectuals to make themselves feel as oppressed (and thus as morally superior) as their European counterparts. They would talk about such heinous crimes as "cultural genocide," "liberal fascism," or "relative poverty" as a means of skating over the fact that real genocide, fascism, and poverty were less prevalent in the United States than anywhere else on earth. He called this process the "Adjectival Catch-up."

Wolfe describes a debate at Yale, back in 1965. Speaker after speaker rose to denounce the neofascist police state of America. One of the panelists was the German author Gunther Grass, author of *The Tin Drum.* After a while he remarked, "For the past hour I have my eyes fixed on the doors here. You talk about fascism and police repression. In Germany when I was a student, they come through the doors long ago. Here they must be very slow."

The point, of course, was that there was no comparison whatever between the fascist fantasies of a few American academics and the terrible realities of a real police state. Yet fifteen years after Wolfe's piece, with Marxism in ruins all over the world, it is the catch-up crowd that's winning the academic debate in America. In place of Marx's idea that the bourgeoisie, as a class, oppresses the proletariat, as a class, they have proposed the notion that men, as a sex, oppress women, as a sex.

As the British author Neil Lyndon has argued in his controversial book *No More Sex War: The Failures of Feminism*, the parallel between Marxism and feminism is a telling one. In 1843 Marx wrote, "For *one* class to represent the whole of society, another class must concentrate in itself all the evils of society. . . . For one class to be the liberating class *par excellence*, it is essential that another class should be openly the oppressing class."

One hundred and twenty-seven years later, in her book *Sexual Politics*, the feminist writer Kate Millett claimed that men oppressed women by means of "interior colonization," which was more powerful than any form of class distinction. Lyndon remarks, "The dominion of females by males is, she said, our culture's most pervasive ideology, providing it with its most essential ideas and conceptions of political power. . . . The long wander of the Marxist Left through the institutions and societies of the modern West, in search of the class which would be the head and heart of society, the class which would be the dissolution of all classes had culminated in the definition of 'the birthright priority whereby males rule females' . . . Karl, meet Kate. Kate, this is Karl: you two were made for each other."

Lyndon surely does not mean to suggest that all feminists are Marxists, and even if he does, I do not. The point is that feminism arose in part (and only in part) from the ideology of the New Left and borrowed the idea of scapegoating a particular group of people as the source of all oppression. The term that was used to define this group was "the patriarchy," which was the ideological embodiment of male, paternal, oppressive power.

From this it followed that men were, by definition, the bad guys. The British feminist Rosalind Miles has written about "the penis rampant" stalking through history, spreading destruction wherever it goes. She sees all violence as male and all men as violent. In *The Women's Room*, Marilyn French famously stated that "All men are rapists and that's all they are. They rape us with their eyes, their laws and their codes." In the words of the American Adrienne Rich, writing in her 1979 book *On Lies, Secrets, and Silence*: "I am a feminist because I feel endangered, psychically and physically, by this society, and because I believe that the women's movement is saying that we have come to an edge of history when men—insofar as they are embodiments of the patriarchal idea—have become dangerous to children and other living things, themselves included."

Andrea Dworkin, the controversial activist and author, has gone even further. In her 1987 book *Intercourse* she claims that "normal, ordinary men commit acts of forced sex against women, including women they know, in the same way that most women are beaten by the men they live with—that is ordinary sexual relations." For Dworkin, men are, by definition, both physically and sexually abusive. In her world there is little possibility of a relationship between a man and a woman that is both loving and mutually sexually satisfying. She states as a fact that "women do not really enjoy intercourse," and that "intercourse remains a means, or the means, of physiologically making a woman inferior: communicating to her cell by cell, her own inferior status."

In a later work, the novel *Mercy*, Dworkin's central character Andrea muses, "I've always wanted to see a man beaten to a shit bloody pulp with a high-heeled shoe stuffed up his mouth, sort of the pig with an apple. . . . " Now, imagine that you take out the word *man* and replace it with *nigger*, or *Jew*, or *faggot*. Obscene, isn't it? Or just add the two letters *wo* and consider what the reaction of the literary world would be to a male author who fantasized about smashing women to a bloody pulp.

Mercy, it must be said, is fiction, and any author is entitled to claim that the words he or she writes in such a context represent the views of his or her characters, rather than his or her personal opinions. Yet when Brett Easton Ellis wrote *American Psycho*, a similarly unpleasant study of male violence, critics were in little doubt that he should be held responsible. One publisher rejected the manuscript. Many bookstores refused to stock it, or kept it out of public view. Why then should we feel so much more comfortable with such clear evidence of one woman's hostility toward men?

Ms. Dworkin is much more militant than the vast majority of supporters of the women's movement. Yet many of the ideas she proposes—the notion, for example, that pornography consists solely of the exploitation and objectification of women for the benefit of oppressive males—have been accepted, in somewhat diluted form, by a vast swath of progressive and liberal opinion.

A culture of victimization has grown up in which women are perceived to be the helpless targets of an extraordinary range of male malevolence. In *The London Review of Books*, dated July 23, 1992, Margaret Anne Doody, Andrew Mellon Professor of English Literature at Vanderbilt University, reviewed *Backlash*, by Susan Faludi, and *The War Against Women*, by Marilyn French. During the course of the review, which ran over several thousand words, she set out the full list of crimes committed by society (i.e., men) against women.

She told her readers that short skirts were an evil male conspiracy designed to infantilize women (of which misconception more anon); that "advertising portrays women as helpless, vulnerable, feckless, silly, so that they will have the humility necessary to take upon themselves the chains of marriage"; that Third World men waste UN handouts on transistor radios; that "the background to all women's lives is fear"; that "individual 'nice' men must . . . collude in woman-bashing in order to preserve the status of manhood"; that people who are opposed to the British monarchy are really woman-haters who want to remove a female head of state; that "the family is where social control of women must take place"; and that men believe "the proper attitude to women is one of contemptuous control, of never-ceasing vigilance, of, in short, permanent hostility."

What comes across in this extraordinary diatribe against male misogyny is an equally powerful anger toward and hatred of men on the part of Professor Doody herself. This would not be of any great concern—*The London Review of Books,* for all its prestige, is not a publication likely to inflame the general public—were it not for the fact that these extreme ideas are influential far beyond the boundaries of university campuses and literary magazines.

THE LEGISLATIVE EFFECT

The idea that men monopolize violence has become a basic assumption of modern public life. In 1991 Senator Joseph Biden proposed a Violence Against Women Act, the first federal legislation specifically designed to combat the problem of domestic violence. The act would make male abusers subject to federal criminal penalties, which could also be imposed against any man crossing a state boundary in search of a fleeing partner. States would be given incentives to arrest wife-batterers, and federal financing for women's shelters would be tripled.

With the possible exception of incentivizing arrests—a principle that throws up a mass of potential difficulties and abuses of power, irrespective of the crime involved—I do not believe that any of these proposals is inherently objectionable. Anything that can be done to free people from the shadow of domestic violence deserves support. Yet the underlying presumption of the act, which is that only men commit acts of violence in the home, and only women are the victims, is repugnant and discriminatory. Domestic violence is inexcusable, irrespective of the gender of its perpetrator or victim. A beaten husband deserves just as much sympathy as a battered wife.

A straightforward Domestic Violence Act, which set forward penalties for abusers and granted funds for counseling and protection services in a non-gender-specific manner, would be a genuinely valuable piece of legislation. It would also, as I shall endeavor to demonstrate in a later chapter, bear a much closer relationship to the truth about violence in the home, which is that it is practiced by both sexes. Yet the chances of such even-handed legislation being adopted are virtually nil, so completely have legislators bought the notion that violence is a uniquely male phenomenon.

Any campaigners who attempt to dispel this notion can expect to come up against three immediate difficulties. In the first place, they will be accused of misogyny. Here I speak, regretfully, from experience. Articles accusing me of waging a campaign against women and women's rights appeared in several British newspapers in the eighteen months prior to this book's publication. As often as not, the writers concerned had never met me or even spoken to me. Invariably, they had not seen a single word of my manuscript. It was simply presumed that any man who spoke in favor of men must, by definition, be speaking against women. The notion that one's ultimate aim might be to help both sexes by acknowledging our shared humanity was never for one moment considered.

Second, there is the matter of vested interest. Jaundiced campaigners for the rights of battered men, such as the Minnesotan George Gilliland, contend that there are now thousands of jobs and millions of dollars tied up in women's shelters, domestic abuse counselors (ditto child abuse, sexual harassment, rape counselors, etc.), academic programs, court officials, lawyers, law enforcement officers, and so forth, all of whom are dependent upon the notion of the victimized woman. Any suggestion that the truth of the situation might differ from the accepted version is perceived as a threat to funding, jobs, and power. It is therefore resisted with the utmost energy.

A more charitable view would be that there are very few people getting rich out of violence and sexual abuse. Many women's shelters have to turn away mothers and children who are in dire need of help. If they are resistant to the idea of sharing their funding with battered men, it is only because there is not enough of it to begin with. Whatever the rationale, however, the end result is the same: a resistance to the idea of male victimization.

The final barrier, which may be the biggest one of all, is public incredulity. Most of us have opinions formed from a confused mass of inherited prejudice, jumbled information, and contemporary beliefs. The idea of women's oppression makes sense to us on two levels. In the first place it fits with everything we have been told by the women's movement. And in the second, it strikes an older, more conservative chord, which is our instinctive feeling that men are stronger, more aggressive, and somehow more impervious to pain (both physical and psychological) than women. Most people, no matter how progressive they claim to be, are pretty old-fashioned when it comes to gender. Surely, we suppose, a woman can't really harm a man. And, in any case, any man who allows himself to be harmed by a woman can't really be a man at all.

These beliefs are irrational, as a moment's reflection demonstrates. When we stop to think about our own experience and that of the men and women we know, we can all think of plenty of examples in which men have been on the receiving end—the divorced father who has lost his family and his home, for example—just as we all know women who have had a raw deal. Yet our preconceptions are awfully hard to shift.

In June 1992, *Life* magazine—which is hardly a banner-waving publication for the feminist Left—ran a cover story entitled "If Women Ran America," which illustrated the degree both to which men are painted as villainous and to which women are idealized. The article's author, Lisa Grunwald, painted a depressing picture of life in a country run by men, noting that "In 1990 an estimated 683,000 women were raped; at least two million were abused each year by husbands and boyfriends."

The use of the word *estimated* is crucial here: According to official U.S. government statistics, there were 94,500 reported rapes, or attempted rapes, in 1989 (again, the last year for which I had published figures at the time of writing). That figure is less than one-seventh the quantity cited by Grunwald. Similarly, the total number of all violent crimes against the person—including murders, assaults, and every manner of bodily harm—was 1,646,000, of which the majority were committed against men, rather than women. The most dangerous thing you can be is not female, but black. A black man runs more than twice the risk of becoming the victim of violence than does a white woman.

Needless to say, it is not only possible, but probable that the number of actual offenses far exceeds the number of those that are reported. And assaults against women are unacceptable and inexcusable, irrespective of their frequency. Even so, you have to wonder where *Life* found the extra 588,500 rape victims and at least 1.5 million battered wives. And you also have to ask yourself how we came to the point where numbers like that can be cited—*and people assume that they must be right.*

If men are bad, women are—so the public believes—far better. An opinion poll of "1,222 Americans, a representative sample of the population," commissioned by *Life* revealed that if women ran America childcare would be more available; maternity leave would be guaranteed; government would be more attentive to the needy (but not, respondents agreed, the work-shy); abortion would be legal; there would be greater equality for working women, and greater sexual tolerance; finally, gun control would be stricter and the law would be tougher on crime.

The irony is that almost all of those conditions already exist in Europe, where—with the possible exception of the Scandinavian countries—the penetration of women into political life is not much more advanced than it is in America. The key difference between the two political cultures is not sexual but ideological. All the major European nations have been governed by socialist parties for prolonged stretches of the postwar period. All have assumed a level of social provision involving such issues as free health care, maternity and paternity rights, worker protection, and so forth, that goes far beyond that experienced by Americans.

The one European leader seriously to challenge those ideas was also the one European woman to walk the world political stage, Britain's former prime minister Margaret Thatcher, who was notably tough about putting the needs of business before those of social justice. She repeatedly drummed into the British electorate that it was not possible to pay for the welfare state unless the economy was healthy. She was no friend of gay or lesbian minority groups. And although she did nothing to alter Britain's tough gun laws, she did commit British troops to two foreign conflicts, in the Falkland Islands and against Iraq. When it came to policy decisions, Mrs. Thatcher was a right-wing Conservative politician first, and a woman second.

SUGAR AND SPICE?

Many critics have argued that Thatcher behaved in that way because she was reacting to a patriarchal society. The contention is that women would behave differently were they able to influence the conduct of events as a whole. I wonder. The hostility and fragmentation within sections of the women's movement itself suggests that women are not immune to the rivalries and power struggles that dog male organizations.

Sally Quinn, who is married to the former editor of *The Washington Post*, Ben Bradlee, wrote a column in that newspaper on January 19, 1992. It was headlined, "Who killed feminism?", and during its course Quinn remarked, "The sad part is that the movement today is more and more perceived as a fringe cause, often with overtones of lesbianism and man-hating. . . . Many women have come to see the feminist movement as anti-male, anti-child, anti-family, anti-feminine. And therefore it has nothing to do with us."

The piece had been prompted in part by the declaration made by Patricia Ireland, the president of the National Organization for Women, that she had a "love relationship with a woman," which she intended to maintain alongside the one she had with her husband. Ireland responded by saying that Quinn's piece should have been headlined "Who killed journalistic standards," but that was not the end of the affair. As the *New York Observer* reported, Gloria Steinem then wrote that Quinn was "a water bug on the surface of life [who] has disqualified herself from any serious consideration as a commentator about women's issues unless she apologizes."

Speaking for the younger generation of third-wave feminists, Susan Faludi said of Quinn, "Who is she to be commenting on feminism? Where has she been all these years during the struggle for women's rights? She's just been sailing along on the coattails of her husband."

Barring the specific references to Ms. Quinn's marital status, this all sounds pretty much like the sort of verbal flak we've come to expect from male commentators. It's eerily reminiscent of one of Norman Mailer and Gore Vidal's little literary spats. On the political front, a similar point was demonstrated in the 1992 Democratic primaries for the New York senatorial election. Geraldine Ferraro and Elizabeth Holtzman slung mud at one another with a glee that any macho, booze-swilling, secretary-fondling congressman might have envied.

A belief that women are somehow immune to the evils that beset men can prove costly. In Australia, a female fraudster called Robin Greenburg used state government backing to start the Women's Information and Referral Exchange, a financial advice company for women whose slogan was "You can't trust a man with your money." As her unfortunate depositors discovered, you couldn't trust Ms. Greenburg, either. She spent more than $3.5 million of her clients' money on shopping binges, as a result of which she was subsequently jailed for seventeen years by a court in Perth, Western Australia.

Interestingly, U.S. government figures show that while women commit far fewer reported violent crimes than men (once again, "reported" may turn out to be a key word here), they commit 46 percent of all frauds and 39 percent of all embezzlements. These figures are roughly parallel with women's penetration of the work force, which suggests that where women are able to commit crime, they will do so just as frequently as men.

This idea is an extremely threatening one, which many people do their very best to deny. Traveling through America in the summer of 1992, I repeatedly encountered writers and editors who would preface a conversation with a phrase like, "Of course, I don't believe in political correctness," or, "No one takes that correctness shit seriously," before launching into a conversation through which the fear of incorrectness ran like the red stripe through a tube of toothpaste. Whatever they may say, no serious, liberal commentator, in Britain or America, would dare make a head-on challenge to the basic premises that underpin contemporary feminism.

Meanwhile, government legislation, on both sides of the Atlantic, is hugely influenced by a desire on the part of male legislators to be seen as pursuing correct policies. Needless to say, those who shout loudest are heard the most clearly. Furthermore, a great deal of sociological and psychological research into gender-related issues over the past few years has been conducted by people who have, a priori, determined where guilt lies.

Over the next few chapters, I intend to question many of the assumptions upon which we base our picture of male/female relationships, particularly those relationships which are in some form dysfunctional or abusive. In some instances, most notably the subjects of child abuse and domestic violence, I will attempt a head-on challenge to current public and legislative prejudices, based on various forms of research which suggest that the truth is very different. First, however, I would like to examine two contemporary issues—those of workplace sexual harassment and acquaintance rape—to see whether there are different ways of looking at them that might yield alternative, and possibly helpful, interpretations. In none of these cases do I wish to deny that men harm women, nor do I wish to excuse or justify the actions of those men who are abusive. It's just that the picture may not be quite as black-and-white as it is painted. There may be shades of gray.

CHAPTER 5

The Rules of
Harassment

There were times during the writing of this book when I wondered whether my efforts were not going entirely to waste. Sometimes I would hear stories about which one could only conclude that the sole mistake made by Andrea Dworkin, Marilyn French, and the rest was to understate the extent of male depravity or insensitivity. One evening, for example, I was talking to a female attorney. Highly respected and at the very top of her profession, she was sympathetic to the difficulties faced by men in family disputes. So even-handed were her opinions, in fact, that she had been strongly attacked by the radical feminist members of the world-famous law school at which she was a visiting professor for selling out to the male establishment. She remarked of that campus, "I'm frightened by the level of feminism. I can't stand it and I find it appalling. I like men." And yet, as she said with a tone of regret, things happened. . . .

She told me about a meeting between the senior partners of two prestigious law firms at which she had been the only woman present. By way of setting the scene, she explained, "I'm fifty-four. I'd like to think that I have kept myself in good condition, but I'm not a sexpot. I was wearing a suit." Everything had been going smoothly until she suffered a sudden coughing fit. In between coughs and gasps for air she attempted to lessen any embarrassment her colleagues might be feeling at her discomfort by making a lighthearted remark. "If I die right here, make sure to give me a decent burial," she said.

To which one of the men at the table replied, "Not before I've fucked you first."

Looking back, the woman asked, "So, did it drive me nuts? No, because I didn't give a damn. But if I'd been a twenty-two-year-old secretary I wouldn't have felt that way."

On other occasions one caught a glimpse of the assumptions that governed people's working lives. At the beginning of November 1992, it was revealed that Bruce Soloway, head of the promotions department at ABC-TV news in New York, had been suspended pending an inquiry into allegations that he had sexually harassed members of his staff. One former member of Mr. Soloway's staff, quoted by the *New York Observer*, said that she had been surprised by the charges, given that Mr. Soloway was by no means the worst offender at ABC: "Bruce is one of the last people around here who should be penalized," she said. "There are others who are legitimate sexual harassers. He had a foul mouth, but he was definitely not a lascivious guy." The woman added that a typical Soloway comment might be something like,"Hey, nice dress. Makes your tits look good."

What are we to do with people who casually make remarks like that? How can I, or anyone else, possibly defend or condone them, still less the legislators who grope their research assistants, or the navy flyers who try to strip female officers? The very least that can be said against them is that they are ill mannered, insensitive, and crude. Somewhere along the line, someone should have told them that a gentleman simply doesn't behave like that. But maybe I'm being old-fashioned.

On October 29, 1991, as Anita Hill's allegations against Judge Clarence Thomas rumbled around Capitol Hill, Helen Gurley Brown, the editor in chief of *Cosmopolitan* magazine, gave *The Wall Street Journal* her opinions on workplace harassment. In a piece entitled "At Work, Sexual Electricity Sparks Creativity," the author of *Sex and the Single Girl* and conceiver of that classic slogan, "If I have only one life, let me live it as a blonde," recalled her days as a young woman working at Radio KHJ, Los Angeles.

Ms. Brown wrote, "I know about sexual harassment," before telling the denizens of Wall Street about "a dandy game called 'Scuttle' " which her male coworkers used to play. The game consisted of chasing a secretary through the office, catching her, holding her down, and removing her panties. The most Neanderthal workplace chauvinist would concede that this went beyond the line that divides acceptable office behavior from blatant offensiveness, but Ms. Brown retained an open mind about it all. She noted that, although they protested about the game, "the girls wore their prettiest panties to work." Indeed, her only complaint was that she herself was never scuttled.

So was *Cosmopolitan* magazine, with its bizarre admixture of feminism and flirtation, just Brown's way of getting back at men for their refusal to scuttle her as a young working girl? Only she and her analyst can say. Certainly her tolerant view of sexual shenanigans in the office is not one that would be shared by most career women. Harassment at work is rapidly becoming a cause célèbre all over the Western world. Even in Japan, the *seka hara* inflicted upon innocent *o-eru*'s (or "OL's"—office ladies) by their *salaryman* bosses has become a talking point. This is a global issue.

SACKABLE, OR SEDUCTIVE?

Here are two stories, told in the first person, dealing with the subject of office sex. One originates in Britain, the other in America. The first, which appeared in the London *Daily Mail*, dated October 17, 1991, is the story of Colin, a thirty-seven-year-old father of three. It appeared under the headline, "I made a girl's life a misery for a year—what an idiot I was."

"Right from the very first day I liked Maggie . . . she was not only an extremely attractive 25-year-old with long copper-red hair and a lovely figure, but was also very bright. The real trouble was that I never admitted, either to myself or to anyone else, how fascinated by her I was. So instead of behaving naturally with her, I was self-conscious and ill-at-ease.

"One way of dealing with that was to make suggestive remarks. Although as an older married man I was initially quite shy, and found it hard to think of things to say to Maggie, I soon discovered that teasing seemed to have the desired effect of getting her attention and making her notice me more than others. I wish someone had stopped me there and then. Not one of my colleagues ever hinted to me that I might be making a fool of myself. She said later that I had made her life a misery—making it an ordeal even to walk to the office in the mornings. I never realised that, or I would have stopped it straight away. I always believed that Maggie enjoyed my teasing and even fantasised that she found me attractive."

Colin only realized the extent of Maggie's distress when her boyfriend walked into his office and punched him in the jaw. He then resigned from his job the following morning, after a meeting between Maggie and his boss. When told of what had happened, his wife "lost respect for me which I can never regain," his teenage sons teased him for being a dirty old man, and his daughter said she was disgusted and would never kiss him again.

His reaction? "That hurt me deeply, but I knew that it was probably less punishment than I deserved . . . there was nothing I could say to defend myself."

The second story was told by the pseudonymous "Susan White" in the January 1992 edition of *New Woman* magazine. She was working at a magazine when "Tom" joined the staff as a senior editor. When she was introduced to Tom at an editorial conference, "I felt a rush, a hot river surge through my body. When I heard my name, my face burned, my knees turned to liquid and when I looked up I knew why. Tom was staring dead center into my eyes."

Following this somewhat disconcerting introduction, Susan took pains to ignore Tom as best she could. "I tried to fade into the woodwork and part of me wished Tom would also disappear. . . . Then my vision became a reality.

"I was working late at the office, hunched over my computer, when I heard a knock at my door. Assuming it was my assistant, I didn't even bother turning around as I said, 'Come in.'

"But once the door was opened, I knew it was him. When I turned around and looked up, without speaking a word, Tom bent over my desk and pressed his lips on mine. I opened my mouth and encouraged his passion. Our embrace felt like a lifetime of longing had been born, given flight. It seemed an eternity as we . . . " and so on, and on, and on.

Let's just compare those two stories. One is the agonized, guilt-ridden cry of a man who has lost his job, the love of his family, and his self-respect. The other is a bodice-ripping true-life drama that might have stepped straight from the pages of a Sidney Sheldon blockbuster. But are the scenarios all that different?

Clearly the men are of a different caliber when it comes to their animal magnetism. Colin, the harasser, comes across as shy, insecure, and sexually unsuccessful. We cannot form any opinion as to his physical attractions, but Maggie clearly found them perfectly resistible. Tom, on the other hand, turns out to be a regular office hunk, at least in Susan's eyes, to wit: "[He] had startling good looks, thick wavy hair flecked with the same shade of gray as his eyes. He dressed in corduroys and tweeds and had a smile that was at once charming and wry. His humour and intelligence danced across his face." No one but Harrison Ford or Kevin Costner will do when the time comes to make *Tom: The Movie.*

Tom is also far cooler when conducting his pursuit of Susan. Whereas Colin thrashes around in a swamp of misguided dirty remarks, Tom plays it smart. He says nothing at all for a month and then cuts straight to the chase, tongue-wrestling with Susan right there and then on her office desk. You have to admire the man's élan.

But in the end, the only substantive difference between one man's actions and the other's lies in the reactions of the women concerned—reactions which might have been very different. What if Susan had said, "No"? After all, we know that she had done her best to disguise her feelings by going out of her way to avoid Tom. He, being the very paragon of a modern ladies' man, correctly interprets this as a paradoxical form of come-on. But what if he had been wrong? Or, just as possible, what if she had been leading him on, but didn't want to admit it, not even to herself, and so feigned repulsion and horror at the arrival of his tongue in her mouth, even though she was really longing for it?

Under these circumstances, Tom might very well have found himself on the wrong end of a sexual harassment suit. He too might have been out on his ear, with the additional penalty of a court action to follow. One Wall Street secretary sued her boss for $107 million, claiming sexual harassment and the intentional infliction of emotional distress—an action that was subsequently dropped without money changing hands. Tiffany, the jewelers, were hit with a $12 million claim when one of their diamond buyers alleged that a manager had tried to rape her. And an Ohio company was forced to pay out $3.1 million when a female employee claimed that her supervisor had demanded she perform oral sex on him, or face dismissal.

That final case sounds like straightforward extortion. You don't have to be Gloria Steinem to see that bosses who tell staff, "Blow my dick or you get the sack," are asking for even more trouble than sex. Similarly, the Geffen Records executive who, allegedly, stuck his penis into his secretary's ear, fondled her buttocks, and ejaculated onto a magazine that he had placed in front of her was, even by the notoriously lax standards of the record industry, behaving repellently. Those cases sound cut-and-dried. But when you get down to more mundane levels of interaction between two adults of opposite sexes, the waters become much, much murkier.

In 1991 an appellate court ruled that the test of harassment was whether a "reasonable woman" would be concerned by the behavior under examination. This effectively suggests that harassment is harassment whenever a woman wants it to be so. Thus Susan was not harassed, because she wanted Tom to kiss her, but Maggie was harassed, because she did not want Colin to pester her with juvenile remarks. The problem arises, however, that Tom did not know for sure that Susan was ready for action until he tried his luck that night in her office. And Colin received no indication that his filthy juvenilities were not regarded as a charming antecedent to physical activity until Maggie's boyfriend whopped him in the face.

So harassment, as defined by the appellate court, is a crime of which the perpetrator may be unaware. Anyone who rips off a car or mugs an old lady knows that he is committing a crime that may, if the police are lucky and the courts tough, lead to some sort of punishment. On the other hand, a man who makes a pass at a woman in an office does not necessarily intend to inflict any harm. What appears to his victim to be an unwanted intrusion upon her may to him just be the first stage in a conventional courtship. He may just be behaving in the way he believes society, including its female members, expects of him.

Even now, men are still supposed to initiate sexual or romantic activity. As a result, men become used to playing the percentages. In the same way that even the best baseball player goes to bat knowing that the odds are against his scoring on that particular occasion, so men try out their arsenal of sweet-talk and suggestion in the full knowledge that rejection will outnumber acceptance by a pretty substantial margin. In the cases mentioned above, the only moral difference between Colin and Tom is that Tom picked up the sexual curveball more skillfully than Colin. The consequences of their actions, however, could not have been more different.

Until recently, there have been quite a few successful Toms about. Some 35 percent of all sexual relationships begin in the workplace—hardly surprising, when you reckon that the workplace is where we spend about 35 percent of our adult lives. But how many men still reckon that the unlikely upside of a sexual encounter is worth the probable downside of an ignominious firing? The very same behavior that, in a man whom they find attractive, is seen by women as being acceptable, not to say compulsory, is regarded as harassment coming from a man in whom they have no interest.

The more educated a woman is, according to a London *Sunday Times* poll on the subject, the more likely this is to be the case. A successful lawyer is far more likely than a mere sales assistant to perceive a wide range of activities, from physical contact right down to unwanted invitations to dinner, as potentially constituting harassment. Under these circumstances, in an age in which the opinions of a "reasonable woman" are the test of misbehavior, no man can afford to make a mistake. Not when that mistake is considered to be a crime.

THE HARASSED MAN

Men might be best advised to forget all about sex and live in an atmosphere of monastic paranoia. According to a survey by The Communications Group, published in 1992, 78 percent of major companies expect their work force to be affected by the need for politically correct behavior. In the office of the future, for example, men will neither compliment women on their dress, should they approve of it, nor suggest that it is inappropriate, if they do not. Nor will physical contact, under any circumstances, be appropriate. Sex, of course, is right out of the question.

The trouble is, it isn't. As my grandmother used to say, "Nothing propinks like propinquity." Or, to put it another way, if you jam lots of members of opposite sexes into a confined space for a minimum of eight hours a day, nature is bound to take its course. And the truth about sex in the workplace is that, just like sex anywhere else, it takes two to tango. Many's the time when the women are dancing just as hard as the men— or so the men, at least, believe.

Few subjects evoked more indignation among men to whom I spoke while researching this book than the use of female sexuality in the workplace. As far as many men are concerned, for every male pest there is a female flirt; for every woman who's being groped there is a prick that's being teased. In the words of Michael Bywater, writing in *Punch* magazine, "The woman who shuffles around at home in a pair of condemned and meaty jeans will dress like a mistress or a $1,000 hooker for the office and exert all the sexual charms to go with it; the batted eyelids, the little gestures, the turning of the wrists, the touching of the sleeve. She will do this to get what she wants."

Alex Kershaw, writing in the British edition of *GQ*, put it another way, when he quoted a friend, Mike, complaining to his fellow bachelors: "We've got all these babes in little black dresses and high heels at work. You ask them out, you know, ask them if they fancy a drink sometime, and they get really fucking aggressive. When they don't fancy you, they think you're hassling them. If they do fancy you and you don't make a move, they think you're a wimp."

Commenting on the record industry, which, as we have seen, is not known for the sensitivity of its male employees, one female publicist told *Entertainment Week* magazine, "I've seen more women eager to look like bimbos or sexually service someone than I have encountered men who are sexual harassers in this business." But are these women exploiting their sexuality, or are their actions simply being misinterpreted by those around them? Do men have the right to complain about women's alleged misbehavior?

The same question arises in the low-level vulgarity that is at the heart of so many harassment cases. We all know about the men who put dirty pictures on the wall or make remarks about women's breasts, but some would claim that it's by no means one-way traffic. Take the case of Donna van den Bergh. She's a British legal secretary who won $8,500 (we Brits go in for bargain-basement judgments) in a harassment-related suit for wrongful dismissal. She claimed her boss, Anthony Hammett, had told a risqué story during an office lunch and subsequently fondled her breasts, a charge he strenuously denied.

It emerged in court that at the same lunch, Mr. Hammett had been encouraged by various other secretaries to eat a seven-inch chocolate penis covered in cream. This is the sort of scenario that anyone who has ever worked in an office may recognize. Just as the guys can't be trusted once they've downed a couple of beers, so the typing pool descends to unimaginable depths of depravity once the cocktails have started flowing at the annual office party.

Mr. Hammett, one imagines, did not feel particularly happy about the prospect of sucking on a seven-inch chocolate schlong. He may very well have felt embarrassed by a confectioner's parody of his own genitalia, just as a woman might when confronted with, for example, a breast made out of Jell-O. To add to this, the act of simulated fellatio would be enough to confuse and even upset the most open-minded male heterosexual, touching as it does upon the deepest-seated fears and taboos concerning homosexuality.

All in all, a "reasonable man" might very well conclude that Mr. Hammett was being harassed on the occasion of the lunch in question. Indeed, the tribunal itself commented that the secretaries who had bought the penis had been "crude" and guilty of "inappropriate conduct."

That Mr. Hammett did not sue was, presumably, due to the ignominy that he would have brought upon himself for so doing. After all, he's a man. And, what's more, he's a boss. As with so many other instances in which the man is on the receiving end of an action that is interpreted as reprehensible when done to a woman, any protest is seen as being unmanly.

Female contempt for men who *do* protest appears to be universal. It's as if women suffer from a failure of the imagination. They simply don't understand that men are just as likely as they are to be hurt by offensive actions. A man is meant to be invulnerable. Once he has revealed the possibility of weakness, he is somehow less than a man.

Yet 10 percent of men in an American survey claimed to have been sexually harassed at work (one British survey put that figure at 37 percent). And Britain's leading agony aunt (as advice columnists are called), Claire Rayner, maintains that there is little difference in the effect upon men and women of repeated, oppressive sexual taunting or victimization. "The men are as hard put-upon," she remarks.

"I remember a letter I ran in the paper from a young man who was going through hell because he was the only feller at work, working with women. They de-bagged him [i.e., pulled his pants down]. They covered his penis with paint. They stuck feathers over his bottom. They put him through hell and all anyone could do was laugh and fall about. He said, 'If I don't laugh I'm a misery and I don't know what to do. I'm getting scared to go to work and I can't get another job. What do I do?'

"It was a terrible situation because he was eighteen, working with women in their thirties, forties, and fifties. I was furious. How dare they treat him like that? The other way round there'd be all hell let loose."

Courts have tended to take a different line when victims are male. A

Rhode Island court awarded a man damages of just one dollar after he claimed that his boss had coerced him into having sex with his (the boss's) secretary. In another case, a Michigan jury awarded a paltry one hundred dollars to a man whose bottom was fondled by female colleagues who also sent him suggestive sex notes.

As long as women still have much less power than men, they can claim a certain license because they are the underdogs. But in their 1992 book *Megatrends for Women,* Patricia Aburdene and John Naisbitt predict that the next decade will see women CEOs of numerous Fortune 500 corporations. As women rise to the top in ever-increasing numbers, that justification by virtue of handicap will wear thin.

The first cases are already emerging of powerful female bosses making it plain to ambitious young men that their careers will greatly be helped by a spot of corporate sex. According to a survey conducted by Continental Research and reported by *Company* magazine, one man in every thirty has been told by a female superior that his career would benefit if he agreed to have a relationship. Of the men who said "Yes," some 50 percent found that the woman in question was telling the truth.

Maybe social attitudes are changing too. As the final proofs of this book were being prepared, a Los Angeles jury awarded $1 million damages to thirty-one-year-old Sabino Gutierrez, who had been sexually harassed by his female boss. She would lock him in her office and demand to be kissed and cuddled. When he rejected her advances and married another woman, he was demoted, his office was demolished, and his personal belongings taken away. Mr. Gutierrez was represented by an attorney described as "the feistiest feminist lawyer in the West." Right on, sister.

THE ARMOR-PLATED MALE

Inequality is not the only factor that has always underpinned the hypocrisy of harassment. Burned deep into our minds is the idea that no man should really allow himself to be hurt by a woman. The wife betrayed by her husband, for example, may be humiliated, but she can expect the sympathy of all who hear her story. The man betrayed is merely a cuckold. For all that women discuss the fragility of the male ego, there seems to lurk in their hearts the idea that men remain fundamentally immune to their actions. Indeed, female contempt for male fragility could be held to imply an expectation of, and even a need for, male invulnerability.

Watching my small daughters, I have begun to wonder whether this does not have its roots in the relationship between a little girl and her father. At the beginning of her life, a girl learns that Daddy *is* invulnerable. She can jump up and down on him, kick him, punch him, say what she likes, do what she will—it makes no difference. He isn't really hurt and he always loves her.

Similarly, it is absolutely vital for a little girl to be able to flirt with her father, secure in the knowledge that he will respond positively to her, reinforcing her self-confidence, without taking advantage of her in any way at all. It is quite disconcerting, in these days of child abuse and social workers, to discover that your two- and three-year-old daughters will behave in ways that are overtly sexual. But they do.

As they grow up, could it be that women carry with them this memory of their father's immunity? Throughout this book, we will come across the inability of intelligent women to draw parallels between what hurts them and what might hurt a man, whether physically or emotionally. This theme of denial, of the refusal to empathize and of the absolute unwillingness to assume responsibility, will reappear again and again. Many women *need* to be able to blame men for their predicaments. To accept their own responsibility or complicity would be to admit to a series of desires, whether for self-advancement, admiration, or simply sexual excitement, that they have been conditioned to deny or repress.

This is a process that begins on the playground. As Deborah Tannen has observed, girls' conversations, games, and social structures tend to be centered on a search for intimacy, inclusion, and popularity. While boys compete for status, girls aim for acceptance within a group. Of course, little girls can be vicious to one another, but studies suggest that that rarely takes the form of face-to-face verbal or physical action. Since, however, girls' fundamental desires may well be as strong as any boy's, they have to learn the ways in which a good girl gets what she wants without actually admitting it.

Much is said about the way in which men perceive powerful, assertive women to be bitches. Less often is it admitted that women are just as critical as men when other women step out of line. The demand for self-effacement originates from the moment little girls learn to play with one another.

A similarly conformist pressure applies to sex. For all the propaganda of the women's magazines, which portray the modern woman as a creature in control of her own sexuality and unabashed about the demands she makes for its satisfaction, there are still strong forces that demand that a woman deny her sexual desires. Just as her mother may have told her that nice girls don't, so a certain puritan strand of the women's movement seeks to persuade her that any sexual encounter—and certainly any encounter that goes wrong—can only be interpreted as a form of male oppression. The politically correct woman is as defenseless in the face of a big, strong, beastly man as any tremulous Victorian maiden.

Just to make matters worse for modern, working women, the signals they send out to the particular man in whom they are interested may be picked up and misinterpreted by a hundred men toward whom they are entirely indifferent. When this happens, a telling combination of upbringing and ideology insists that they must claim they weren't sending out any signals at all.

Women are left with a mass of mutually contradictory impulses and instructions. The idea that women can only be considered as passive victims of male abuse has prevented discussion of their own active participation as agents of sexual harassment. Given the relative scarcity of situations in which women both outnumber men in the workplace and control executive power, it is unlikely that there are many examples of the type of overt harassment described by Claire Rayner. But, as with many issues in the sexual debate, the fact that there are not mirror images of misbehavior between one sex and another does not mean that there are not traits in women that are equivalent to, if not the same as, those in men.

DRESS FOR EXCESS

The two men quoted earlier, complaining about the way some women dress for work, speak for many of their male counterparts who feel that the overt sexuality of some women's clothes—the "Executive Tart" look, as it is known in the British advertising trade—constitutes a form of what one might term passive harassment. It exploits a man's sexual responses, despite the women's claim to have quite different intentions. Are the men being fair?

Most males in white-collar occupations come to work in clothes that were specifically designed to give away as little information as possible about their bodies. A suit may be smart, but it carries few sexual overtones. Meanwhile their female colleagues can, they believe, parade before them in high heels and even higher skirts, both of which broadcast a clear sexual signal.

Over the last few years, as Michael Bywater suggested, garments that were once considered to be the preserve of call girls have been turning up on the backs of career girls instead. The power of the erotic was demonstrated by a female friend of mine who applied for the post of editor of an English national newspaper. She arrived for her interview with the paper's proprietor wearing a tiny skirt and stiletto heels, both of which showed off her slender physique to its best advantage.

Her would-be boss suggested that they conduct the interview on his office sofa (the suggestion, it should be said, was that they be placed next to, rather than on top of one another; this was no casting couch). He sat there next to this vision of loveliness, asking her questions and puffing on his cigar. The more the interviewee preened upon the sofa, the heartier the puffs became. He eventually generated a cloud of cigar smoke so intense that it set off his fire alarm, whereupon a minion had to be summoned to reset the building's alarm system, lest the water sprinklers burst into life and drench both the proprietor and his luscious would-be employee.

The newspaper magnate may have reacted in a way that is characteristic of his generation as much as his gender. Younger men have become increasingly accustomed to female company. After a while, the chocolate factory principle applies and even the most ardent consumer loses his sweet tooth. The presence of attractively dressed women becomes a delight, but not, with any luck, a distraction.

That, however, does not necessarily diminish the resentment that some men feel. This is motivated, in part, by sheer jealousy of a woman's sexual power, and partly by the fact that, in any discussion of harassment, the very mention of female complicity or encouragement is ruled out on the grounds of political incorrectness. Many women, including the fashion writers and commentators on newspaper fashion pages, will strenuously deny any responsibility for the effect that their style of dress may have on their male colleagues. Their appearance, they say, has nothing whatsoever to do with wishing to appeal to men. Are they sure?

This is an area where caution is required. No one wants to give an excuse to a man who mistreats a woman and then claims, "She was asking for it." But, at the same time, the belief that it is unacceptable to draw a connection between a grown woman's actions and their possible consequences is fundamentally childish. Yet it repeats itself time and again and will resurface continually throughout this book. Nor is it something that can be allowed to pass without serious comment, since the way in which women are absolved from responsibility directly impinges on another repeated phenomenon, namely the criminalization of male behavior.

Men continually carry the buck. In *Backlash*, for example, Susan Faludi devotes a fascinating and entertaining chapter to an account of the way in which the moguls of the fashion world attempted to force women into miniskirts and fancy underwear during the 1980s in the hope of reducing their status as independent, intelligent human beings. All American women really wanted to wear, claims Faludi, who has copious statistical evidence with which to back up her assertions, were basic cotton panties and sensible suits with knee-length, size 16 skirts.

Yet many of the garments Faludi regards as unacceptable were the creation of female designers, who wore their feminist credentials with pride. Katharine Hamnett and Donna Karan, for example, sold their miniskirts as dashing clothes made *by* independent women *for* independent women. The staple sexy garment of the late eighties—the diminutive black Lycra mini—was introduced to the world, not by sexist businessmen intent on the oppression of women, but by Debbie Moore, a former model turned entrepreneuse, whose Pineapple label epitomized female enterprise and freedom.

Wherever the look first emerged scarcely matters. What is certain is that to walk down city streets, on either side of the Atlantic, at any time between about 1987 and 1992, was to be confronted with huge numbers of women whose supposed enslavement to the short skirt looked as enthusiastic as it was voluntary.

In the fall of 1992, when the fashion industry was busily promoting the new long skirt as the definitive look for our time, I happened to be traveling extensively in the United States and Europe. I also addressed a conference of working women in London. The vast majority of the women I met or observed were still wearing variations on the short skirt, whether neat and businesslike, or tight and sexy. Retailers stocking the long look may have been taking a bath that season. But they knew that gradually women would decide to treat themselves to something different, not because they were foolish, nor because they were enslaved by a male conspiracy, but because they were human. And most of us like a little novelty in our lives. In a year or two, everyone may be wearing long, at which point—naturally—a brand-new short look will reemerge.

Women, then, are active participants in the fashion game. But how powerful can an artfully stitched piece of cloth be? Do men have a right to be as bothered by women's clothes as women seem to be by men's jokes, or their pinups? Most women do not choose to appear at work as if dressed for the bordello. In the words of Sally Vincent, writing in the London *Independent*: "All women believe themselves to be variously deformed. This is why when they try something on they're not thinking, is this an asking-for-it dress, or does it send out signals I'd be unwilling to deliver on? They're thinking, will it camouflage the enormity of my butt?"

When they go to work, they're also thinking, "Will this enable me to be taken seriously at this month's sales meeting?" Even so, women know that certain items of clothing are overtly sexual and so do men. You only have to look at the language of the fashion pages to see that clothes are frequently promoted on the basis of their sex appeal.

Cosmopolitan magazine would be the first to echo the line that clothing is unrelated to male response. Yet the headlines on the fashion pages of the twentieth-anniversary issue of British *Cosmo* tell a very different story. They read, "Fun-loving . . . heartbreaking . . . traffic-stopping . . . pleasure-seeking . . . eye-catching . . . show-stopping . . . breathtaking . . . attention-grabbing . . . head-turning."

Underneath these headlines, *Cosmo* girls are enticed with copy like, "Be flirty and funky with fringes . . . Wear the ultimate in eye-catching cling . . . If you've got it, flaunt it in the ultimate, must-have catsuit . . . Be stunning . . . Be the centre of attention."

A February 1989 feature in the American edition of *Cosmo* was even more specific about the sexual subtext of women's clothing. Titled "How to make an impact on a man," it advised readers to "Wear body hugging styles, lots of jewelry, vivid eye make-up and lipstick. A lush style is a sexual signaler. . . . If you have good legs, wear a very tight short skirt and very high heels. Bend over with your back to a man to pick something up or look in a file drawer, etc. . . . Always wear perfume . . . Every woman seriously interested in attracting men should invest in a short black leather skirt and wear it with heels." Moving from clothing to behavior, the story continued, "Run your fingers lightly over a man's knuckles. It will send shivers up and down and all around him . . . Feel his muscles . . . Cross and uncross your legs at lot . . . Talk sexy or at least suggestive . . . Drop anything as you pass his desk, then stoop down to gather it up. He'll help. Lean close to him, put your hand on his shoulder to steady your balance."

These extracts were read out by Lawrence Diggs, a member of the board of directors of the National Council of Free Men—a nationwide men's organization—in a lecture at San Francisco State University in February 1990. He went on to say, "If this article was isolated and if women did not use these tactics to put constant pressure on men to have sex, and if they didn't work, we could laugh it off. If time permitted, I could quote from hundreds of such articles. If all these articles were combined into one text, it could be called, 'How to rape a man, have him feel responsible for your orgasm and get paid for it.' "

To which most men would reply, "Hey, I should be so lucky." Because what man is ever going to admit that he agrees with Mr. Diggs? What man is ever going to say that he doesn't like it if some foxy babe in a tight leather skirt bends over in front of his desk? And what woman is ever going to believe him?

Men, after all, are supposed to be primed to have sex any time, anywhere. Anything less than that, and they are not fully male. Of course, if they actually go ahead and act upon their urges, then they may very well be called harassers, or even rapists, which puts them in something of a bind: damned if they don't, and double-damned if they do.

Personally, I do not feel myself to be under siege in the way that Mr. Diggs appears to. But I do wonder whether there is any moral difference between the imposition of female sexuality upon an unwilling or uninterested man, and the imposition of male sexuality upon a woman. Any man who is being honest, as opposed to saying what he thinks he is supposed to say, will admit that there is little fun to be had from being continually propositioned by a woman in whom he has no interest. It's just that we are not supposed to admit it.

Enough has been written by authors such as Naomi Wolf about the pressure imposed on women by the images in glossy magazines for us all to be aware that beauty is a two-edged sword, the demand for which can be more of a burden than a blessing. But many of these images are created, not by men, but by women. At the time that its twentieth anniversary issue was published, there were only two men on the editorial staff of British *Cosmopolitan*. And one of them was the editor's secretary.

Women "trap" their sisters by the perpetuation of the so-called Beauty Myth, because the wearing of revealing clothes and seductive makeup is an exercise in female power. And as long as men are susceptible to the seductive charms of an attractive woman, this will continue to be the case. In her recent book, *Women on Top,* Nancy Friday comments upon the struggle between a woman's delight in exhibitionism and her need to deny that delight, or its consequences.

She remarks, "I am not sure whether women's new sense of the power of their beauty extends to a sequential awareness of their responsibility for the erotic wheels they have set in motion by drawing attention to themselves. . . . What we have today is a war not just between women but within the woman herself: how consciously should a woman admit to beauty and use it to get what she wants? . . . Perhaps we are . . . close to admitting to women's ancient competition for the eye of the beholder, not as a mindless sport devised by wicked men to set women against one another, but as a powerful force in natural selection, one that is built into the species. What has always made the competition so deadly is women's denial that it exists."

They may not have the option for very much longer. On January 23, 1992, Jeremy Campbell reported from America for readers of the London *Evening Standard* as follows: "In New York [this week] a bevy of reputable psychiatrists outraged feminist orthodoxy by blaming sexual harassment on women's willing enslavement to fashion designers and the erotic clothes that are a must for the nineties. The psychiatrists poured scorn on the pretensions of designers to promote 'female empowerment' with their Madonna-inspired, underwear-out look. Business consultants have even started telling female employees: if you want more respect from your male colleagues, put some clothes on."

Here we have an equal and opposite force to that which demands that men make no compliments toward their female colleagues, lest any inadvertent offense be caused. In order to ensure that no man be charming, no woman will be attractive. Thus will the sensibilities and weaknesses of both sides be protected. The Ayatollah could not have done a better job of making life miserable for us all.

GET A LIFE

There is, of course, an alternative. It's called growing up and learning some manners. A man who feels obliged to be offensive to women is not just a man who is oppressive: He is quite simply beneath contempt. A man who is not self-controlled enough to temper his hormones at the sight of the first well-turned leg to pass before him across the office carpet is (a) too immature to be trusted with any sort of executive responsibility, and (b) a loser.

Equally, any woman tough enough to handle a responsible job should also be tough enough to tell a man when to get lost. In the words of Camille Paglia, speaking to Leslie White of the London *Sunday Times* in May 1992: "There is absolutely nothing we can do to desexualise the workplace, so women must be constantly signalling what their intentions are and how they wish to be treated. When a man has crossed that line and said something vulgar, she must stop it immediately. The Clarence Thomas thing was just a crock . . . you're telling me that this guy said he liked her breasts and she went home and cried? Oh, puh-leese, give me a break. The idea that women are victims of men and have to get help from committees is absurd."

Surely the route to a happy relationship within the workplace lies in a genuine equality of both opportunity and responsibility. The more each side feels that it is getting a fair deal, the less it is likely to complain. America's twin obsessions with litigation and political correctness, together with the self-defining nature of sexual harassment legislation, may point the way toward a hellish vision of a repressed, neopuritan workplace, but there is an alternative.

French law makes harassment (irrespective of the gender of perpetrator or victim) punishable by fines, or even imprisonment, but it is very specific about what constitutes criminal harassment. This is defined as "a word, gesture, attitude or behavior by a superior with a view to compelling an employee to respond to a solicitation of a sexual nature."

In this context, bad manners are not enough. There has to be an element of coercion, blackmail, or abuse of power, any one of which constitutes an undeniable violation of the trust that an employee has placed in his or her superiors. Faced with the question of a woman who is confronted with dirty pictures, stupid remarks, or unwanted passes from colleagues of equal rank, Veronique Neiertz, the French minister for women's rights, remarked, "What is wrong with *un gifle*—a slap round the face? Be clear, it is blackmail to make sexual advances to someone who depends on you for their work. . . . In the case of blackmailing harassment the state has something to say. Otherwise, the relations between men and women are merely part of life."

In other words, the proper response for a Maggie, faced with a sniggering Clive, is simply to tell him to stop. No one, irrespective of gender, should force unwanted attentions on another person *once that person has made it clear that the attentions are unwanted.* But the obsessive hunting down of real or imaginary sexual misconduct in the workplace will result, like all witch hunts, in far more pain, suffering, and damage than the problem itself could ever cause.

Helen Gurley Brown is right, up to a point: The presence of men and women can bring spice and creativity to a workplace, but it depends on everyone being in on the deal. If men act like brutes, women have every right to get offended. But if women insist on assuming a spurious sense of moral self-righteousness, they should not be surprised if the atmosphere they engender is less than inspiring.

CHAPTER 6

Crying Rape,
and Crying Wolf

According to official government figures, the average American woman currently stands a 1-in-2,630 chance of being raped during the course of the year. This figure varies dramatically, however, between one part of the country and another. The vast majority of rapes and attempted rapes take place within major metropolitan areas. Within the entire rural and small-town population of the United States, there have only (and I am aware that *only* is an unfortunate word in these circumstances) been about 7,000 reported rapes per annum in recent years. In a typical twelve-month period, 1 North Dakota woman is raped for every 8,333 members of the state's female population, while the risk in Atlanta, Georgia—the most dangerous city in the country—shoots up to 1 in 617.

If we take the sexual lifespan of the same Ms. Average to be from fifteen to eighty, a total of sixty-five years, and factor that into 2,630, the odds against her being raped during that time currently stand at about forty to one. Yet even that greatly exaggerates the risk, since the vast majority of rapes are committed against women aged sixteen to thirty. If government figures are accurate, a woman who has reached her thirties unscathed runs a negligible risk of assault thereafter. Her chances of being involved in a serious road accident, or of suffering from breast cancer, are far, far higher.

But that begs a big question: Are government figures accurate? It is commonly believed that the rapes reported to the police are only the tip of an iceberg of sexual assaults. In an earlier chapter I quoted the *Life* magazine report that claimed that there were 683,000 rapes per annum in the United States. This is more than seven times the reported figure. If it were true, the odds on a woman being raped at some point in her life would fall to around one in five. Yet that is not the end of the story. A study of 930 "randomly selected adult women" conducted by the National Institute for Mental Health in San Francisco in 1978 found that 44 percent of those women had endured a rape or an attempted rape at least once. Within that figure, there may be a very wide variation in the seriousness of the events referred to and the effects upon the women concerned. But even so, if it is an accurate reflection of the truth, we live in the midst of a maelstrom of sexual violence.

Whom are we to believe? Looking at the official figures again, there is little sign of the frequency of assaults upon women that campaigners claim to have identified. There certainly was a rapid rise in the number of reported cases between 1970 and 1980. This was the period during which the women's movement first alerted society to the prevalence of sexual assault, and the difficulties faced by women seeking to report it (they were not believed, they were assumed to have been responsible for the attack, and so forth). In 1970, there were 37,990 reported cases of rape and attempted rape. In 1980, there were 82,990. This rise of more than 100 percent far exceeded those for violent crime in general, or for murder (the murder rate for women rose by some 20 percent during the same period). So it is possible that it was largely due to an increased willingness among women to report their victimization, rather than an increase in victimization itself.

During the 1980s, the number of reported rapes rose much more slowly, increasing 14 percent and reaching 94,500 by 1989. Given that the same period saw an increasing awareness of the importance of rape as a social and political issue—typified by films such as *The Accused,* for which Jodie Foster won the 1988 Academy Award for Best Actress—it might be thought that the reported figure was getting ever closer to the total. Certainly, the number of women murdered—and murder is a crime that is almost impossible to conceal—actually dropped during that period. Research to which I will return later also suggests that, contrary to public myth, the rate of domestic violence against women actually declined in the 1980s. So there is little concrete evidence of a general rise in serious violence against women, a category under which I would include rape. Yet researchers on both sides of the Atlantic still maintain that the true rape figures are far, far higher than anything produced by any official agencies.

The one thing we can be sure of is that the fear of rape is all-pervasive in our society. Vast numbers of women tell researchers that they feel unsafe on the streets after dark. They are terrified by the prospect of being alone in a railway or subway carriage. In London, even the city's famous black cabs—once considered the one place in the city in which a woman was absolutely safe—have been sullied by reports of attacks on female passengers.

The problem appears to be universal. Holland is a country of astonishing tolerance. The age of consent is twelve; many drugs are legal; pornography and prostitution flourish free of government interference. Yet following research revealing that one Dutch woman in three had suffered some form of sexual abuse, and one teenager in five had experienced some form of sexual violence, the government launched a multimillion-dollar TV advertising campaign designed to alter male sexual behavior. Marie Jose van Bavel, the campaign's spokeswoman, commented, "We want to make men aware of the unsolicited side of their sexual behavior and the stereotypes upon which this is based. We also want to prevent sex crimes by getting youths and men to realize their responsibilities."

The degree to which men are now seen as a hostile force can be judged by a piece of advice issued by Men Stopping Rape, Inc., a group at the University of Wisconsin. It suggested, "The man who finds himself walking down a street behind a lone woman should go to the other side of the street in order to relieve her entirely reasonable fear that he will rape her."

Similar suggestions have also been made by local authorities in Britain. When I first read about them I felt disgusted and offended. The notion that a man's very presence on the same street as a woman constitutes a potential threat degrades him. It suggests a form of sexual apartheid, in which men—being violent, unclean, second-class citizens—must predicate all their actions on the assumption of their potential guilt.

And yet, no sensible man could deny that a woman walking alone along a sidewalk might very well be frightened by the sound of his footsteps behind her. So what is a man to do or think when confronted with female fear? How is he to respond to the accusations about the ways in which male sexuality is being used as an offensive weapon in the war against women? Most of us are afflicted by a mass of different, often contradictory, opinions and emotions. In the first place, one feels shame. Then comes a sense of denial. Like revisionist historians disputing the existence of Auschwitz, we tell ourselves that it can't be true. We question the basis on which research was carried out. What were the questions? How was rape defined? Who replied? Did they have an axe to grind? And what was the researcher's hidden agenda?

In February 1992, the British columnist Bryan Appleyard, writing in the London *Sunday Times*, quoted a guidebook from the London Rape Crisis Centre called *Sexual Violence: The Reality for Women*, as follows: "Rape is all the sexual assaults, verbal and physical, that we all suffer in our daily contact with men. These range from being 'touched up' and 'chatted up' to being brutally, sexually assaulted with objects. Throughout this book we use rape to describe any kind of sexual assault."

Appleyard attacked the Rape Crisis Centre's view that "While men may choose not to commit rape, they are all capable of it." This he described as "sexual fascism." He admitted that "the objective fact of rape is appallingly common," but wondered whether "we want the police and courts probing into every contested bedroom scene. Should we drag every movie-crazed, sexually incompetent, adolescent date-rapist through the courts?" Finally he concluded that "the feminists are right when they say that women have often suffered in silence, but they are stupidly wrong when they use that as a simple, brutal tool of global social analysis or as an indictment of all men."

Appleyard did not have the space to amplify why the feminists are "stupidly" wrong, but I do. The first stupidity is an elementary error of logic: All buttercups are yellow flowers, but not all yellow flowers are buttercups. Similarly, all rapists are men, but that does not mean that all men are rapists. This is, of course, part of an attempt to induce guilt by association, the second half of which rests upon a linguistic trick, namely the use of the word *capable*.

The notion that all men are "capable" of rape is either, as Appleyard points out, absurdly prejudicial, or meaningless. Given that I, for example, am six feet tall and weigh around 180 pounds, I could theoretically overpower most women. So why don't I? Answer: because in the more meaningful sense of the word *capable*—a meaning that takes account of psychology, conditioning, desire, and so forth—I am not remotely capable, let alone desirous, of such an act.

Nor are the vast majority of men. To brand us with a stereotype that is profoundly negative and carries with it the suggestion of automatic guilt for a series of dreadful crimes is an act that may not be "fascistic" in the most pedantic sense of the word—there being no authoritarian state involved—but it certainly is unscientific, extremist, obscurantist, and antisocial, which should be plenty to be getting on with.

That does not, however, get away from the fact that many women have horror stories to tell. When a man comes to think about these stories and attempts to discuss them, he will, however, encounter a further difficulty, which is this: How can a man talk about rape without either accepting the blame that is thrust upon him by campaigners such as those from the Rape Crisis Centre, or, on the other hand, appearing to condone the actions of the rapist?

I was given an illustration of the problem when asked onto a British television debate with a representative of Women Against Rape. During the course of the broadcast, which took place in the wake of the Mike Tyson trial, we took pains to keep our conversational tone as reasonable and nonaggressive as possible (somewhat, I suspect, to the disappointment of the program's producers).

Afterward, we had a brief conversation in the studio's greenroom. I mentioned that I was writing a book about men and would be interested in talking to members of Women Against Rape at greater length to discuss the social or psychological pressures that might be acting on the two people involved in a supposed date-rape. It seemed to me that it might be an oversimplification to see the event purely in terms of his assault upon her.

Not to that woman it wasn't. Any time that a man had sex with a woman without her express consent, no matter what the circumstances, it could only be seen in one way: He raped her, and that was the end of it. There could only be one interpretation because there was only one form of oppression, the male oppression of women. Men oppressed women because their economic superiority gave them power over women. For instance, she said, men had more cars than women. So women were put into a position of dependence upon them at the end of an evening. This meant that a man was given an opportunity to go to a woman's home, where she might be vulnerable to his assault.

The WAR spokesperson was unwilling to accept that women were ever anything other than victimized. She finished our conversation by saying words to the effect that there was really no point in discussing the subject further. By the way, it might be best for me not to spend too much time writing about the subject because people might then conclude that I was trying to defend rapists. And I wouldn't want that, would I?

I could not have been warned off more effectively if Vito Corleone had left a horse's head in my bed on a Sunday morning. The message was clear: This is our turf and you're not welcome.

Well . . . it's not that simple.

YOUR SEXIEST SEX

The traditional idea of a rapist is a Jack the Ripper–style madman in a dark alley with a knife. One of the few generalizations that can be made about him with any degree of confidence is that, far from being the living embodiment of an oppressive patriarchy, he is likely to be lonely, insecure, and inadequate in his relationships with other people. He may have been a victim of abuse as a boy. Yet whatever the psychological background that may have led him to commit acts of sexual violence, few of us would be inclined to forgive him and I have no intention at all of attempting to justify or excuse his actions. But what of Bryan Appleyard's "movie-crazed, sexually incompetent, adolescent 'date rapist' "? What are we to make of him?

To the members of Women Against Rape there is no controversy here, either. The adolescent is a rapist, just as surely as the maniac. Their crimes are the same. There is no difference of nature or degree. Rape is rape, period.

I would suggest, however, that it is not. Of course, no woman should ever be forced to have sex when she does not wish to do so (and the same applies to men). Within the boundaries of the law, all of us have the fundamental right to determine how and with whom we wish to share our bodies. But there is as wide a variety in the forms of sexual assault as there is in physical assault as a whole. To take a parallel phenomenon: The law distinguishes between murder, manslaughter, and self-defense even though all those events end in a death. The difference between these various offenses is largely concerned with questions of motivation and/or the degree to which the victim's own actions may have contributed to his or her eventual demise. Much, for example, has been written and broadcast about female victims of domestic violence who finally kill their husbands. Many people feel that these women have been every bit as victimized as the men they murdered.

Why, then, should we refuse to distinguish between various forms of nonconsensual sex, even though those events all end in the unwanted penetration of a woman's body by a man's penis? There is surely an enormous gulf between the experience of a wife who has sex with her husband on a night when she would rather not have done so, and the woman who is held at knife-point by a stranger in a leather mask. En route, there is an infinite number of permutations of violence or coercion. So why are the very women who insist on the need to examine the possibility of provocation or mitigation in the case of a woman who commits murder the first to deny such consideration to a man accused of rape?

Once again, I am not trying to blame women for their misfortune. In fact, if at all possible, I would like to remove for the time being any consideration of guilt or blame for either party and merely look at the context in which both people find themselves. This is vitally important if there is to be any understanding of date-rape since, as matters stand, the whole phenomenon is overloaded with value judgments.

After all, when a woman makes a claim of date-rape, one of two alternative opinions has to be proved. Either he wanted sex and so did she, in which case she is blamed, both for the act itself and for bringing the case to court; or, he wanted sex and she didn't, in which case he is a criminal. Under those circumstances, objectivity soon vanishes and, as was amply demonstrated in the differing fortunes of Messrs. Tyson and Kennedy Smith, any court proceedings rapidly become a form of beauty contest. Jurors openly base their judgments upon entirely nonlegal criteria suggested by their personal response to plaintiff and defendant.

I would suggest, instead, that the phenomenon of date-rape is an entirely predictable result of the extraordinarily confused state of contemporary sexual morality. Both men and women are being asked to cope with contradictory demands, which can only—as matters stand—end in women enduring the pain and trauma of unwanted sexual experience, while men find themselves treated as criminals.

No one profits from the situation. The woman's relationships with other men may be poisoned for years to come. The man may have his life ruined by a jail sentence for an act regarded as despicable by the whole of society. Meanwhile, debate on this most complex of issues is stifled by the heavy hand of political correctness, whose massive ideological influence is in no way merited by the shoddy, illogical, and psychologically inaccurate nature of its arguments.

Taking those points one at a time: It is a cliché to say that we are surrounded, more than ever, by images of sexuality. Wherever we go, we see advertisements, TV shows, rock videos, newspapers, and magazines that flaunt sexual imagery, the vast majority of it based upon the desirability of women.

Something very important has happened, however, over the past decade or so. The woman is not merely the passive sex object of days gone by. Nowadays she is also an active protagonist. Madonna, for one, has made an entire industry out of the exploitation of her own body, and every possible sexual permutation to which it can be put. The modern woman is in control, and she is often photographed in advertisements or fashion pages surrounded by submissive and adoring men, as if James Bond had been replaced by Jane. Young women, leafing through their glossy magazines, are bombarded with articles and photographs exhorting them to greater sexual activity and achievement.

In 1991, for example, British *Cosmopolitan* magazine promoted 102 different features on its cover. Of these, just over half were specifically sexual, including:

How come you're in love after one night of sex?

What men do wrong in bed

Great sex is crazy positions, silly noises and other undignified things

Addicted to sex: Is he your hero or your heroin?

Yes, yes, oh yes! Men fake orgasms too

Keep it up! The care and feeding of his erection

When your mind wants sex but your body says no

101 uses of sex

The new sexual fantasies

His ego, his sex drive

The formula clearly works, because *Cosmo*'s circulation soared by more than 48,000 copies a month, taking its audited monthly sales above 450,000 and deservedly winning its editor, Marcelle D'Argy Smith, the title of Magazine Editor of the Year. More to the point, those cover lines represent a philosophy that has long been central to popular feminism. This is that women have every right to be actively sexual, just as much as men have always been. There is no reason for a woman to be ashamed of her sexuality, nor need she be shy in setting forward her demands for satisfaction.

In this chapter, as in others, I have singled out *Cosmopolitan*, but there is nothing remotely unusual or unique about its preoccupation with sex. Every young woman's magazine in the Western world thinks in exactly the same way. In the words of British *Elle* magazine, introducing its April 1992 sex survey (sponsored by Durex, a condom manufacturer), "For a growing number of women, the battleground for equality has shifted to between the sheets and they consider it a playground as much as a battle-zone. . . . They work hard and play hard (but not hard to get); they know what they like and they make sure they get it. . . . 'I just won't settle for sleeping with a man who doesn't bring me to orgasm on a regular basis,' stated one London woman. 'I tell my boyfriends exactly what to do, where to go, which buttons to press and, if they're not getting there, I'll tell them that, too.' "

The August 1992 edition of *Company*, a magazine for young British women, which is advertised as "The magazine for your freedom years," came with a free supplement, whose cover read as follows:

THE BEST SEX YOU'LL EVER HAVE

YOUR SEXIEST SEX GUIDE EVER

(give it to him—it's what you really want)

Revealed—we show you the 12 hottest sex positions

Sexual appetisers—how to fine-tune your foreplay

Oral sex—the pleasures, perils and techniques

Sex toys—we separate the hot from the hype

Raw passion—the glorious abandon of quick sex

16 wonderfully uncensored pages

A similar preoccupation with sex governs the fiction read by women. Writers such as Jackie Collins and Judith Krantz turn out gold-embossed paperback potboilers that compete with one another in the quantity, variety, and perversity of the sexual fare on offer. The vagina becomes a receptacle for an extraordinary range of implements, animal, vegetable, and mineral. Heroes are masterful and hung like donkeys. Heroines are gorgeous and insatiable.

This manic sex-obsession has no direct parallel in the male universe. The top shelves still groan with tit'n'ass magazines, but these are clearly seen as unsuitable for right-on, liberal men. Nonpornographic men's magazines such as *GQ* and *Esquire* may have the occasional sexy photograph of a hot young starlet. But, by and large, they seem much happier with tales of Hollywood actors, business scandals, and sporting heroism. One editor of a British men's magazine even revealed to me that all his publication's features on sex had to be written by women: If they ever published anything by a man that was even remotely honest, it was always condemned as offensively sexist by their ever-alert audience.

Men's fictional equivalents to Mesdames Collins, Krantz, et al., are such hard-boiled thriller writers as Robert Ludlum, Tom Clancy, and Frederick Forsyth, for whom women are an incidental diversion from the real issues of power and paranoia. The typical woman's heroine is a beautiful ingenue who proceeds to acquire copious quantities of orgasms, money, and clothes, not necessarily in that order of importance. The typical men's hero is a solitary outsider, faced by a host of enemies, who wins through despite them all. He is expressing men's fears and fantasies, which are all about independence (or the loss of it) and the ability to make one's mark in a hostile world. Sex, as a priority, comes remarkably far down the list. Clancy's hero, Jack Ryan, is given a beautiful wife. But he is far too busy saving the world to have much time left over for action between the sheets.

Perhaps it has always been so. From Medusa through Messalina to Madonna, men have always been fearful of unbridled female sexuality. Ancient myths and modern psychology speak of man's terror of the *vagina dentata*—the wound that has teeth, that leaves a man castrated and diminished. For however erect a man may be when he goes in, by the time he comes out he is flaccid and spent. In a bizarre repudiation of female power, feminism chooses to think of the phallus as the source of all threat, but in the battle between cock and cunt, the cock always comes out the loser.

This was the hidden agenda behind many a social convention. During the 1930s, my grandfather Bernard lived in Buenos Aires, the capital of Argentina. He once had dinner with a friend, whose daughter wanted to

go out to the movies with her boyfriend. In order to do this she had to
have a chaperone, who, in this case, was her aunt. The aunt was unexpectedly delayed, so the young couple pleaded with the girl's father to let
them go out without her. They were in danger of missing the start of the
film, they said. They would buy the aunt a ticket and she could join them
later. But the father stood firm. Until the chaperone arrived, which she
eventually did, he would not let them out of his sight.

Over dinner, my grandfather asked his friend why he had been so strict.
"Don José," he said, "your daughter's friend is an honorable young man.
He comes from a fine, respectable family. I am sure that your daughter
would have been quite safe with him."

The Argentinian laughed. "But Bernardo," he replied. "I have not the
slightest doubt that you are right. I am not concerned with what this
charming young man might do to my daughter. My only worry is what
she might do to him."

Now I am perfectly well aware that the fact that a woman might want
to dress or behave in a manner that is overtly sexual does not entitle a
man to abuse her, or to presume any consent on her part unless she has
actually given it. But a young, inexperienced man who flicks through his
girlfriend's books or magazines could be forgiven for thinking not only
that women were—to use a phrase—"aching for it," but also that he
would be falling down on the job of being a man if he didn't give it to
them, with orgasmic knobs on. Yet we remain convinced that it is men,
not women, who are obsessed with sex.

Society persists in believing that delicate, asexual women have to be
protected from the insatiable lusts of men. Supposedly radical feminists
are only too happy to portray women as eternal victims, helpless in the
face of male oppression and sexuality. It's almost as if the radicals want
to enshrine the victimization from which they derive their moral justification, even at the risk of undermining female power. The traditionalists
want to retain the gentle, submissive image of women. There seems little
difference between Andrea Dworkin announcing that no women like intercourse, and Barbara Bush telling Larry King, "We ought to tell children
that sex is . . . is death." From radical feminists to family values, the message is the same: Sex is bad and it's not our fault. It's all those horrible men.

BLAMING THE BOY

The fight to establish the innocence of the rape victim has been a long
and vital one. For too long, her suffering was doubled by the attitude that
she was as much at fault as her attacker. Even now, a woman giving
evidence against her attacker can expect his defense counsel to do every-

thing possible to suggest that she is a loose-living hussy only too eager to have sex with as many partners as possible. This is not a remotely acceptable or satisfactory situation. But are we any better off if we go to the other extreme and see her as being entirely without responsibility, particularly when all the punitive consequences descend upon the man?

College campuses have become the focus for concern in the date-rape issue. An April 1991 article in *Harper's Magazine* by Philip Weiss reported that Phyllis Riggs, the former coordinator of Dartmouth College's Sexual Awareness and Abuse Program, had found that 125 women were raped at Dartmouth every year. In this context, rape was defined as "unwanted completed sexual intercourse." In Weiss's words, "The trouble is that she set out to record *feelings* of being violated: she defined 'unwanted' sex to include situations in which a student, while 'certain at the time that s/he did not want to engage in the sexual experience . . . did not communicate her/his unwillingness because of a feeling of intimidation.' "

The use of word-structures such as "s/he" or "her/his" in this context is highly disingenuous. Increasingly, counselors on sexual issues are not employed to provide balanced judgments or advice. They are there to act upon allegations of bad behavior by men against women.

Such allegations are not hard to come by. At Dartmouth, a student accused of fondling one student and kissing another found his face plastered on posters across the campus, on which were the words, "a warning to all dartmouth womyn. beware this man. how many more ????? you may be next!!!!!" At Brown, the names of alleged sex-offenders were posted on bathroom walls. At the University of Wisconsin, men were ordered to "stop fantasizing about rape." Note the assumption that they were bound to have such fantasies.

Categories of "rape" and "attempted rape" have been broadened to include nonpenetrative sexual events, such as kissing and heavy petting. These can clearly lead to full sex, but they do not necessarily do so. A man who forcibly kisses a woman may, indeed, attempt to have sex with her as well, but it may equally be the case that he goes no further (just as it may be the case that he did not think that he was forcing himself upon her). None of this excuses the man's behavior, but it does mean that the nature of the event is not so easily defined as current orthodoxy might suggest.

Moreover, as Weiss remarks, "Respect for students' civil rights does not seem to be of primary concern to the activists, not when they see human rights being abused. The literature of the campus brigades contains definitions of proper and improper speech that smacks of thought control by the politically correct." Repeatedly, rape is considered to be one element in a patriarchal system that ranges from sexual harassment to male domination of class discussions. In such a context, an individual man—no matter how innocent he may believe himself to be—is guilty by virtue of his membership in an oppressive group—i.e., men as a whole. Comments Weiss, "The individual man is always responsible for the general problem, whether or not the woman he is with expresses her fears."

Details magazine organized a seminar on date-rape for its October 1991 issue. Four experts were invited to give their answers to a series of questions on the subject. They included Dr. Alan Berkowitz, who runs rape prevention clinics for students at Hobart and William Smith Colleges in New York, and Rikki Klieman, an attorney who has defended several men accused of date-rape.

Throughout their dialogue, Klieman and Berkowitz took very different views on the issue. Ironically, the latter was far stricter toward men in his interpretations. One wonders whether he was in some way comforted by the idea that the men were fully responsible for what went on: After all, if they bear the full burden of responsibility they must be very much the senior partners. Klieman, on the other hand, saw women as being much more active, much less innocent, and, by implication, much more equal.

One of the questions, for example, asked the respondents to imagine a scenario in which a woman invites a man to her apartment. They kiss. They have sex. She never says yes or no. In the morning she claims he raped her. Could she be right?

Berkowitz responded, "It could be rape, depending on the specifics of what happened. Many men believe that if a woman invites you to her apartment and kisses you, she wants to have intercourse with you and that it's okay to do it because she took the initiative. That's not right."

Klieman, however, asks, "How in heaven's name is a man supposed to know that it was against her will unless in some way or other she tells him?" On the other hand, she observes, "If they are kissing and petting and she says, 'No, I don't want to do this. I want you to stop,' and a man continues to act after that communication, in this day and age he is acting at his peril and would likely be arrested and, I think, probably convicted of rape."

A similar division occurred over the issue of whether a woman was a rape victim if she had given in to psychological pressure to have sex.

Berkowitz: "That would still be rape because the perpetrator did not make sure that she was consenting."

Klieman: "That's preposterous. Usually these cases tend to fall among young people—late adolescence, early twenties. There's a lot of ambiguity that goes on with young people in those stages. They're not quite sure what is exactly right and what is exactly wrong. It seems to me that to criminalize that conduct by calling the young man a rapist is never what the law intended when it enacted rape laws to protect women."

What happens if the alleged victim was drunk? Klieman, who is, re-member, a woman, and so may be expected to have had some experience of the female side of the mating game, remarks, "I cannot imagine a situation where I have been drinking that I would ever come close to a point of not being able to say no."

Berkowitz has less faith in a woman's ability to hold her drink: "If she was drunk, then he didn't have her consent. How can you consent if you're drunk?"

Berkowitz and others are trying to shift the definition of rape. To them, rape does not occur when a woman says "No," but a man carries on regardless. It occurs whenever a woman has not positively said "Yes." One begins to understand how rape activists are able to come up with the figures they like to bandy about.

Dr. Berkowitz tells the readers of *Details*: "The research suggests that anywhere from one-third to half of college women will experience an acquaintance rape or some other form of sexual assault." Can this be the case? If Dr. Berkowitz is right, far, far more rapes take place on campus every year than are currently reported for the entire nation. Maybe what he really means is not just that some college women will be the victims of genuine assaults, but also that lots of coeds will have bad nights and will then wake up the next morning with a sore head, look at the guy lying next to them and think, "Oh, shit." This he wishes to define as rape.

As matters stand, most young men and young women are socialized to behave in ways that increase the risk of a man being accused of rape. For young men are still expected to take girls out, pour a couple of drinks down them, plead everlasting love, and then make a pass. Young women are taught to expect some effort at seduction: It is almost an insult to them if a man does not at least try. To complicate the matter, they are also expected not to be too "easy." A certain degree of resistance is a sign of femininity and moral worth. Does a "nice" girl ever actually say, "Yes"? Or does she merely indicate her compliance? The final decision, of course, is hers, even if—and here is a crucial point—there may never be a moment at which anyone actually asks, "May I?" or gets a positive answer back.

What if the question is asked, however, and the answer comes back "No"? In the words of Rikki Klieman, "If there are young men around today who think that no means yes, they're in for trouble." Clearly she's right. Any man should work on the assumption that no means no. The consequences of misinterpretation are too drastic to risk. So it is merely as an aside that I observe that in a 1991 poll, conducted among female students at the University of Texas's psychology department, and reported in the London *Sunday Telegraph,* nearly 50 percent of all students admitted that they said "No" to sex when what they really meant was "Yes," or "Maybe." Their reasons for so doing ranged from a feeling that it was more feminine to be seen to resist, to a wish to see a man prove his desire by making him work a little bit harder for what he wanted.

To Barbara Amiel, the Canadian columnist who writes for the London *Sunday Times*, the date-rape controversy epitomizes the activities of a movement that "has moved from the liberal goal of equality between the sexes to the political goal of power for women, and is now well on the road to legislating out of existence the biologically based mating habits of our species. . . . "

Amiel continued, "Feminists wish male sexuality to be immaterial in criminal law. Women should be free to engage in any type of behavior that suits their own sexuality without regard to the consequences. This approach views men as vibrators: women may pick them up, switch them on, play around and then, if the off-switch doesn't work, sue the manufacturer for damages."

She concluded that the hidden agenda behind political attacks on male sexuality could be found in the fact that the National Organization for Women had just announced that its senior leaders were lesbians. I, however, would not claim that lesbianism is the key to the whole thing. But I wonder whether the motivation might instead be fear.

After all, leaving aside the horrifying, but still small, possibility of random assault, why should college women need to be protected from their peers? We are constantly told—indeed it is a cliché that has almost acquired the status of a truism—that teenage girls are far more mature than boys of the same age. Some might even suggest that teenage girls are incomparably more mature than boys of any age, right up to seventy and beyond. But, letting that pass, we can agree, I think, that they are certainly not less mature.

We also know that students at a university are all of roughly the same age and have approximately the same amount of money—usually very little. The male of the species has none of the social or financial advantages that might accrue to him in the outside world. So the notion asserted earlier by that representative of Women Against Rape, which saw the man as being in an inherently superior, oppressive position, simply does not hold true among young people in any sense other than physical strength.

In which case, if the girl is so mature, and suffers from no obvious economic or social disadvantages, why can't she look after herself? Of course, if she has been physically overwhelmed by someone using overpowering force, then she has every right to expect the law to act with utmost vigor on her behalf. And her assailant deserves the full weight of its disapproval. I've got no argument with that. But what if the date-rape panic isn't about real violence? What if it's about a fear of sex?

This is demonstrated most obviously as fear of the male. But its roots may lie elsewhere. Could it be that, understandably enough, some young women are afraid of their own sexuality? Could they feel unprotected, now that the taboos which once limited their activities, but protected their honor, have disappeared? We are, after all, only thirty years into the greatest shift in sexual patterns ever known to humankind: the freedom from pregnancy caused by the arrival of the Pill. We should not be surprised if young women still feel profoundly dislocated, not to say overwhelmed, by the new demands that have been placed upon them. Not everybody wants or is able to be the swinging, demanding, superconfident sex kitten put forward by the glossy magazines. It's much easier to retreat from the fray and blame it all on men.

The assertion that women blame men for problems that are really to do with themselves is increasingly being made by women writers, many of whom have come through the feminist movement. It helps to explain why such an apparently modern movement so often expresses itself in terms that are so traditional. Now we know why some women dress their bodies in jeans, but put their minds into crinolines. For women faced with the pressures of an entirely new responsibility, a reversion back into the role of the passive, helpless victim must seem comforting and secure.

More than that, a culture of victimization has grown up that seeks to treat every unpleasant aspect of life as a problem requiring treatment, counseling, and the apportioning of blame. One of the difficulties in writing this book has been the need to walk a fine line between the reasonable desire to recreate what I believe is a lost balance between the competing claims of the two sexes, and the unreasonable wish to appear more-victimized-than-thou.

As each side battles to put out competing claims of unfair treatment, there is a real danger that society will simply sink into a pit of sulky self-pity. The college women who claim that they are being assaulted by men are now being met by men who claim that they are harassed by women. In the speech given to San Francisco State University by Lawrence Diggs, to which I referred earlier, Mr. Diggs cites "A study at the University of South Dakota by Professor Cindy Strickman [which] showed that 16 percent of the male students, compared to 22 percent of the female students, felt that they had been coerced into sex. Half of those men said that they were psychologically coerced. The other half reported tactics such as being locked in cars, fondled and even blackmailed until they gave in."

Half of me responds to that much as Camille Paglia did to Anita Hill: "Puh-leese!" Be a man, I feel like saying. Grow up. But then the other half responds, "Yes, but why shouldn't these young men expect the same protection that is afforded to women? Why shouldn't they be allowed their insecurities and their uncertainties too?" The guiding principle behind this book, however, is that men and women should be treated as equals. They deserve equal amounts of compassion and sympathy. And they should accept equal amounts of responsibility.

LOVERS' TALES

Here is a story about young lovers on a summer's night. It may be apocryphal, although it was told to me as fact by Renate Olins, director of London Marriage Guidance. She had herself been told it by a female lawyer involved in the case it describes, who was appalled by its outcome. Its veracity hardly matters: What counts is the principle of the thing, which illustrates the double standard with which we tend to judge sexual behavior by men and women.

Let's begin. Two students went to a ball on a fine English summer's night. They drank champagne. They danced. They laughed and chatted away. One thing led to another and the boy suggested that they go outside, find a secluded spot, and see what happened next. The girl was only too willing to agree. So out of the ballroom they went, arm in arm, until they came to the sort of quiet, well-camouflaged garden hideaway in which, for centuries too numerous to count, swains and their maids have been getting to know one another just that little bit better.

As bad luck would have it, however, no sooner had they lain down next to one another on the grass than someone else, another courting couple perhaps, happened to pass the same way. So our two lovebirds got up, straightened their clothes, and went off to find somewhere else. Finally they found another little nook. It was by now getting late and the ground was dewy. So the boy, being a chivalrous sort of chap, put his jacket down on the ground and invited the girl to lie down on top of it, facing upward, while he lay down on top of her.

Once again, she consented with alacrity. They kissed, fondled, and fumbled. We've all been there, have we not? Clothes were removed and elastic twanged. But then, just as he was about to enter her, she suddenly changed her mind and said, "No." The young man had not read *Details*. He was not aware that when a girl says "No," he had better assume she means it. He thought she was just teasing. So he went ahead and had sex with her. The next day, she reported him to the police for rape.

He was arrested and charged. His lawyers advised him to plead guilty. Their reasoning was that there was no dispute that an act of sex had taken place. If the boy pleaded not guilty and the court found against him, he might face a severe sentence. If, on the other hand, he pleaded guilty, but was able to show both mitigating circumstances and a suitably contrite heart, he should get away with little more than a slap on the wrist. He had a completely blameless past, had never been in trouble, and, after all, the girl had hardly been seized at knifepoint. So the boy pleaded guilty. He was sent to jail for two years.

Now, I do not want to set up a charter for college sex-pests, but it is worth examining this story to see whether the young man it involves was really a criminal as the court's verdict suggests. Why was it appropriate for him to go to jail? As a convicted rapist, his chances of finding a good job or leading a successful adult life are now practically zero. His whole future has been thrown away because of one impetuous act. But when one examines that act, it is hard to see any crime that matches so terrible a punishment.

To the best of my knowledge, the young woman suffered no physical injury. She may very well have been traumatized—as much, perhaps, by all the legal proceedings as the act of sex itself—but is the trauma of a one-night stand that goes wrong so totally devastating that it requires the jailing of the other protagonist? And what of his reactions and his emotions? What if he was not the sex-mad beast of feminist myth? What if he was a young man who, if only for that one night, really was in love with the girl he was with? What if he was swept away by his emotions?

After all, a woman's supposed helplessness in the face of her emotions is thought to justify her actions. Susan Christie, a British army soldier who killed her lover's wife by slashing her throat with a butcher's knife, was originally sentenced to just five years imprisonment because she was considered to be in the grip of passions beyond her control. In court she said, "I did it for Duncan. I was so in love wth him I would do anything. That love was so strong, it was like a drug that you can't do without."

Nancy Friday points out that being swept away is the Nice Girl's excuse for sex for which she does not wish to be held responsible. In the American *GQ* feature on "What Women Really Want," referred to in an earlier chapter, the six feisty New York women who are being interviewed agree that they want to be "swept away" by an "aggressive male sexuality."

This idea is a staple of romantic fiction, too. When Scarlett O'Hara is picked up by Rhett Butler, carried upstairs and flung on her bed, before (once the bedroom door has closed) being ravished to within an inch of her life, what we have witnessed is an act of marital rape. Her look the next morning, however, suggests that she is the true victor. She has driven her man to act in this passionate way, despite all his attempts to stay cool. And, judging by the success of both book and film over more than half a century, the women of the world agree with her.

A man, however, is under no such freedom to be swept away. No matter how caught up in an event he may be, and no matter how hotly his blood may be running, he must be ready to switch himself off like a light, the very instant his partner commands it.

What is it about the undoubted trauma of nonconsensual sex that makes it so much more significant than any of the other wounds that men and women can inflict upon one another? Many people, male and female, are devastated by the everyday wounds of love. Many men suffer at the hands of emotionally manipulative women. Yet we consider their pain, no matter how deep or long-lasting, to be far less than that of a woman who happens to have had sex on an occasion when she did not wish to have it.

This places an extraordinary significance on the act of penetration. It implies that nothing that any woman does to a man, short of an act of physical violence, can possibly traumatize him as much as his penetration can traumatize her. And that trauma is so great that its infliction must be considered a criminal act.

This further implies that the female experience of sex is so profoundly different from that of the male that she needs to be protected by a specific series of laws for which there is no equivalent for men, despite increasing evidence that they, too, are the victims of forcible sexual assaults by both men and women. Yet if women are so different in this central area of human experience, then how can they not be different in other areas, too? And if they are different, then how can one justify the raft of legislation that is predicated on the sexes being exactly the same?

To this, one may reply that the act of insertion is also accompanied by a string of other brutalities. A woman may be menaced with a weapon, beaten, held against her will. Of course these are criminal acts. A penis can, in its own way, be as offensive a weapon as a clenched fist. If one is attacked, it matters little how one's assailant chooses to make his, or her, assault.

We do seem to be moving toward a situation now in which the legal definition of rape as "penetration of the vagina by the penis when the victim is unwilling" can be taken to apply to an occasion whose real dynamic may be one of mutual misunderstanding, or shared complicity in an act that may be grubby and even unpleasant, but is certainly not criminal.

There is, however, no equivalent protection given to men against the manipulation of their feelings or sexuality. I came across an example that illustrates this point when appearing on a television discussion on date-rape in 1991. A brief studio conversation was followed by a phone-in, during which victims of assault recounted their stories. Most of these victims were, naturally enough, women, some of whom had clearly suffered greatly as a result of their experiences. But one caller was a man.

His story was that he had gone for a drink after work with three women from the office. They were all good friends and there was no advance suggestion that this was anything other than a pleasant, social occasion.

As the evening wore on, however, it became clear to the man that one of the three women was more interested in him than he had supposed. One thing led to another and they ended up at her flat, where they made love. The man left her place in the early hours and went back to his own home with a song in his heart. Not only had he enjoyed the sex, but he felt that this could be the start of a serious relationship. He had always liked the woman. Now they were going to become lovers.

He turned up for work the next morning bearing a bunch of flowers, only to find that the woman to whom he was intending to give them, and with whom he was hoping to start a long-term affair, had accused him of date-rape. He was devastated. Quite apart from the seriousness of the allegation, and the consequences it could have upon his career, not to mention his freedom, the accusation was a bitter blow to his emotions. He felt utterly betrayed and humiliated.

In the end, the accusations were dropped before any legal action could be taken, but the effect upon his feelings toward that woman in particular and his relationships with women in general was far more long-lasting. His pain, however, had no legal significance (it never occurred to him that it might). He had no means of redress. Faced with a psychological assault from a determined and malevolent woman, he was entirely defenseless.

What, though, is the view from the other side of the fence? Not long ago I went out for a drink with an old friend. She's funny, attractive, and flirtatious—good company, in other words. And, as friends do over a glass or two, she was telling me about her recent exploits, one of which ended with the sight of a man leaving her flat in the early hours, simultaneously pulling up his trousers as he tried to hail a cab. It was all good stuff, but the most interesting thing was the reason why the man was leaving.

My friend, you see, had picked him up at a club. "I just wanted a really good snog," she said (*snogging* being the English slang for kissing). So, after they had smooched around the dance floor, she invited him back to her place for a snog and a stroke and just about everything else . . . except the actual act of sex itself. As soon as her needs were satisfied, and at the point when he looked as though he might be about to go further than she desired, he was out the door and onto the pavement, with his trousers in his hands and a sorry expression on his face.

He had, to put it bluntly, been used. She wanted a "really good snog" and once she'd gotten it, she had no further use for the snogger. Barbara Amiel would have every reason to use this as an example of women who use men as vibrators, to be picked up, played with, and discarded as they see fit, but men can hardly complain. After all, they've been using women as sex aids for centuries. The only difference is, men haven't gone running to the law whenever things went wrong.

Suppose, however, that the man my friend picked up had had a different agenda? Suppose he had not meekly walked out into the night, but had stayed and had sex regardless of her wishes—it would be a criminal act all right, but could you really say that she was entirely without responsibility for what had occurred? Let me put it another way: Say I walked through the streets of the South Bronx carrying a placard that read "I carry gold American Express and Mastercard." If I were to be mugged, I would still be traumatized and it would still be a crime. But do you really think that anyone would have very much sympathy for my predicament?

RESPONSIBLE ADULTS

This is where we are now: Political activists see all acts of sex into which a woman has entered unwillingly as rape. They interpret this as an embodiment of men's oppression of women.

Meanwhile, the mass media—often the ones whose content is determined by women for other women—pump out a message of aggressive female sexuality. A continual theme of this message is the inability of men to satisfy the needs or demands of women.

Men are told that their masculinity is, in part, determined by their ability to satisfy these needs, often by being masterful and assertive.

However, should these aggressively sexual women have sex on an occasion upon which they did not want it, the man with whom they had sex is a criminal.

The reason we say this is because we place an enormous emphasis on penetration of the woman's body, thus suggesting that male and female experience of sex is profoundly different.

Except that we legislate on the basis that, in every other area of life, there is no difference at all.

My view is that nothing will be solved until responsibility is shared equally. Men should be responsible for their own behavior and I do not condone any acts of brutality or unreasonable coercion. But women cannot be raunchy sex kittens on the one hand and delicate virgins on the other. If they want to be as free as men, they may have to accept that they will end up being as unprotected.

One final thought: Is this issue really one that turns, not on the maintenance of male power, but on a much more fundamental level of female power? Could it be that what women are really fighting for is the continuation of their monopoly on the ability to control sexual activity through their power of acceptance or veto?

Claire Rayner places date-rape in the following context: "Women initiate sex, really. It's the woman who's in charge. We make all the choices, we make the decisions, because we invest all the time involved in producing a baby."

I asked Ms. Rayner whether one could, on that basis, define date-rape as an occasion on which a man has made the decisions.

"Yes, that's all," she replied. "He's misread the signals and he's fed up with her being in charge. So he's decided to be in charge instead."

And that is his first mistake.

CHAPTER 7
Battered Husbands

George Gilliland points to a cutting, pinned to a bulletin board in his modest suite of offices in St. Paul, Minnesota. It is an advertisement from *Marney's Shopper*, a publication in Hibbing, Minnesota. In capital letters, a headline reads, OCTOBER IS DOMESTIC VIOLENCE AWARENESS MONTH. Underneath is a childish drawing of a man with devil's horns and, in what is meant to be a kid's handwriting, the words:

> *My Daddy is a monster*
> *He hurts my mommy*
> *He hurts me too*
> *Sometimes he hits*
> *Sometimes he says things*
> *that scare me and*
> *make my mommy cry*
> *after he leaves*
> *Sometimes I wish he*
> *won't come back . . . ever.*
> *I love my daddy.*

Just next to it is a series of letters, cut out of the *Minneapolis Star Tribune*, dated March 17, 1991. One of them, from a Diane Ostoj of Brooklyn Park, Minnesota, reads: "Where are the shelters and support for men who are abused by women? A male friend of mine went to the police for help because of being threatened with a knife by a live-in girlfriend; she changed the locks on his home, cut up his clothes and slashed the tires on his truck. He was told by police to 'go home and grow up and be a man.' Later she filed a false domestic assault charge against him, obtained an order for protection from the court and he was put out of his house."

That's the sort of thing that drives George Gilliland mad with anger, despair, and frustration. He's a recovering alcoholic. Gray-haired, stocky, of a medium height, and with a ruddy complexion that testifies to his former drinking problems, he has been accused of violent behavior by two former wives (one of whom has withdrawn the accusations) and a former girlfriend. Two of his sons went on the *Geraldo* show to allege that he had mistreated them when they were boys. He has a conversational style that starts out confrontational and works upward from there. He makes twenty grand a year, tops, and lives in a small house in an area he describes as upper-middle-class, but which looked a lot less desirable than that to my foreigner's eyes. He works out of a small, untidy suite of offices atop a cash-register shop on a windswept avenue. And right now he is the best hope, in fact the only hope, for America's male victims of domestic violence.

For Mr. Gilliland is the founder and executive director of the Domestic Rights Coalition, a nonprofit organization that claims to be America's only counseling service for men who have been attacked by their partners. There are, of course, hundreds, possibly thousands of homes, shelters, and advice centers, and so forth, for female victims, a fact that reflects both society's views on the subject of domestic violence and the efforts of all the activists who have campaigned on behalf of the bruised and beaten women who fall victim to male aggression.

Gilliland's view of the current state of domestic violence legislation can be summed up by a quote he gave to a weekly newspaper called the *Twin Cities Reader* in November 1991: "If Jesus Christ himself were accused of domestic abuse or domestic assault, and he walked into a courtroom with the twelve apostles behind him for character references, he'd be dead. Hung. Because when it comes to domestic assaults, domestic abuse and rape, that man is guilty until he can somehow prove his innocence, and men have a helluva time overcoming that."

His office is packed with files, each of which contains a story that, he believes, supports his contentions. He shows me a police arrest report. (In the account that follows, I have changed the names and addresses of the people involved; all other quotations are exactly as originally written.) It deals with a routine domestic incident.

> Squads were sent to 545 Lincoln on a domestic call. When I arrived, the victim, BROWN, MICHAEL BRADLEY, was standing in front of the house. I stopped my squad and Scott said, "She is going crazy." The suspect then ran from the house and yelled, "You are fucking dead." She then began to slap and punch the victim. I told the suspect, SMITH, CAROL JANE, to settle down and

have a set in my squad. When I went to open the door, SMITH
said, "Fuck you." She then turned and hit me on the chest with
a closed fist. I then grabbed her arms and got behind her. She
continued to turn back and forth attempting to hit me with her
elbows.

I then placed my Nova Spirit stun gun in the kidney area and
pulled the trigger for 23 seconds. SMITH was then handcuffed and
placed in the rear of my car.

BROWN then said that he was laying on the couch when the
very drunk SMITH attacked him punching and scratching him.
BROWN stood up and SMITH kneed him in the groin. BROWN did
have scratches and a small fresh cut on his left wrist. He said
that she doesn't drink often but when she does she gets very
violent. He said that they have been living together for 3 years.
BROWN signed the report.

SMITH was then taken to HQ where she was issued crime tag
(a number follows) for domestic abuse and booked. While being
booked SMITH complained of a sore jaw and said that BROWN had
hit her on the jaw (no marks). SMITH was taken to SPRH. SMITH
agreed that her 2 children should stay in the home for the night.

Four weeks after Smith was arrested, so was Brown, following another
violent argument. Smith was granted a protection order, forbidding Brown
access to herself or her two children. She alleged that he had threatened
her, kicked at her, and told her that she had better not try to make him
leave or he would kill her and her children. She further stated that he
had previously attacked her repeatedly, causing black eyes, possible broken bones, and a grand mal seizure due to being struck in the head.

A few days after that, Brown filed a counterclaim on behalf of himself
and Tammy and Ken, his two children from a previous relationship. The
notes to his petition, in which Brown is referred to as the petitioner, and
Smith as the respondent, give his account of the events leading up to his
own arrest. "While petitioner was away from home, respondent threatened to spank Tammy and sent her to her room. Tammy was hysterical.
Petitioner's brother then took her to petitioner's mother's home. Petitioner
learned later that Tammy attempted suicide on this date and had scratches
on her arm. When petitioner came home and learned of the above incident, petitioner and respondent argued. Respondent told petitioner to
leave. She called police and made allegations of abuse and petitioner was
arrested."

Brown's request for a protection order lists two more incidents upon
which Smith attacked him. It adds that he has a heart problem caused by
the stress of his relationship and that Smith sees a psychologist and a

psychiatrist. In addition to protection, the claim requests domestic abuse counseling, chemical dependency counseling, and psychological evaluation for Smith, along with assistance for Brown from the police department and the sheriff. At the top of the five-page form is written one word: *Denied.*

To Gilliland, such a story is clear evidence of the way in which men are attacked twice over, once by their partners and then again by the system. His opponents might retort that he is simply encouraging abusive men to deny their guilt and offload it onto women who finally summon up the courage to fight back. To me, it all looks like one more reminder of the infinite number of ways men and women can find to harm one another. Having listened to more tales of heartache over the past two years than I thought I would hear in a lifetime, I no longer care about who is right and who is wrong. I just want all the people who claim to care about violence to stop fighting among themselves long enough to take a long, calm look at the situation as a whole.

Before that can happen, however, the existence and the status of the male victim has to be acknowledged. In public, the subject of female violence is still taboo. In private, however, it is a very different story. One of the earliest battered men to whom I spoke told me that, in his experience, once the subject was introduced an astonishing number of men began to talk about the attacks that they had suffered. I did not really believe him, but I was soon forced to change my mind.

I remember one ten-day trip to the States in the late fall of 1992. I was writing a bunch of features for a London Sunday newspaper. Wherever I went, I tried to start conversations on the subjects in this book in the hope of getting feedback from potential American readers. To my amazement, one person after another recounted stories about female aggression. One photographer told me that he had won custody of his two daughters after ten years of assaults by his wife. A woman said that her current partner had divorced his ex-wife on the grounds of her violence.

An old friend in New York revealed that his former girlfriend, whom I knew, had regularly attacked him. She had repeatedly started fights, then called the police and accused him of assault. The cops had refused to believe that he had been the victim. It had reached the point where he would stand with his hands clasped behind his back, refusing to react or retaliate in any way, while she attacked him with her fists and her nails. He began to wonder whether there was something wrong with him: "Once you've been accused of being the aggressor, you're always haunted by the ghost of it. You never go back to thinking, 'I'm not an aggressor.' You're not a virgin anymore.

"It's the same for the victim. In these situations, it's almost as though there is no victim and no aggressor. You switch sides. It's a pernicious distinction. Both people are the victim. You've been victimized by your inability to resolve conflict by talk."

I would have found such stories incredible, were it not for the fact that I had already had exactly the same experience in London. These sorry tales were comparable to those told to me by female friends who had started conversations with their friends about their experiences of sexual abuse and the shocking frequency with which that, too, had happened. I began to wonder whether I had been wrong to question the claims reported in earlier chapters about female victimization. Perhaps all of us, male and female, carried around far more bad memories than we ever cared to admit. Perhaps it was not that men were not guilty, but that we were all—male and female—both victims and perpetrators.

But let me return to that first victim. I'll call him Donald. We met in an office in London and the account that follows is what he told me on that day. Over the next several months we met on a number of other occasions. He documented his case for me in thorough, not to say obsessive, detail. His first words to me were to prove uncannily prophetic. To readers of early drafts of this book who had not experienced the horrors of long-term domestic violence, the details of Donald's stories seemed unbelievable: "Grotesque" was one editor's comment. Grotesque is, indeed, exactly what they are. But to anyone involved in an abusive relationship, I suspect that they would prove all too credible. I have certainly heard many similar stories since.

Donald said, "This is a story you will have difficulty believing. It will test your credulity beyond belief. But there are plenty of others like it." The man before me was not a particularly prepossessing sight: narrow-faced, with a sallow complexion and thinning hair that was turning to gray, scraped back off his forehead across his scalp. He sat hunched up in his chair, pulling on the cigarettes that he chain-smoked as he told his tale.

He was not by any means insubstantial, maybe five-ten and about 170 pounds in weight. But he held himself in such a way, hunched up and round-shouldered, as to diminish his physical presence to the point where one would, at first glance, have taken him for a far smaller, weaker man. He was a highly qualified professional. But he was entirely bereft of the middle-class self-confidence that one might have expected.

He looked, in short, like a beaten dog. It was entirely appropriate. For Donald had suffered years of physical abuse at the hands of his wife, Mary. It began, he said, right at the very start of the marriage.

"Three days after we got married, we went out for the evening. When we got back to the flat, I went to get something to eat. She suddenly became enraged. She hit me with a flurry of fists. I didn't know what was going on. I was dumbfounded. What she wanted was sex. She was annoyed that I hadn't jumped on top of her the moment we were alone. We had sex. I assure you, if someone is wielding a hammer, or any number of other objects at your head, you will have sex."

This first explosion of rage was the start of a pattern in which his wife's obsessive jealousy came to rule their entire lives. "I've been accused of having heterosexual affairs, homosexual affairs, incestuous affairs—anybody and everybody. It's not about sex. It's about control. There was a time when I could hardly get to work. The front door was barricaded. She'd be up against the door. I could have flung her out of the way, but I didn't want to. I didn't go out for two years, apart from work. My wife would even come to my work to check up on me, so that she'd know where I was."

If her suspicions were ever aroused, her retribution took the form of violence—both physical and verbal. "There was one night, she had been hitting me and my chest was covered in bruises. I didn't notice them. In fact, she was the first person to see them, when I had a bath the next day. She said I was covered in love bites. I must have been seeing another woman. So she attacked me again.

"Once when she attacked me with a hammer, I snatched it and held it above her head. She just kept on hitting me with her other hand. When I grabbed that, she went for my testicles. I've played rugby all my life and I've never been scared of a rugby player in my life. But I am terrified of my wife. Trying to restrain her is no good. Even verbal restraint pushes up the level of violence.

"At the end of an attack, the only way that the violence would stop was that my wife would demand that I get down on the floor and beg forgiveness. Why didn't I retaliate? I didn't want to hit a woman. And if I had retaliated, that would have been the final humiliation."

There were, however, plenty of other humiliations in store. "One of the things my wife did was that she would want me to make love to her to prove that I had not been unfaithful. After making love, she had the habit of checking her vagina to see if there was 'enough' semen there. She thought that if there wasn't it would prove I had been with someone else.

"I could always have sex with my wife if I initiated it. It was no problem. She would always accept it. But if she wanted to make overtures to me, she couldn't do it in any way other than jealousy or control. For example, if I did the washing-up wrongly, that would lead to an argument, a tirade, and the final demand would be, 'Have sex with me.'

"One night we made love, fine, then she gets up. Suddenly, like someone had thrown a switch, she said, 'Do it again!' Of course I couldn't. I have to wait a certain time. She started to attack me. She seized my penis and started trying to masturbate it. I had fingernail marks on my penis.

She sat on top and tried to have intercourse. Now, okay, my penis was nothing like totally erect, but it was not totally flaccid either. There was still some residual engorgement. By that time I was in tears. I couldn't retaliate."

The violence was not confined to attacks upon Donald. He alleges that his wife forcibly restrained their daughter, Jane, when she was still a baby; force-fed her to the point of vomiting; and then, when she was sick, slapped her so hard around the face that she fell out of her high chair. On other occasions, she hit the child powerfully enough to leave substantial bruising, and later, when the little one was two, knocked her off her feet, bursting her eardrum in the process.

Jane was taught, "You are not to call your father 'Daddy.' He is not your father. He is a bastard." So intimidated did she become in the face of her mother's assaults that she would run and hide in a cupboard, rather than face the risk of punishment. Despite this, Donald said, "I have my suspicions she's training her to say I've hit her. I've only ever smacked her once. I believe you should never use force on a two- or three-year-old little child."

WHY DON'T YOU HIT HER BACK, SIR?

Faced with a story like this, it is hard to know how to respond. Some people might find it irrelevant. The battered husband is so rare, and the battered woman so common, they would say, that it is offensive even to contemplate the male victim in the face of endemic female suffering. Others might find it hard, reading Donald's testimony, not to suppress a laugh at the thought of a man being terrorized by a woman who is, as a matter of fact, pretty, delicate-looking, far smaller, and, apparently, weaker than he. For goodness sakes, one might think, pull yourself together, be a man.

But put yourself in the victim's shoes and a very different picture emerges. The vast majority of men who are attacked by their wives or partners never report the fact to anyone. They feel so humiliated and emasculated that they dare not tell anyone what has happened. When they do, they are confronted with a mixture of indifference and disbelief.

The first time that Donald rang up his local police he was told that his wife was probably just asking for it. "She is just trying to wind you up, sir," said one woman police officer, an opinion shared by a health visitor, who had been called to examine the physical evidence of his wife's abuse of their little daughter. "Why don't you hit her back, sir," opined another police officer, helpfully. When Donald tried to warn the Social Services of what was being done to his daughter, the social worker assigned to him walked out of their meeting in mid-sentence. When Donald's parents voiced their concerns, the same social worker walked out on them, too.

Nor were counselors able to help. Despite psychiatric reports that diagnosed Mary as having a personality disorder, liable to lead to maladaptive and even psychopathic behavior, there seemed little that anyone could or was willing to do to remedy the situation. One counselor advised Donald to get a divorce, forget about his daughter, and start again with a new family. "I wasn't going to take that abuse," he told me. "I'd had enough already."

In any case, divorce is the very last thing that a battered husband can afford, particularly if he is worried about the safety of his children. A battered woman will often be advised to institute divorce proceedings, accompanied by court orders evicting her partner and preventing him from seeing her again. A man, however, knows that a divorce will almost certainly lead, not to his wife's eviction, but to his own.

In Britain, as in America, no matter how great the degree of abuse meted out by a wife to her husband or child, courts almost never find in the husband's favor. The wife is almost certain to be given custody of the children, and with the children comes the family house. So a battered man who divorces his abusive spouse stands to lose everything he has. First he's attacked by his wife, then he's finished off by the system.

Donald, like all battered men, faced the continual threat that he would be reported to the police at the first sign of retaliation. On one occasion, in March 1992, his wife said she would accuse him of marital rape. "There she is, with her arm over my windpipe, holding my balls and saying I've got to have sex with her or she'll accuse me of rape. And I remember saying, 'If I don't have sex with you, how can you accuse me of rape?' "

Such claims are entirely par for the course. At the height of the attacks against him, Donald was visited at work one day by a representative of Families Need Fathers, a British pressure group that campaigns for paternal rights. "The man came to my office and asked about my personal situation," he recalls. "I told him I was thinking of getting a nonmolestation order against Mary. Without batting an eyelid, he said, 'How are you going to cope when your wife makes malicious allegations saying that you've been abusing your child?' That had happened to him. He was a battered man."

In Donald's case, matters came to a head a few weeks after the "rape" incident. "Over the previous month I'd been standing up to my wife and saying, 'Mary, you are a bully.' That morning we'd had a row and she was in a foul mood by the evening, although there'd been no violence. During the TV news, Jane went off to the toilet—the only training that Mary had given her was to hit her when she missed or was sick; I've done everything for my dughter. My wife noticed that Jane had closed the door, so she went off to see what happened. I could hear a tirade and Jane being slapped—one, two, three—I thought, 'Uh-oh, what's going on?'

"I went to the bathroom and said, 'What's going on? Slapping's not the way to deal with it.'

"Mary said, 'I'll hit my child if I want to.'

"Then there was an argument. My wife was getting aggressive. I said, 'If you do that again, I'll call the police.' She immediately thumped me again. I dialed 999. The operator put me through to the police. I said I wanted to complain about an assault by my wife on my daughter. My wife put the phone down and bundled me out of the way. Well, there are two phones in the flat, so I went to the other one. I couldn't get a line. I didn't think anything of it because the phones were dodgy, but when I went back to the other room, Mary was on the phone, screaming that she was terrified.

"I decided to go to the police, so I grabbed my jacket and went to the nearest police station. I saw the guy on the desk. He said to phone their Domestic Violence Unit in the morning. But I was worried about Jane, what could I do?

"I drove back to the house. When I got there, there was a police Metro parked outside. I knew when I walked up the stairs that I would be arrested. In the living room were my wife, my daughter, a police constable, and a WPC [female police officer]. I said, 'This is a long-running thing,' and named two WPCs that I'd talked to about it in the past, but the copper had me pinned down as the guilty party and he came on very strong. He said he'd seen my daughter in sheer terror of me as I had walked in.

"I was nervous. My wife was still in the room and I was reluctant to give full vent. But then the WPC took my wife and daughter into the bedroom. I leaned forward towards the PC and told him I'd put up with four years of this and that I considered I had been indecently assaulted.

"He was very unhappy about the situation. He said, 'I know there'll be further violence tonight and we'll be called back.'

"I assured him several times that there would be no violence from me. He tried to say I ought to leave the premises. He said, 'If we have to come back here tonight, I will have to arrest somebody for breach of the peace and you know who that will be . . . you.' In effect he was saying that no matter how violent my wife was, don't call us, because we'll arrest you.

"However, I could see he was beginning to get perturbed. He said he ought to call on higher authority. So he called up and said, 'We've got a battered husband syndrome here.' Another car arrived and a gentleman got out and chatted to the policeman for five minutes. The copper came back upstairs and there were all four of us in the living room. My wife said she wanted me out. He said I had a right to live there and he wanted to make a full report. Then she made allegations that I had been sexually abusing her. The police paid no attention to her and left."

The next day, Donald tried to make a formal statement to the police. Despite a series of phone calls and letters, some to senior officers, no such statement was ever taken. The last time I spoke to him, he had just been served with divorce papers by his wife. The divorce was being sought on the grounds of his cruelty and violence toward her. "If you think my story's bad," he said, "it's not half as bad as some blokes. I've had it comparatively easy."

The threat of legal action is one faced by all the battered men to whom I spoke. In every case, their divorce had been brought about by their wife's claims that she had been the victim. And in every case, the police, social services, legal advisers, and courts had found it impossible to conceive of the idea that the woman might have been the instigator, rather than the victim, of the domestic abuse. Why should they? For years, they have been told that men are the violent sex. To be told that they can be the victims is as shocking as it would be to discover that apples, in fact, fall up.

NICE GIRLS DON'T

In part, this is a matter of social conditioning. We naturally assume that women—being both smaller and, we imagine, less inclined to violence—cannot possibly do harm to big, strong, aggressive males. They are forced, we believe, to resort to other stratagems if they want revenge against a partner. When a British aristocrat called Lady Graham-Moon cut up her adulterous husband's suits, covered his BMW with paint, and gave away his wine to other people in the village, she was hailed by columnists who saw this as typical of the acts of minor defiance to which women must resort in the face of their menfolk's overwhelming physical strength.

One newspaper, *Today,* published an article on March 18, 1992, entitled "Twenty delicious ways to get even with your man," which included scrawling "Scum" on his car, destroying his most treasured possessions, and kidnapping his new lover. On the same day, the London *Daily Mail* ran another feature headlined, "Why women will always throw more than abuse." The writer, Diana Hutchinson, began her piece thus: "The tension is mounting. He's not listening, beginning to shout. Your hand strays almost of its own accord towards that ugly heavy cut glass fruit bowl his mother gave you. Crash! Satisfyingly, the shards of glass sprinkle over the TV set. Why is it that when a woman gets mad, really mad, she invariably ends up throwing something?"

Ian Grove-Stephenson, a "psychologist and counsellor," was quoted in the same article. He saw throwing as "the straightforward David and Goliath syndrome," the woman, of course, being David. He concluded, "Throwing things means, 'I consider this relationship worth fighting for.' "

Would that, I wonder, apply to punching, kicking, scratching, or biting? Would it apply if it were the man who was doing the fighting?

Cathy Lever is the administrator of Move (Men Over Violence), a counseling service for violent men in the English town of Bolton, Lancashire. The service aims to help batterers come to terms with what they have done, accept full responsibility for their actions, and learn not to act in that way again. Ginny Dougary, a journalist who watched a counseling session in action, reported that the men involved "talk with raw, smarting candour. They castigate themselves so much it is like a form of masochism."

I asked Cathy Lever whether any of the men who came to her reported being in relationships in which their violence was just one element in a general dysfunction. She replied, "When men initially come to us, they invariably won't take responsibility. They say, 'She made me,' or, 'She said this or that.' But after a few sessions they take the whole responsibility for their actions."

Was that entirely fair? Was there no possibility of provocation?

"We say there are always alternatives," she responded. "He can always get up and leave the room. He has to take sole responsibility for the violence. There's no excuse."

This seemed to me to be an oversimplification of what may be an immensely complex situation. But I could understand that forcing a man to admit his wrongdoing, whatever the reasons for it, might be a necessary first step along the road to understanding it and then preventing further recurrences. I then asked Lever whether there was any evidence of violence against men by their partners. She said, "It's a very, very small problem. You've got to consider the power relationship between men and women. When I argue with my fiancé, I've slapped him round the face because I didn't like what he was saying. But I'm five foot five and he's six foot three."

Oh well, that's all right then.

I don't think that Ms. Lever had any idea of the implications of what she was saying. For example, she knew that she could hit her boyfriend without any fear of his retaliating as he would do if struck by a man. His self-restraint, motivated by the taboo against hitting women that is drummed into boys and young men, was being used as a weapon against him. More to the point, I think she had confused intention and effect. Just because a woman isn't very good at hitting a man, that doesn't make her action any more morally justifiable. Either violence is inexcusable, or it isn't.

This is a perfect example of the double standard that we now have toward men and women. We are told continually that women have all the drive, energy, intelligence, and sheer ambition required to get to the top of any business, army, or political party on earth. But as soon as the focus shifts to their relationship with men, we consider them . . . well, what *do* we consider them?

What do you call someone who has no self-control, who lashes out, but who expects to be forgiven by a big strong man on the grounds that she didn't mean it and couldn't do any real harm anyway? You call that person a child.

But I don't think that women are children. I think that they are fully grown adult human beings. Which means that they have to take responsibility for their actions. They can't have it both ways, however nice it might be to do so. My preferred solution would not be to turn the clock back to the days when women were treated as children in every aspect of their lives, but to move it forward. Once again, what I'm calling for here is more equality, not less.

SHE'S A VICTIM, AND THAT'S OFFICIAL

Whenever the matter of domestic violence is discussed, the assumption is always made that women are the primary, perhaps even the sole victims. That assumption was the basis of Senator Biden's Violence Against Women Act, and it applies just as surely on the other side of the Atlantic.

On page three of the British *Law Commission Report No. 207: Family Law—Domestic Violence and Occupation of the Family Home*, it is stated, "There can be no doubt of the extent of the problem [of domestic violence]. It has been summarised thus: 'All studies that exist indicate that wife abuse is a common and pervasive problem and that men from practically all countries, cultures, classes and income groups indulge in the behaviour' . . . Although both men and women can suffer domestic violence, nearly all the studies have shown that in the great majority of cases, men are the perpetrators and women are the victims."

The report is annotated. Note 5, to which the reader is referred in the last sentence above, remarks, "Whilst a certain amount of attention has been paid to 'battered husbands' e.g. F Bates 'A Plea for the battered husband' (1981) 11 Fam Law 90, other commentators have concluded that whilst some husbands certainly suffer violence at the hands of their wives, this is an individual rather than a social problem. It is uncommon and there is no sound evidence to suggest that any 'syndrome' exists comparable to the problem of battered wives. See M D Pagelow, 'The battered husband syndrome: social problem or much ado about little?' in N Johnson (ed.) Marital Violence (1985).''

Mildred Daley Pagelow's paper is a scholarly attempt to examine the subject of violence against husbands. Or rather, it is a scholarly attempt to prove that such violence is insignificant. Its first half consists of a methodological assault on one of the few other reports on the subject, a paper entitled *The Battered Husband Syndrome* written in 1977 by the American sociologist Suzanne Steinmetz, who claimed a figure of 250,000 annual cases of husband-battering for the United States as a whole.

Having questioned the statistical basis upon which Steinmetz based her conclusions, Pagelow examines evidence from various centers catering to victims of domestic violence and asserts that the true proportion of male victims ranges from 0 to 4 percent. She then cites other experts in order to determine that violence and even murder on the part of women is not only far less common than that by men, but is almost always an act of self-defense when it occurs.

Pagelow goes on to state that battered men are much freer, given their greater economic power and mobility, to leave the family home than are women. She wonders why an able-bodied man would want or need to remain with a violent wife after being subjected to physical abuse, and is unable to come up with an answer.

She claims, furthermore, that female attacks tend not to be serious and concludes, ''The preponderance of scientific evidence leads to the conclusion that the vast majority of victims of spousal violence are female, whether wives or lovers. *Most importantly, in the years since 1977 when the image of the battered husband syndrome was publicised, there has not been a single report of scientific research on a sample of battered husbands.* [Her emphasis]

''In sum there undoubtedly are many violent wives and some battered husbands, but the proportion of systematically abused husbands compared to abused wives is relatively small, and certainly the phenomenon does not amount to a 'syndrome' as popularised.''

But why should the fact that there has been no research into female marital violence indicate that the phenomenon is unimportant? Might it not indicate instead the priorities of an academic and sociological establishment that has an enormous intellectual investment in the idea of an oppressive patriarchy? Alternatively, might one find that—as with sexual abuse—the notion of female violence is simply unthinkable, and therefore unresearched?

Are we really surprised that the WomenShelter in Long Beach, California, which is cited among Pagelow's sources, reports no male victims of domestic violence? If you were a battered man, would you go there? If you did, would they even let you in?

Looking through Ms. Pagelow's notes one finds references to a plethora of works on the battered wife, often given at such occasions as The Second International Symposium on Victimology and including Pagelow's own paper, *Social learning theory and sex roles: violence begins in the home.* She also makes frequent references to the British husband-and-wife team of sociology professors R. E. and R. P. Dobash, whose cited works include their 1979 book *Violence Against Wives: A Case Against the Patriarchy,* and a piece in the radical feminist magazine *Spare Rib* entitled "Battered women: in defense of self-defense."

Without wishing to call their academic credentials into question, one cannot help but wonder how interested any of these distinguished authorities would be in any work that succeeded in overturning their preconceptions. In 1991, an English law student named Stephanie Jeavons decided to write an undergraduate thesis on female domestic violence. She soon realized that there was virtually no research on the subject, so she contacted Professor Rebecca Dobash and asked for her advice.

According to Jeavons, Professor Dobash gave her a reading list and then added, "I had hoped that the British would have more sense than to waste resources pursuing this line," before remarking that Jeavons was "politically naïve" to be tackling such a subject.

As Jeavons began to research female domestic violence, she began to encounter two sets of responses. The first, from friends and acquaintances, consisted of jokes, unease, and then—if those two handicaps could be overcome—serious conversations, often involving personal experience. The second, from feminist academics (in this particular field, there are really no other kind), was one of outright hostility. She came to the conclusion that "Domestic violence has been hijacked by hardcore feminists and used as a political weapon. It's treated as a woman's field, whereas actually it involves violence against children, against men, against old people . . . it's whole families.

"We're always standing up for minorities, but men are the last great taboo. Feminists are putting up the same arguments against them as were put up against women when Erin Pizzey started coming forward in the 1970s. The criticism, the hostility, the trivialisation, the humour . . . it's exactly the same."

I know what she means. At a lunch in March 1992 arranged by British *Elle* magazine, at which my fellow guests included Marilyn French and Susan Faludi, I mentioned that I had just spent several hours interviewing a male victim of domestic violence. I said that I suspected that the phenomenon might be much more widespread than I had previously thought. At this, another one of my fellow guests, the Australian author Kathy Lette, turned to me and said, "You had better get your statistics absolutely right, or we're going to crucify you."

MEN ON THE RECEIVING END

Ms. Lette might be interested in a book called *Violent Men, Violent Couples: The Dynamics of Domestic Violence* by Anson Shure, William A. Stacey, and Lonnie Hazelwood, chapter three of which is entitled "The Violent Woman." The chapter covers some of the issues over which Mildred Pagelow passes so blithely. Why, for example, do men not leave their homes? Well, in some cases they are unable to do so: Their assailants lock the doors and block their exit. Shure, Stacey, and Hazelwood do not, however, mention a much more powerful argument for a man's not leaving, which is: Why should he? If he has spent years living in a house, which he may well have paid for and which contains all his most personal possessions, why should he be forced to leave because of someone else's wrongdoing? Pagelow's casual assumption that a man can just walk out the door only makes sense if she believes that men have no feelings, and that they can discard a home as casually as they might a worn-out pair of shoes.

As for attacks not being serious, Shure, Stacey, and Hazelwood—whose research data is mostly based on reports from Texas police and sheriff's departments, and a counseling project in the city of Austin—cite the case of a man on trial for the assault of his former girlfriend. He denied that he had ever been violent, said that he had ended their relationship because of her drinking and aggression, and revealed that he had been hospitalized with a knife wound to the scrotum, inflicted by her while he was sleeping in bed. She had also slashed the tires on his car. He had never reported any of these or other incidents to the police because he felt that it was wrong to file charges against a woman.

"In one case," the authors report, "an Army sergeant could no longer deal with the private humiliation of his wife's violence towards him. Tears streaming down his face as his family said grace together one night before a meal, he quietly pulled a pistol from his belt, put the barrel in his mouth and pulled the trigger. The daily contrast between his macho parade-ground image . . . and the reality of his being the frequent target of his domineering wife's physical abuse (in front of their children) became overwhelming."

In Texas, 10 percent of all domestic violence victims listed by the police were male. This figure does not, however, include those male victims who were arrested as aggressors—a phenomenon of which Shure et al. found considerable evidence. Women seemed far more willing than men to involve the police, often doing so as part of the war they were waging against their partner. One man had his working life ruined by his former wife's habit of filing assault charges for no reason, forcing him to go to court, and then dropping the charges.

There appeared to be little difference in the factors influencing male and female violence: family background, financial pressures, substance abuse, and so on. The authors also noted that a survey in Austin revealed that two-thirds of all male batterers had had objects thrown at them by their partners, half had been threatened physically, often with being killed, and half had been punched or kicked. As many as three-quarters reported psychological intimidation, including attempts by the woman to limit the man's contact with his family or friends, outbursts of extreme jealousy, and the withdrawal of sex as a punishment. The authors conclude, "There is undoubtedly distortion at work in these reports but we know from previously documented case reports that women's violence cannot be dismissed as sheer rationalization."

They also quote some research done in 1985 among American students by a sociologist named Richard Breen. He interviewed 884 students, male and female, married and unmarried, about their experience of violence within a romantic partnership. His findings were surprising: Far from male victims being in the minority, 18 percent of men and 14 percent of women reported being the victims of violence within a relationship. Breen then asked the married men a series of questions about their wives. Once again, the results were at odds with received opinion:

20 percent had wives who threw or broke household objects when angry

23 percent were punched, kicked, or slapped by their wives

30 percent were pushed or shoved by their wives, either in public or private

9 percent had wives who had attacked them with objects

9 percent had received visible welts, cuts, or bruises as a result of attacks by their wives

10 percent had sought medical aid as a result of attacks

14 percent had wives who had, at least once, threatened either to kill their husband or to commit suicide

5 percent had called the police at least once because they felt that they, their family, or their friends were in danger from their wives

Further evidence of the even-handed nature of domestic violence is provided by "Interspousal Violence," a paper by Professors Merlin B. Brinkerhoff and Eugen Lupri of the University of Calgary, printed in the *Canadian Journal of Sociology* 13(4) 1988. The authors reviewed the then-current literature on the subject, noting that "For an American couple, married or living together, the chances are almost one out of six (16 per cent) that one of the partners engages in [a violent act] at least once a year, according to the first national study (1975) of family violence in American homes (Straus, Gelles and Steinmetz, 1980). The incidence rate for severe violent acts such as 'kicked, bit or hit the other with a fist,' 'beat up the other,' 'threatened the other with a knife or gun,' or 'used a knife or gun on the other,' is about 4 per cent. Surprisingly the statistics on husband beating are slightly higher than those for wife beating (4.6 per cent versus 3.8 per cent)."

If that was surprising, what followed was surely even more so: "A 1985 follow-up study showed a similar incidence rate for couples, but a slight decrease in husband-to-wife violence and a slight increase in wife-to-husband violence. These findings prompted Straus and Gelles to state, 'In marked contrast to the behaviour of women outside the home, women are about as violent within the family as men.'"

Brinkerhoff and Lupri were not, however, content to depend upon the research of other academics. They conducted their own survey of 562 married and cohabiting couples in Calgary. Both members of the couple were interviewed separately. While one member was being interviewed, the other filled in a questionnaire. Both were asked to report acts that they had committed. The authors noted that their figures might represent substantial understatements of the truth because some people thought violence so normal that they did not bother to report minor incidents; because others were too ashamed to report their own perpetration or victimization; and because divorced couples, among whom severe violence may well have been a reason for marital breakdown, were not included in the survey.

The table below reproduces the headline findings of Brinkerhoff and Lupri's research:

During this past year of marriage or living together, I . . .	Wife-to-husband violence %	Husband-to-wife violence %
1. Threatened to hit or throw something at the other		
—once	8.9	10.5
—twice or more	10.8	6.8
2. Pushed, grabbed, or shoved the other		
—once	7.8	9.8
—twice or more	6.2	5.2
3. Slapped the other		
—once	5.2	4.1
—twice or more	2.6	1.8
4. Kicked, bit, or hit the other with a fist		
—once	3.7	2.1
—twice or more	2.7	1.1
5. Hit or tried to hit the other		
—once	7.5	5.7
—twice or more	6.5	3.1
6. Beat up the other one		
—at least once	1.8	1.7
7. Threatened the other with a knife or gun		
—at least once	1.3	0.6
8. Used a knife or gun on the other	1 case	none

You will note that in all but two categories, violence by women exceeds that by men. When the authors looked into their figures more closely, some fascinating trends began to emerge. For example, the more highly educated a man is, the less likely he is to be violent toward his partner. Female violence, on the other hand, increases with education. In fact, college-educated women were nearly twice as likely to assault their partners as college-educated men (14.5 percent versus 8.8 percent).

Other findings suggest that critics of the conventional family may be misguided. Younger, unmarried, and childless couples were all much more likely than older, married couples with children to engage in acts of violence. The only exception to this occurred among couples in which the man was of pensionable age. Perhaps because of the strain imposed by the loss of a job and the increased amount of time spent in the home, men of sixty-five and above were actually more likely than middle-aged men to be violent toward their spouses.

The same pattern of greater female violence appeared in a study of 150 Quaker families (Brutz and Ingoldsby, 1984), which found the incidence of severe wife-to-husband violence to be three times that of husband-to-wife violence. On a more populist level, two surveys conducted by British magazines uncovered similar trends. A January 1992 report by *Chat* magazine revealed that 47 percent of female respondents admitted to slapping or hitting their partners. One-third of the men said that they had done the same. A similar proportion, one-third, of all women had thrown plates or other objects. Just 16 percent of the men had thrown anything at their womenfolk.

British *Reader's Digest* published a MORI poll on attitudes and behavior within the family in its October 1991 edition. The survey consisted of interviews with 2,075 people. Of these, some 1,510 were currently in a relationship. The pollsters asked a number of questions under the heading, *"Which, if any, of the following have you done as a result of an argument between you and your current partner?"* Two of the findings were as follows:

Hit your partner	Male 3%	Female 10%	Total 7%
Thrown something at your partner	Male 6%	Female 20%	Total 13%

Now, the figures from these surveys vary quite dramatically. Yet the preponderance of violent women never alters. One might explain it by saying that—as we have already seen—women do not believe that their actions are serious and so admit to them readily, whereas men feel guilty and stay quiet. But even the most gimlet-eyed feminist would have a hard time claiming that 97 percent of violence was caused by men—not, at any rate, based on these four surveys, covering thousands of people in two countries.

Equally surprising are the findings of M. McLeod, a female academic, reported in her paper "Women Against Men: An Examination of Domestic Violence Based on an Analysis of Official Data and National Victimization Data," printed in *Justice Quarterly*, 1 (1984). She examined six thousand cases of domestic assaults reported to law enforcement officers and National Crime Survey interviewers. Of these, the vast majority (94 percent) concerned crimes against women, a finding that supports the conventional view of male-dominated domestic violence. The unexpected element of

McLeod's work concerned the nature of the attacks and injuries reported by male victims: More than 80 percent of them had been attacked with weapons. Women, on the other hand, were attacked with weapons in only 25 percent of all cases. Men also suffered a higher rate of injury than women: roughly 75 percent, to roughly 55 percent.

McLeod concluded, "Clearly violence against men is much more destructive than violence against women. . . . Male victims are injured more often and more seriously than are female victims."

Further evidence to support McLeod's opinions was provided by the results of research carried out in 1988 among 341 victims of domestic violence treated by the Accident and Emergency Department at Leicester Royal Infirmary in England. The study, which was subsequently passed on to both general practitioners and hospital doctors by the British government's Department of Health, was carried out by Dr. Sue Smith and Dr. David Baker, Mr. Gautam Bodiwala, a consultant surgeon, and Professor Alan Buchan, director of Leicester Health Authority.

The report states that "The commonly held view of domestic violence is of women as the victims and men as the aggressors." In fact, this perception was found to be far from accurate. In numerical terms, assaults were almost evenly divided between the sexes, but the severity of the assaults showed a far greater proportion of serious injuries among male victims.

Some 45 percent of all the men surveyed were attacked with weapons—ranging from knives, scissors, and saucepans through to automobiles—compared with only 19 percent of women who were attacked in similar ways. More than twice as many men as women had been knocked out by their assailant—19 percent versus 8 percent—so that the study concluded: "Assaulted men received more serious injuries than women, lost consciousness more often and required admission to hospitals on more occasions."

These figures directly contradict conventional assumptions about domestic violence. What makes them even more surprising is that the researchers only dealt with cases that had been specifically noted down as being the results of domestic violence. Given that men are even more reluctant than women to report the true reasons for their injuries, one might conclude that, if anything, the study has underestimated the extent of their victimization. That being the case, two obvious questions are begging to be answered. The first is: How do we know that these reports are accurate? And the second is, how come we haven't seen the evidence of female violence for ourselves: If there's so much of it around, how come it's not more publicly reported?

Brinkerhoff and Lupri give serious consideration to the first question. They note that men may well not perceive their actions to be violent.

Even when they do admit to their actions, "husbands tend to perceive the context as mutually violent, whereas wives perceived it as husband-violent." They refer to research that suggests that women are capable of being just as aggressive as men, but only when first provoked or attacked, and thus suggest that "women abuse their husbands in response to being abused by them."

That does, however, beg a further question: Just who is denying what? Do men cover up their own violence by pretending that it is part of a mutual exchange? Or do women escape responsibility for their own actions by insisting that they are the original victims? Anyone observing the behavior of men and women and the propaganda put out on their behalf must be forced to conclude that there is a great deal of pretending going on on both sides.

WHO'S FOOLING WHOM?

How is it that we don't see the victims of female aggression turning up at shelters for men, or looking haggard on the pages of our newspapers, or weeping into the camera on the seven o'clock TV news? To someone like George Gilliland, the answer is that there is a conspiracy of silence. Women's activists suppress the truth about domestic violence because they want to monopolize the money given to the issue. "They get state funding and they get United Way funds, and foundation grants, and donations. They get multimillions of dollars. The name of the game with these women is to keep the money coming in so they can throw the screws to the men some more."

The media are equally to blame: "You've got two rags here in the Twin Cities, the *Star and Tribune* and the *St. Paul Pioneer Press*. They're female-sympathetic, female-dominated, female management—it's all antimale. They don't do anything about male victims of domestic abuse, but they sure splash anything about women that have been assaulted, or raped, or all of this stuff."

Judges and legislators, he claims, know perfectly well what's going on, but choose to remain silent. "Judges don't want to upset the applecart. They don't want to change things because they know damn well that if they piss off the women's groups, they'll go to the polls and get women elected who will make judgments the way they want." Even Minnesota governor Arne Carlson comes in for criticism. "His ex-wife Barbara smacked him over the head with a frying pan. She tried to stab him when he was taking a nap on the couch. She beat him with her fists. He will acknowledge that these things happened, but he will not talk about it in public."

Finally, Gilliland turns his guns on men as a whole. "They're just a bunch of damn crybabies. We are responsible for it. We let women get away with it. Guys won't go out and vote against judges who make screwy decisions. If you think it's bad now, just see what it's like for your sons in twenty years' time."

Gilliland is the men's movement's answer to Andrea Dworkin. His position is so extreme and his rhetoric so angry that he alienates even those people who might feel sympathetic toward him. But, as the old bumper sticker says, just because you're paranoid doesn't mean they're not out to get you. Many of his claims do have at least some substantive evidence with which to support them. For example, whereas Gilliland's Domestic Rights Coalition survives on around $100,000 per annum, raised entirely from members' subscriptions and fees, women's shelters and organizations in Minneapolis and St. Paul received some $2.4 million in 1991 from the United Way alone. The United Way turned down a funding request from the DRC. No one's saying that money should be taken away from battered women, but even if men only make up a fraction of abuse cases, couldn't they at least receive a fraction of the funding?

One of the most distressing aspects of the whole abuse question is the absolute refusal of some—although by no means all—of the women involved in the shelter business to accept the existence of any battered men at all. They perceive all attempts to raise the subject to be deliberate attempts to undermine feminism. The same *Twin Cities Reader* article that cited Gilliland's remarks about Jesus Christ also contained the following quote from Loretta Frederick, legal adviser for the Coalition of Battered Women: "We shouldn't be surprised when there is a significant power shift, as there has been in the past twenty years, that certain men are organizing to stop it. And we shouldn't be surprised that the most verbal, vitriolic proponents of this position are convicted batterers themselves."

In Britain, Sandra Horley, director of the world's first shelter for women, the Chiswick Family Refuge, told *The Spectator* magazine that she would be worried if attacks on men became a serious public issue. "There are resource implications. Refuges for battered women are struggling to survive, and if we put across the idea that abuse of men is as great as the abuse of women, then it could seriously affect our funding." She sees stories about battered men as part of a concerted backlash against feminism: "For some reason, people seem to think that if they can show that men are also abused then violence against women is not a problem they have to think about and they *should* think about it. I'm not saying that all women are angels, but it's clear that the home is a much less safe place for the woman."

Interestingly, that is not the opinion of the person who originally set up the Chiswick Women's Refuge in West London. Erin Pizzey has spent the past two decades campaigning for the rights of the abused and victimized, but she has no doubt that violence is evenly divided between the sexes.

At fifty-three years of age, Erin Pizzey has, like a more fecund version of Germaine Greer, retired to the countryside. She lives in a little village outside Siena, Italy, where she swaps cookery tips with her neighbors, tends to her four dogs and two cats, and keeps in touch with her nine children—seven of whom were adopted—and all their various offspring. She even wears the costume of an Italian mamma, draped in black and decorated with a bejeweled crucifix settled upon her ample chest.

"Retired" in this case is a relative term. She supports herself by writing popular fiction—a trade which she practices sufficiently successfully to enable her to stay, at her own expense, in suites at London's magnificent Savoy Hotel, where our interview was conducted. After five years in the mid-1980s during which she lived and did counseling work in Santa Fe, New Mexico, she is now helping to set up Italy's first two refuges, along with others in the West Indies and South Africa.

Pizzey's manner is friendly and her voice is quiet, but a few moments of conversation reveal that the passion of her convictions has not diminished one jot. The surprising thing is that the target of Erin Pizzey's fire is not men, but women, and, more particularly, what she calls "that whole coven of witches"—the women's movement. She is convinced that the debate on domestic violence has been hijacked by activists whose main interests are political and financial.

Her opinions may have been expressed thousands of miles and several months apart from George Gilliland's, but they sound uncannily similar: "There are as many violent women as men," she says, "but there's a lot of money in hating men, particularly in the United States—millions of dollars. It isn't a politically good idea to threaten the huge budgets for women's refuges by saying that some of the women who go into them aren't total victims. Anyway, the activists aren't there to help women come to terms with what's happening in their lives. They're there to fund their budgets, their conferences, their traveling abroad, and their statements against men."

On the question of female participation in violence, she notes that her unpublished research into the first one hundred women to stay at the Chiswick Women's Refuge indicated that sixty-two were violence-prone, meaning that they were drawn to relationships in which they were both the victims and perpetrators of regular acts of aggression. Some were actually more violent than the men they accused.

"I get nervous saying these things, but the difficulty is that men are fairly straightforward. Certainly you get very feminized men who can be as equally psychologically delinquent as women. I've dealt with thousands of men and some of them were psychotic and dangerous, but on the whole they were very confused. They didn't know what was going on. Whereas I found the women extremely manipulative."

Why then, I asked, did society have such a hard time accepting the existence of female violence? "The only solution I can come up with," replied Pizzey, "was suggested to me by a conversation I had with a friend of mine who is an author. He was having trouble writing his third book and I said, 'The problem is you can't face your mother's role in your childhood. You can be absolutely accurate about your father, but the moment you have to face what your mother did, you fall to pieces.'

"No man wants to admit that his mother was violent, particularly if she was also incestuous. Incest between fathers and daughters is commonplace and written about. Incest between mothers and sons is hardly ever written about, yet my experience is that, unfortunately, far more women are incestuous than men. It's the last taboo, but how many men have to die, and how many have to kill themselves before we'll admit to it?"

The issue of child abuse is one to which I shall shortly return. The point to note here is Pizzey's belief that pain is passed on from generation to generation like a rotten chromosome. People should, therefore, accept and understand their own pain, so that they can learn to come to terms with it and thereby break the ongoing cycle of violence. First, however, they have to admit that it is there.

Ignorance and denial have been part of the problem from the very start. Back in 1971, when Pizzey founded her refuge, discussion of violence against women was still as taboo as violence against men remains today. "I was running a community center in Hounslow," said Pizzey, "when this woman Kathy walked in. She took off her jersey and her body looked like raw liver, she'd been beaten so much. Because I came from a background where both my mother and father were violent, I was outraged. I'd assumed, like everyone else, that all these social workers and health visitors—this huge clan of people—were taking care of victims, but nobody was. There was no literature, even. Nothing. [I took Kathy in and] within a matter of weeks the place filled up. I had nothing. It was just me, and I just decided to take it on."

During the time that Erin Pizzey ran the Chiswick Women's Refuge, it became known as a place that cared for women who were too aggressive or disturbed to be catered to by conventional shelters. In 1975, a study of 400 women who had visited the refuge during the course of the previous twelve months found that 330 (or 82.5 percent) were violence-prone, which is to say that they had been participants in a mutually violent scenario. Yet few could really accept what they had done.

"There was a woman we called Jaws," Pizzey remembered, "because one night she got drunk and got into an argument. The other woman started waving her finger at her, so Jaws bit it off. The next day I said, 'So now do we accept that you are violent?'

"Another woman had had the whole social worker bit about how she was a victim. She had had a row with a man and bottled him. She'd taken half his chin off. I said, 'Are you telling me you're not violent?' "

Was any criminal action taken against this woman? I asked. "No," said Erin Pizzey.

Did the man report his injuries? "No."

Was there any official record of her violence or his victimization? "No."

Pizzey said, "Time and again I've dealt with men who are physically attacked by women. In fact, the ophthalmologist I used to go to in Santa Fe said that one of the major injuries he saw was men who had had bottles and glasses in their eyes. I suppose that at the end of five years in America, in which I traveled and lectured everywhere from Alaska to the South, I just came to the conclusion that not only did I have hardly any American women friends, but they were the most aggressive and dangerous women I'd ever met in the world—terrifying. I had my dog shot at. I had my children shot at by women living in the surrounding areas. And their wimpish husbands—most of them would quietly say to me, 'I'm so sorry this has happened to you,' " but they were too frightened to do anything themselves.

There has, claims Pizzey, been a deliberate attempt on the part of politicians, academics, and journalists to suppress the truth about domestic violence. She is, she says, used to having speaking invitations canceled when the organizers discover that she believes women must take responsibility for their own violence. From the start, Pizzey claims, women who were "lefter than left"—among whom she names one senior British politician—saw the money given to refuges as a useful source of political funding. "I remember sitting in the offices of the women's movement in London, watching the activists coming in, ripping open these letters from desperate women, putting the money in their pockets—because it cost three pounds, ten shillings to join—and then throwing the letters into the back of a cupboard. Many of the early refuges weren't really shelters for battered women and children—sure, they'd have a couple—but a means of getting grants."

Pizzey first set out her views on women's involvement as both active protagonists in and provokers of violence in a book called *Prone to Violence*, published in 1982. It was greeted with extraordinary hostility. "I had said to my editor, 'Please see that the book doesn't go out until the day of publication, because if you put it out early, the women's movement will have time to react and organize.' He didn't believe me. He said I was paranoid. Then he got a phone call saying that if he put the book out, they'd smash the windows at the publisher's offices and they'd kill him. Finally he rang me up and said, 'Well, Erin, you weren't paranoid after all.' "

Her London hotel was picketed by three hundred screaming, banner-waving protesters. "I went downstairs and said to one of the policemen, 'Why don't you just get rid of them?' And he said, 'Because we're scared of them.' I had to have a police escort everywhere I went because there were threats on my life and bomb scares at my house."

There is a certain bitter irony to the notion that feminists would deny the concept of female violence and then threaten to kill the woman with whom they disagreed, but for Pizzey it was no laughing matter. "I finally decided that I couldn't take any more of that intimidation, not for my sake, because I'm used to it, but for my children's sake. So we went abroad."

I put it to Pizzey that her opinions might be taken as evidence, not that she was right, but that she was deeply troubled. She is, by her own admission, the victim of abuse from both her parents, particularly her mother. Was she, I asked, merely working out some deep-seated hostility toward women?

"That argument would be valid if I wasn't known internationally for the work that I do and the women that I've helped. They made a film for [the British TV series] *Cutting Edge* about my work and they found the women that I'd worked with who were violence-prone and whose lives had been in a total mess. They'd come through the therapy and the most exciting thing was to see them all again, leading wonderful lives with their kids."

Few female researchers have stirred up the kind of hostility among their fellow women that Erin Pizzey has provoked, but anyone arguing against the view that women can only be seen as innocent victims can expect, at the very least, trenchant criticism. In 1987, R. L. McNeely, professor of occupational social welfare at the University of Wisconsin–Milwaukee, and Gloria Robinson-Simpson, supervisor of programs for emotionally disturbed children and youth in Norfolk, Virginia public schools, published a paper in the magazine *Social Work* entitled "The Truth About Domestic Violence: A Falsely Framed Issue."

Toward the end of a comprehensive study of the literature on abuse they remarked, "Men are increasingly defenseless when allegations of domestic violence are made. Women increasingly are successfully using charges of past abuse as a justification for assaulting, killing or planning to kill husbands. Women also increasingly escape first-degree homicide convictions when they claim past spouse abuse. The effectiveness of past abuse as a defense results from the popular view of domestic violence as perpetrated only by emotionally disturbed men against women who are physically weak, defenseless, predisposed to passivity and philosophically non-violent . . . this view is supported by women's rights activists and a growing body of academic literature. . . . These facts are particularly interesting given the fact that approximately equal numbers of men and women are killed each year by spouses."

This article provoked a flood of response. Not for the first time (consider, for example, the *Details* debate on date-rape reported upon in an earlier chapter), male academics could be found taking female peers to task for their insufficiently profemale approach. But McNeely and Robinson-Simpson were unbowed. In March 1988, they wrote a second *Social Work* piece: "The Truth About Domestic Violence Revisited." In this, they stuck to their original opinions, reaffirmed their belief that "whereas 1.8 million females will be the victims of severe violence each year, 2.1 million males will be victimized by severe violence during the same reference period," and added an opinion whose every word could be taken as the motto for this entire chapter, to wit:

> Labeling domestic violence as a "women's issue" tends to vilify men simply because they are men, ignores the fact that many men are victimized, creates conditions that diminish the involvement of men in solving the problem and it leads to the development of remedies that do not address the full scope of the problem. . . . It is just not good judgement to conceptualize the problem as the exclusive domain of a single group, one outcome of which is to create conditions that set men and women apart rather than bring us together on domestic violence as *our* problem.

TAKING ACTION

Surely McNeely and Robinson-Simpson are right: Domestic violence is not a woman's issue, or a man's issue, but a human issue. The only way that we can ever help to solve it, or even manage it, is to be as open as possible about all its various aspects.

One of the benefits of this approach would be that it would enable help to be given to violent women themselves. In January 1993, I made a one-hour radio program for the BBC on the subject of female violence. One of the people whom I interviewed was Diane Core, a former associate of Erin Pizzey who now runs a charity called Childwatch, which cares for abused children in the north of England. She remarked that "There are a lot of women out there who are extremely violent and dangerous and who are very destructive to their husbands and their children. They need help and they're not getting it. I have spoken to violent women who are completely lost. They don't know why they're violent or why they do the things they do. They desperately need help and all they get doled out to them in their doctor's surgery is Valium, or some other antidepressant. Nobody actually asks why they are the way they are."

For women such as these, the acceptance of their violence, both by them and by society as a whole, would be a form of liberation. Equally, a public understanding of the equality of violence would end another all-too-common phenomenon, which is the projection by women of their own need for violence onto their partners, so that the man acts out violence whose psychological roots lie in the woman's unmet needs.

Nina Farhi is a senior member of the British Guild of Psychotherapists. In the course of the same BBC recording she said, "Surprisingly enough, I have probably come across and treated violence in women more than I have in men. I don't think that it is easy for women to talk about the level or even the presence of violence, but I think that if there is a safe enough setting, as there generally is in psychotherapy or psychoanalysis, it doesn't take very long for women to talk about their violence, once they've found somebody who can meet these feelings that they've had that have been unacceptable.

"Because society is uncomfortable with the notion of a violent woman, or an angry woman, women have found other means of expressing their violence. And one of them, for sure, is by putting it into the man, who is more acceptable as a violent figure. Quite often it is done unconsciously. People who live together know each other well and they know very well how to trip their partner into a violent channel. Women can put their own violent feelings into the men and say, 'Well, men are like that!' In that sense they rid themselves of the disturbing sense of their own violence."

Women, who are often more articulate than men, can also express their violence verbally and emotionally, particularly if they are well educated. "There are more options open to people who have been educated in a particular way, one of which is to use words in a way that is as painful, as damaging, as frightening as an actual punch, or a blow in the face. Words and language contain all the possibilities of violence and, to some extent, can have a far worse and far longer-lasting effect.

"I would always say that the capacity for violence is equal in men and women and comes out of, and is the result of, unmet needs in an infant's life, even from the word go."

To put it another way: Male or female, the pain is the same. During the course of researching this chapter, I have begun to understand why George Gilliland is so fired up about the abuse of men. It must be devastating to spend most of your working life listening to terrible stories of personal suffering, only to be told that none of these stories is worth anything and that your only interest is in attacking the rights of women and defending the violent male. For the record, Gilliland's opinion on violence is as follows: "Guys get abusive and that is not okay. It is just not okay for a guy to hit a woman, or a woman to hit a man, under any circumstances."

I wouldn't argue with that. And to critics who claim that campaigners for the rights of male victims are solely interested in distracting attention from female ones, I simply say: wrong. All we want is equality. All we want is for everyone to be given an even break, by society, by the courts, by the media, and by the politicians. And there can never be an even-handed approach until we know and accept how extensive the problem of female violence against spouses really is.

Nothing should be done that in any way worsens the position of women who are genuinely victims of abuse. They exist, in huge numbers, and they have a right to be helped in every way possible. But there is a great deal of evidence to suggest that many claims of abuse are themselves abusive, an offensive weapon in an ongoing war against a male partner. What, after all, could be a more effective form of abuse than depriving a man of his house, his family, his money, and possibly even his freedom? It is impossible to be sure about the degree to which claims are fabricated or exaggerated. The only way that we will ever find the answer to this and other hysteria surrounding the subject of domestic violence is to bring the problem—all of it, from both sides—out into the open.

Dr. Malcolm George, a lecturer in neurophysiology at Queen Mary and Westfield College in London, and a member of Families Need Fathers, is currently conducting his own research into the experiences of battered husbands. By working through organizations like FNF and placing advertisements in letters sent out by them and other men's groups, he has contacted a number of male victims of spousal abuse. He, like Stephanie Jeavons, has found that conversations on the subject proceed from nervous laughter to denial and then on to admission. Journalists who have interviewed him, for example, begin by expressing open derision toward the idea of battered men and end by telling stories that begin, "I knew a bloke once who was attacked by his wife." They, of course, may well be the bloke in question. "I can't speak to anyone who doesn't know a case," says Dr. George.

He notes, however, that men are very reluctant to consider themselves to be victims. They will begin stories by saying, "Of course, I'm not a victim, but . . ." and then go on to describe scenarios in which they have clearly been abused. They never say, "My wife hits me." They just say, "I'm volunteering for your research."

It is often left to someone else—a new girlfriend, perhaps, or a parent—

to come forward on the victim's behalf. "Women ring up and say that their man is an ex–battered husband," Dr. George says. "One woman told me, 'We go on access visits to see his kids and we have to take the police. They stand there and do nothing while she hurls abuse and assaults him.'

"Parents will call up and say, 'We know our son is being beaten and we've seen it happen, but he won't talk to us or anyone else about it.' "

As yet, Dr. George has not come to any definite conclusions, but trends are beginning to emerge. The first is men's silence: "For every man that comes forward there's another I know has been battered. I saw one at an FNF meeting. He had a black eye and his face was covered in bruises, but he wouldn't say a thing. I know three people whose wives stabbed them. Not one of them has gone to the police."

The second is that men are extremely reluctant to take advantage of domestic violence legislation. This may be because, if they try to do so, they receive no help at all from police, social workers, or even their own lawyers. The latter are a vitally important group because violence often occurs toward the end of a relationship as a means of forcing the husband to leave the family home. "The men are all scrambled up emotionally, but they have to work it all out by themselves. Their solicitor as sure as hell isn't going to help them," comments Dr. George.

Finally, as the Austin, Texas study also illustrates, it is often the men who end up on the statistics as the attacker. "Several battered men admitted to me that they had retaliated. One said, 'Yeah, we all hit back in the end,' then, bang! He's gone. He's looking at assault charges, non-molestation orders, ouster orders, whatever. . . ."

It is vital for male victims to be able to have somewhere to go where they can discuss their problems in a safe setting. The Everyman Centre, which is close to the Oval cricket ground in London, is one of the very few places in the country where men can meet to talk about the issues affecting them. Domestic violence was originally dealt with—as it is in most American counseling services—by asking men to come to terms with the violence instilled in them by their upbringing and their expectations. Claims of male victimization were seen as attempts at denial by the men for their own culpability. Increasingly, however, counselors are coming to realize that the situation is far more complex than they had imagined.

Robert Hart, the Centre's assistant director, told me, "It really does appear that violence is the expression of a dynamic in a relationship, and it goes both ways. We had a bus driver here who had battered his wife. He attended our counseling program and by the time he'd finished he'd changed many of his attitudes an beliefs about sexism and women. We were very pleased.

"He came back a few weeks later very distressed. He was crying. He said he'd been beaten up by his partner. We were very taken aback and we asked why she attacked him. He said a bloke down the pub had been bothering her, so she asked him to beat the guy up. When he refused, she beat him up instead.

"It makes me wonder who really wants to control the power in relationships. The old idea of the patriarchy is a very unsophisticated idea of how people relate."

Dr. George has been attempting to find a more sophisticated model. In October 1992, he submitted some preliminary findings from his research to the British Parliament's House of Commons Select Committee on Home Affairs, which was considering domestic violence. His sample size—thirty-eight volunteers—was tiny and all his statistics possess sizable margins of error. Nevertheless, they confirm that women need no lessons from men when it comes to violent assaults.

Noting that the typical abusive relationship lasted seven years, with violence occurring within six months of its start, Dr. George observed, "Over 80 per cent of the men reported that violence inflicted upon them involved the use of household objects or the like. Examples of objects used as a weapon included knives, scissors, hammers, bottles, vases, sticks, a baseball bat, an iron bar, a frying pan, and various other kitchen instruments. . . .

"Most men reported that they had experienced attacks which varied from a single blow, to a sustained attack over several minutes. In some cases attacks would consist of a series of separate assaults lasting over some hours. In over 90 per cent of the cases, these men considered that violent assaults could be unprovoked . . . a few [stated] that they had been attacked in their sleep.

"The most common injuries were bruising or lacerations and abrasions, but three men reported that they had been stabbed . . . three reported that they had been knocked unconscious and others reported injuries such as broken noses or fingers, being scalded by boiling water, and black eyes.

"A majority (80 per cent) reported that they had been taunted to hit their partners back and all stated that they experienced a high level of general abusive behaviour [including] verbal abuse and threats, destruction or disposal of their personal possessions, damage to the home, sleep deprivation, being locked out of the matrimonial home, and defamatory remarks to family, friends and even employers. Several men reported that they had lost their job . . . because of their marital situation.

"Approximately 50 per cent of men told their GP of the problems of their marital situation, but only 33 per cent sought medical attention for injuries received. . . . In only two cases did the men not confide in anybody, although all men said that they had also passed their injuries off as something other than a result of their partner's attack. . . . Over 60 per cent did not seek police involvement. . . . In only one case did a man report that any action was taken by the police and in the majority of cases these men considered that the police attitude to them was indifferent.

"Less than 20 per cent actually petitioned their wives for divorce. In contrast, 70 per cent of the women petitioned their husbands for divorce, all on the grounds of unreasonable behaviour, with 25 per cent also obtaining non-molestation and/or ouster orders against their husbands. In six cases, these were taken out after husbands had eventually retaliated, but in three cases an order was obtained even though the husband stated categorically and strenuously that he had not used physical restraint or retaliated.

"All men with children expressed concern that they might lose their relationship with their children upon separation or divorce. In only two cases was the man granted custody/residence and all the other men reported that there had been . . . frustration or even repeated denial of access visits under a court order. In some cases, violence or abuse by the women occurred in relation to access visits to their children."

I found this one of the two most distressing sections of this book to write and research (the other one, sad to say, follows next). It has been hard at times not to feel consumed with emotion at the suffering and injustice faced by men who are victims of domestic violence. But anger solves nothing. It merely perpetuates problems that are crying out for objectivity and balance. We desperately need official understanding of the plight in which battered husbands are trapped. To those women who persist in denying that the problem of domestic violence by women even exists, I can only say this: Twenty years ago, you asked for society's understanding of the harm that was being done to women. Now, when it is men whose pain is ignored, is it too much to ask for your tolerance in return?

CHAPTER 8

Suffer Little Children

Women are not the only supposed victims of man's inherent aggression. I quoted Adrienne Rich earlier saying that "men—insofar as they are embodiments of the patriarchal idea—have become dangerous to children," and she is by no means the only person to hold that opinion. Toward the end of the 1980s, Britain, along with numerous other Western nations including both America and Australia, was gripped by a sense of moral panic on the subject of child abuse and molestation. A clutch of self-appointed experts, ranging from doctors armed with controversial diagnostic techniques to fundamentalist Christians on the lookout for devil worship, managed to persuade us that the land was rife with suffering, sexually abused little children.

Finally, in the summer of 1992, this social issue, like so many before it, found its very own celebrity scapegoats. What William Kennedy Smith, Mike Tyson, and their respective accusers were to date-rape, and what Anita Hill and Clarence Thomas were to sexual harassment, Woody Allen and Mia Farrow were to child abuse: the focus of blazing publicity and speculation. At this point, I do not know, nor would I care to speculate, whether there is any truth in the allegation that Mr. Allen abused Ms. Farrow's daughter Dylan. By the time of publication more may be known, but this may equally be one of those cases in which the full truth is never uncovered. Whatever happens, one thing is clear: If it is possible to believe that a man famed for his intelligence, his humor, and his sensitivity toward women might conceivably have abused little children, then it is possible to believe it of anybody. And with every case that emerges, the temptation to presume guilt, rather than innocence, will become ever stronger.

Now, the crime of child sexual abuse as it is popularly conceived—to wit: forcible, nonconsensual sex with an underage child—is so shocking

to most ordinary people that anyone who commits it should not be surprised to receive the full force of society's wrath. We know that abusers
tend to be people who have themselves been abused. It is also true that
abusers are, increasingly, to be found among the ranks of children as
young as eight, boys and girls who are already passing on the virus of
pain with which they have been infected. Yet to most of us, especially
those who are themselves parents, the thought of little children being
sexually assaulted and penetrated is almost unbearably repellent. Do not,
for one second, suppose that I condone the action of the male child abuser.
What has become increasingly clear, however, as one horror story has
given way to another, is that the hidden agenda behind the activities of
many self-appointed guardians against abuse is at least as destructive, and
as harmful to the children, as the abuse itself.

In Britain there have been several cases over the past few years in which
mass seizures of children have been made by public authorities following
allegations of sexual abuse. In the northeastern district of Cleveland, one
doctor, Marietta Higgs, claimed that her use of reflex and dilation tests
had uncovered hundreds of cases in which children had been anally
abused by men. In the Lancastrian town of Rochdale, one council estate
(the British equivalent to a municipal housing project) was said to be the
scene of systematic mass abuse. And on the lonely Scottish isle of Orkney,
a priest was said to be conducting satanic sexual rites in which children
were the victims of unspeakable acts.

In every case, gangs of police and social workers made dawn raids on
families, abducted their children, and denied any contact between parent
and child. In Cleveland, children were being woken from their sleep in
hospital wards for anal and genital examination in the early hours of the
morning. In all three cases, children were interviewed in ways that owed
more to the Gestapo than to any responsible notion of child psychology.
Children were verbally assaulted until they gave the "correct" answer,
which is to say the one that the investigators wanted to hear. (There is
reason to believe that the investigation into at least one celebrated American abuse case—that of the Wee Care Nursery in Maplewood, New
Jersey, was grievously distorted by similar interrogatory tactics.)

Parents were consistently denied the opportunity to act in their own
defense. They were not allowed to see their children, write to them, or
give them Christmas or birthday presents. They were refused access to the
media, the courts, or even their local MPs. Only thanks to the determined
action of MPs such as Stuart Bell, in the Cleveland case, and newspapers
like the *Mail on Sunday*, which broke the Rochdale scandal, was the public
at large alerted to what was going on. In each case, judicial reports,
commissioned after the event, revealed a catalogue of incompetence and
obsession. In the Orkney case, for example, a disturbed fifteen-year-old

girl alleged that the priest had been holding satanic ceremonies at a quarry. Her word was accepted as the basis for immediate action without any checks on the priest—who suffered from a heart condition—or even on whether there was such a quarry on the island. In actual fact, there wasn't.

By the time these findings appeared, an unlikely alliance of antifamily and antipatriarchy ideologues, fundamentalist religious fantasists, and misguided media celebrities, ever eager for a bandwagon upon which to jump, had managed to persuade the nation that one in three children suffered from sexual abuse administered by men. What they did not reveal was that their conclusions were a deliberate distortion of research that defined abuse in an extremely general sense. Far from consisting exclusively of the forcible intercourse which most of us tend to imagine, however disgustedly, in these circumstances, the term was applied to any unwanted sexual experience of any kind. So any little girl who had seen a flasher in the park had, by that definition, been abused. Any little boy whose math teacher had put his hand on his knee had also been abused.

Penetration by a man's penis formed a small proportion of total cases of abuse. Of those cases, many occurred between stepfathers and teenage daughters. Of the rest, most involved vaginal, rather than anal, penetration. Only a minute fraction within a fraction comprised the activity alleged by the doctors at Cleveland—the anal penetration of small boys and girls by their fathers.

In my view, the obsessive search for evidence of such perverse behavior tells you more about the people doing the searching than it does about those being searched. But, lest anyone doubt the harm that such obsession may bring, let me quote from a letter that was published in the *Solicitors Family Law Association Newsletter,* November 1991. It was written by a lawyer, whose name and gender were not revealed, although I presume from the account given in the letter that she was female. It ran as follows:

> I was sexually abused over a period of approximately two and a half years by a male near relative who had been adopted into my mother's family. The sexual abuse has, so far as I am aware, had little discernible effect upon me. The discovery of the sexual abuse and the trauma of the investigation by professionals have had a profound effect upon me.
>
> I will never forget the ordeal I was put through at the age of seven. I will never forget the feelings of shame, degradation and intense physical invasion when examined by a paediatrician. I have no doubt that the same paediatrician would, if questioned, have stressed the consideration, tact, kindness and understanding he showed to me on examination.
>
> My views were not sought as to whether I should be examined.

I doubt that I would have had the knowledge or understanding to express or hold my own views. In retrospect, of course, I have strong views, but those are formed only with the knowledge of hindsight. I was seven: these were "grown ups" who knew best what should be done with me.

How much needless suffering is caused to children who have been sexually abused by the professionals? . . . In my own view, the sexual abuse I suffered was, to quote a judge in a rape trial, "a pretty tepid affair." The subsequent sexual abuse I suffered at the hands of a paediatrician will live with me for the rest of my life.

The children weren't the only ones blighted by the child abuse panic. In May 1988, shortly before the publication of the Butler-Sloss report on the Cleveland case, a book was published called *Child Sexual Abuse*. Written by Dr. Danya Glaser, a consultant child psychiatrist at Guy's Hospital, in London, and Dr. Stephen Frosch, a lecturer in psychology at Birkbeck College, it was a handbook for social workers dealing with child abuse. Its central proposition was that the family was founded on patriarchy and the ownership of women and children by men. Family life was, consequently, inherently destructive: "There are elements in all families that are potentially abusive—that is something inherent in families themselves," the authors wrote.

Furthermore, the abuse of children by their fathers was the inevitable result of men's "emotional illiteracy," which meant that their "ability to form emotional relationships is restricted." Sex, in this worldview, was little more than a means by which men dominated their partners: "The link between such a form of masculinity and sex abuse is apparent."

This is weasel-worded prejudice, disguised as rational opinion. To get its full flavor, simply repeat the exercise of substituting the words "black people" and "blacks" for "their fathers" and "men's" in the paragraph above. Now imagine that it ended with something like, "The link between such a racial background and sex abuse is apparent." These apparently sober words suddenly sound like blatant racism. So why did they not seem particularly offensive in the first instance? Because we are so used to pseudoscientific denunciations of men and masculinity that we have ceased to notice how repulsive they actually are.

Note, for example, the use of the word "potentially." The argument here is the same as for the use of "capable" in earlier claims about men's inherent propensity for rape. If by "potentially," the good doctors mean that I possess the strength "potentially" to abuse my children if I were so inclined, then of course it is true. I have the same physical equipment as any other man. But such a truth is so trivial as to be worthless. If, on the other hand, "potential" is taken to mean an *actual,* if unfulfilled, urge or inclination to commit an act of depravity against my own children, then it is as offensive as it is inaccurate.

If men are, by definition, incapable of expressing the full range of human emotions, then they are clearly less than fully human. If they are less than human, then they do not deserve to be treated in the same way as those people—i.e., women—who are. And if that is the case, then you might as well start stoking up the ovens right now.

I do not for one moment believe that the authors are proposing a Final Solution for the gender problem. But I am quite certain that they express— perhaps unknowingly—a prejudice that is far more common than one might imagine. Lots of otherwise normal, rational people sincerely believe that men are far less sensitive or vulnerable than women, as if they walked around in a permanent state of emotional anaesthesia. Over the past few chapters, I have been discussing several different, but related, social phenomena, including sexual harassment, date-rape, and domestic violence. In each of those areas examples were given of policies and conventions that only make sense if one presupposes that men do not feel pain, or fear, or emotional distress.

To this readers might say, "But you told us yourself that the male brain is different—it's got all those inhibitors, or whatever they're called, that prevent men feeling." Well, up to a point . . . the male brain may be structured in such a way that it does not permit the continual intermingling of thought and emotion that takes place in the female brain. A man's cerebral wiring is designed to limit distractions. It acts a bit like a Dolby system, which cuts out the hiss that might otherwise cloud a tape recording. But that does not mean that emotion is not present in men, nor that it cannot be just as acute as it is in women: It is simply handled in a different, more compartmentalized way.

One hesitates to think what might have gone through the mind of any impressionable young social worker who read, and believed, *Child Sexual Abuse* back in the dark days of 1988. How, for example, could one possibly write a favorable report on a father seeking increased contact with his children, knowing that such a father was, by virtue of his maleness, an emotional retard who was liable to translate his frustrated sexual urges into abuse at any moment? How could one be dispassionate about a man accused of abuse if one knew, as a matter of faith, that such abuse was "potentially" present in every man?

These theories of male inadequacy are the intellectual equivalent of toxic waste. They poison the ground around them. And they need to be cleared away. Until they are, they will continue to distort official thinking on a sensitive subject, and the feelings of individual human beings will continue to be corrupted. At the time that *Child Sexual Abuse* was published, my first daughter was four months old. Her birth had been, for me as for so many other parents, the best thing that had happened in my entire life. I was overwhelmed with love—an unconditional love that required no analysis or calculation. It had nothing to do with patriarchy. It was in no way emotionally illiterate. I just loved my child, end of story.

Except that these people, it seemed to me, wanted to sully and pervert that love. They wanted to strip it of any nobility or altruism. They wanted to interpret my actions as those of a pervert. An extreme reaction? Of course, but you have to remember the extraordinary atmosphere of the time. You have to consider the fear that the knock on the door in the middle of the night might be coming to your house next. I knew parents who were refusing to take their children to the doctor in case sore bottoms, brought on by upset stomachs, were interpreted as signs of abuse. I knew fathers who dared not bathe their children in case they were accused of improper conduct every time they washed their private parts. There was real evil abroad in the land.

Worse than that, in the hysteria surrounding abuse of children by men, abuse by women was ignored. Indeed, it was actively denied. It was, after all, as impossible as it was politically incorrect.

THE FEMALE ABUSER

Over the last few years, however, a different view of mothers' abuse of their children has begun to emerge. It has always been accepted that much of the general abuse of children—from the occasional smack around the ears to full-blown violence and/or deprivation—has been carried out by women. Now, very gradually, and with extreme caution, researchers are coming forward who suggest that maternal involvement may stretch to sexual abuse as well. Clearly, women don't do this in the same way that men do. They don't have penises with which to penetrate their children. What they do instead, as those who have suffered it will tell you, is envelop and overwhelm their little victims. The experience can leave them psychologically crippled.

For Kerry, a sufferer from maternal abuse whom I met at a men's group outside Sydney, Australia, the effect of his experiences had been to leave him as one of life's automatic victims. His mother had regularly got into bed with him, lain over and around him, and fondled his genitalia. Now an adult, he was the sort of man who seemed always to be getting ready to cower in the nearest available corner. All through his childhood and teens he had been mercilessly picked on and frequently beaten up by gangs at school and in the street. Teenage boys can be like animals: They smell weakness and prey upon it. It is often said that if you do not act as if you are in danger, you will not be, even in the roughest parts of town. Your body language will protect you. Kerry's body language screamed out his defenselessness. In the urban jungle, he was easy meat.

How common, then, is abuse by mothers and other women? Official Home Office figures show that only 2 percent of sexual abuse cases in Britain involve female suspects. Of those convicted for abuse, 3 percent are female, half of whom are charged together with a man. But how much is undetected or ignored?

As with so many other phenomena in which the woman is protagonist, rather than victim, no one really knows. The victims are extremely unwilling to come forward. They feel suffused with guilt about their own suffering, as if they themselves were to blame. Our instinctive denial of the possibility of such a crime—our atavistic revulsion at the thought that the Madonna may turn out to be a whore—combined with the politically correct refusal to accept the concept of female wrongdoing, have left this whole subject festering under a rock of ignorance.

The academic literature on the subject appears confused. In an American book on the subject, *The Sexually Abused Male, Volume 1: Prevalence, Impact and Treatment,* edited by Mic Hunter and published in 1990 by Lexington Books, Anthony J. Urquiza and Maria Capra confidently assert that "Most boys and girls are victimized by male perpetrators who know them."

Turning specifically to the question of sexually abused boys, the authors note that "The literature specifically addressing or identifying sexually victimized boys strongly identifies males as the primary perpetrators. Published studies report the percentage of male perpetrators as 97 percent (Friedrich, Beilke and Urquiza, 1988), 88.9 percent (Showers et al 1983), 86 percent (American Human Association, 1981), 66.7 percent (Urquiza 1988) and 53.3 percent (Risin and Koss, 1987). Separating the abuse into three levels of severity—exhibition, fondling and penetration—Risin and Koss (1987) identified male perpetrators in 49.3 percent, 60.9 percent and 46.8 percent of the cases, respectively."

Well, hold on a minute. Just how strongly *does* the literature pin the blame on males? Urquiza himself shows a 30.3 percent swing in his opinion between two studies published in the same year. And the only study that is quoted as categorizing forms of abuse appears to suggest, staggeringly, that men do *not* commit the majority of cases of penetrative abuse, although this particular finding is not deemed worthy of comment by the authors. The same 1987 study by Risin and Koss is subsequently said to have found that 42.7 percent of abusers were female (the missing 4 pecent were, presumably, not known), "many of whom appeared to be baby-sitters, teachers, neighbors and parents' friends."

Note that only one of these studies, all of which were carried out in America, appears to support the British Home Office's belief that 98 percent of abusers are male. Either Americans have habits that are very different from those in Britain, or the British government is way out of line. As we shall see, the latter is by far the most likely proposition.

One of the best ways of bringing the subject out into the open is by publicizing the existence of both male victims and female perpetrators through stories in the media. In June 1991 *The Spectator* published an article by Sandra Barwick in which she suggested that child abuse may not, as had always been thought, be a purely male crime. This was, of course, a dangerous proposition. One female therapist told Barwick, "I have had some feminists walk out of a talk when I have suggested that women also sexually abuse their children." The therapist asked not to be named, "or I may never be allowed in another support group."

One researcher who would be named was Tilman Furniss, professor of child psychiatry at Munster University and author of *The Multiple Professional Handbook of Child Sexual Abuse.* He said, "At first it was thought that sexual abuse was all by men against girls. . . . We have increasing knowledge of female abusers assaulting children for the same reason as men— for sexual relief—though my feeling is that the total will turn out to be less than 50% of all abusers."

As Barwick remarked wryly, "The guess of 'less than 50%' is a long way from the received wisdom of 2%."

Barwick went on to detail further examples of cases involving abuse by women, including the penetration of children's anuses with objects held by the mother or even, in one case, by the family's much-loved female doctor. She also cited one therapist who calculated that about a quarter of all her patients were victims of sexual abuse by women. The therapist commented: "It is no longer a surprise to me when children mention women as the assailant, but what is a surprise is this figure of 2%. If that is true then the whole 2% workload for the country is somehow ending up on my casebook."

The *Spectator* article was read in Australia by Lyndall Crisp, editor of the prestigious *Bulletin* magazine. So astounded was she by its findings that she decided to investigate sexual abuse by women in Australia. Professor Kim Oates, who for fifteen years was in charge of the sexual abuse unit at Sydney's Royal Alexandria Hospital for Children, told Crisp: "We used to think that most abuse happened within the family. Now, the indications are it's happening in pre-schools where women have the most access . . . babysitters . . . you don't want to think about that. . . . There's never been any argument that the main physical abusers are women. So there's a view around that you can say women cause physical abuse, but you're not allowed to say women sexually abuse."

It should be noted at this point that antipatriarchal feminists are by no means the only people who deny the possibility of female abuse. In Britain,

I know of many men who have found it impossible to persuade conserv-ative judges—brought up to believe in women as angelic, domestic fig-ures—that the women with whom they live could be capable of abusing their children (or their partners, as we have seen). Equally, Crisp mentions the case of a judge in the United States, who dropped meticulously pre-pared abuse charges brought against a woman by a social worker, detec-tive, and lawyer on the grounds that "Women don't do these kinds of things. Besides, the children need their mother."

But what kind of mother would abuse her own children? Lyndall Crisp interviewed Elizabeth McMahon, a doctor from Denver, Colorado, now working as a counselor of abuse victims in Melbourne, Australia. McMahon told her: "In the case of women who sexually abuse, the victim is in years of sexual bondage before telling anyone. The mother is a fairly ruthless, dominating woman. Whereas with female victims it is anger that motivates them to report a male abuser, the male being sexually abused by a female is usually a very vulnerable personality who feels absolute shame and worthlessness. There isn't much publicity, it isn't talked about, so it's very hard for them to report it. They don't think they will be believed.

"Thanks to the women's movement, women have formed support groups for each other, but that hasn't happened with men. . . . The prog-nosis for males who have been sexually assaulted by their mothers or another female is not good for three reasons. One, because there are no clinics to deal specifically with their problem. Two, it has been going on a long time. Three, child victims of abuse who do best are those with strong, supportive mothers."

TURNING BLIND EYES

Crisp published her story in August 1991. On March 31, 1992, Kidscape, a British childcare charity, organized a conference on female sexual abus-ers. It was prompted by the extraordinary response to a single phone-in program on women abusers on a London radio station, which had resulted in a flood of calls from victims. How did journalists respond? Well, Sarah Nelson, writing in the London *Guardian,* got her retaliation in early. In a piece published before the conference she asserted that this interest in "a tiny minority of women" had emerged not because of any genuine public concern, but because "During the eighties professional literature strove to show the preponderance of male abusers was accidental or incom-plete. . . . It ignored any implication that sexual abuse was a problem of male attitudes. . . . Powerful establishment forces merely went into brief retreat under the weight of feminist evidence. Today's stress on female sex offenders is part of the fight back on behalf of 'gender-free' theory [as opposed to] demanding a radical look at men's responsibility to challenge other men's behaviour and at power relations between the sexes."

Over the next few hundred words, Ms. Nelson considered the professionals' "anti-woman basis," the "dynamics of male-female power and domestic violence," and the need to consider our "deep-rooted prejudices about women." She ended, "Many child protection staff will feel this conference is fiddling while Rome burns and will ask that the urgent interest lavished on it is also given to 95% of the problem of sexual abuse."

The London *Independent*'s report on the conference, while perfectly fair in itself, concluded with a quotation by one Jan MacLeod of the Glasgow Women's Support Project: "There has been a disproportionate amount of interest in female abusers. There is a danger that attention will be distracted from the main abusers: men."

I wonder whether the Glasgow Women's Support Project has a copy of a fact sheet called *Child Abuse and Neglect Data* published by The American Humane Association, whose offices can be found at 63 Inverness Drive, East Englewood, Colorado. Admittedly, it comes from America, rather than Scotland. But the members of the GWSP would surely agree that men in America are not likely to be any less satanic than their Scottish brothers. Please forgive yet another piece of number-crunching, but it is the best guide I have found to the numbers of all forms of abuse, on all types of children, by all forms of perpetrators.

The following is a summary of data prepared by the AHA's children's division, the American Association for Protecting Children (AAPC). It concerns reported cases of child abuse and neglect collected throughout the United States between 1976 and 1987, the latter date being when the Reagan administration—you remember, the one that cared so much about family values—cut their funding. By the time this book appears, there will be new information covering the period until 1990, assembled by the National Center on Child Abuse and Neglect in Washington, D.C.

Preliminary estimates from that information indicate that the total number of abuse cases reported in 1990 was approximately 2.5 million, a 267 percent rise on the figure for 1976, which was 669,000. As always in these cases, one has to be careful in drawing apocalyptic conclusions from such an apparently horrendous increase: Much of it may be due to improved reporting, rather than an actual increase in activity.

In 1987, the last year for which accurate statistics are (at the time of writing) available, 2.2 million children were reported to have been abused or neglected. Of these reports, some 40 percent were substantiated after investigation. The remaining 60 percent were not, it should be added, dismissed as false, they were merely not proven, or were not fully investigated.

Going back one further year, 1986 was the last year in which the AAPC was funded to collect data on each individual case. In that year, 2.1 million children were reported, of whom 737,000 were shown to have been maltreated. Of these, the form of maltreatment was broken down as follows (N.B.: the figures add up to more than 100 percent since some children suffered multiple forms of abuse):

Type of Maltreatment	Percent of Children	Actual Numbers
Major Physical Injury	2.6	(21,000)
Minor Physical Injury	13.9	(115,000)
Other (Unspecified) Physical Injury	11.1	(84,000)
Sexual Maltreatment	15.7	(132,000)
Deprivation of Necessities (Neglect)	54.9	(429,000)
Emotional Maltreatment	8.3	(71,000)
Other Maltreatment	7.9	(61,000)

The AAPC's figures, however, do not stop with the forms of abuse; they also cover characteristics pertaining to its victims and perpetrators. They conclude that:

The average age of a child involved in an abusive or neglectful situation is 7.23 years old

The victim is female in 53.5 percent of the cases

The perpetrator of the abuse is a parent in 81 percent of the cases

The average age of the perpetrator is 31.7 years and is male in 46.7 percent of the cases

Stress factors acting on abusive families include health problems (42.8 percent of cases), financial worries (40.8 percent), and family interaction difficulties

You will notice that one finding of this research, while it is clearly implied by the figures above, is not actually stated in explicit terms; in fact it is specifically hidden. The finding is that, according to an authoritative study of every single case of child abuse in the entire United States— a study that requires no extrapolation whatever since it covers 100 percent of the population, and whose findings I have personally checked with staff at the American Humane Association—slightly more than half of all child abuse (53.3 percent, to be exact) is carried out by women.

Let me run that by you one more time: More than half of all child abuse in the United States of America in 1986 was carried out by women.

Suzanne Steinmetz, the chairwoman of the sociology department at the University of Indiana, whose controversial research into battered husbands has aleady been mentioned, has gone even further. She has claimed that women are 62 percent more likely than men to abuse children and that boys are more than twice as likely as girls to receive physical injuries. These findings are thought to reflect women's greater access to and time spent with children, rather than any inherent female malevolence, but they certainly challenge the picture of feminine innocence and masculine guilt.

It could still be that men commit the majority of acts of sexual abuse. But that begs another question: Why are we so obsessed by that particular means of doing harm to a child? Is a child who has been beaten, or starved, or verbally humiliated any better off than one who has been sexually assaulted?

It is generally agreed that a child who is compelled to have sex with an adult against his or her will suffers lasting damage. Certainly that would be the commonsense view, and one with which, as a parent, I would instinctively agree. But in August 1992, the British political weekly *The New Statesman* departed from its traditional liberal-left stance and published a special issue devoted to opinions that were politically incorrect. One of its articles, by Edward Barrie, suggested that the aftereffects of sexual activity might be less traumatic to children than had previously been supposed.

In particular, he said, "An enormous investigation was carried out for the German police by Dr. Michael Baurmann, who reported his findings in 1983. His team carefully assessed 8,058 young people of both sexes (more girls than boys) involved in illegal sexual relationships. They found that in many cases no harm was done—neither emotional nor physical. About 1,000 boys under the age of 14 took part in the study, and not one of those was found to have been harmed. Harm to the girls, when it occurred, was sometimes (not always) a result of the sex act itself, and sometimes the result of heavy-handedness by police, parents and others in the aftermath. Baurmann has shown conclusively that a child may well become a victim purely because victimization is expected. More recent police department follow-up studies have confirmed the findings."

Those findings, astounding though they seem at first glance, tally with the experiences of the lawyer whose letter about her experiences of abuse I reproduced earlier in this chapter. They make me question whether the important social issue that both British and American society needs to confront is not abuse itself, but our apparent obsession with it.

Barrie remarks: "Perhaps most sinister of all, a young woman university graduate working on a doctoral thesis and pursuing the 'harm done' aspects of abuse, with help from . . . overseas experts, was denied a grant unless she came up with findings that would help the authorities detect paedophiles.' She found this distortion of her views unacceptable."

At this point, the truth is so clouded by exaggeration and confusion that one cannot do anything other than speculate about what is really going on. But when celebrities queue up to reveal ever more lurid accounts of their childhood experiences, or publicize abuse helplines, the sickness to which they bear witness may just be the profound suspicion with which Anglo-Saxon society regards sex. That, and the belief that the quickest route to public approval is to label oneself a victim—even if one happens to be a millionaire rock star, or a candidate for the presidency.

Consider, specifically, the determination with which some women seek to paint a picture of rampant sexual abuse, practiced entirely by men. Is this motivated by an altruistic desire to cure a social malaise, or just a fearful hostility toward male sexuality as a whole? Are they simply projecting their own terror onto children? Is there anything to choose between the dysfunction that causes an adult to seek out sex with children, and the dysfunction that persuades a doctor or social worker that she is surrounded, on every side, by a raging sea of sex abuse?

Meanwhile, why won't anyone have the courage and the honesty to confront and deal with abuse carried out by women?

Perhaps they assume that it isn't serious. Perhaps the women, trapped with their kids all day long, just inflict minor injuries. Maybe there are single moms who, desperate to get out and earn some money, leave their children unattended, or neglected in an inadequate day-care center. It's a plausible scenario and it would, after all, ill behoove those of us who live in comfort to criticize the behavior of women on the breadline. Perhaps the really serious assaults are committed by men.

Fair enough, we'll look at the fatalities. In 1986, the AAPC was only able to collect figures on infanticide from twenty states, representing about 50 percent of the total U.S. child population. The following statistics are not, therefore, complete, but they come from a sample size sufficient to satisfy the most critical statistician; the margin of error is so minimal as to be negligible.

In the twenty states surveyed there were 556 child fatalities as a result of maltreatment.

The average age of the victims was 2.8 years.

The victim was male in 53.7 percent of cases.

The perpetrator was a parent in 76.4 percent of cases.

In 62 percent of the cases, the cause of death was a physical injury, while neglect was the cause in 44.3 percent of the cases.

The perpetrator was on average 27.3 years old and was female in 55.7 percent of the cases.

So, in cases of child fatality, perpetrators are actually more likely to be female than in lesser cases of abuse. And their victims are more likely to be little boys. In the words of "Child Abuse and Neglect Fatalities: A Review of the Problem and the Strategies for Reform," a working paper published in the *Monograph of the National Center on Child Abuse Protection,* "Active victims [of infanticide] are typically males, under two years of age, living in low socioeconomic status families with multiple young siblings, and who die at the hands of a single mother." This is, in other words, exactly the opposite of the line spouted by activists, parroted by the media, and taken as gospel by legislators.

Figures for 1990 from the National Committee for the Prevention of Child Abuse and Neglect show that there was a nationwide total of 1,211 childhood fatalities in America as a result of maltreatment. Assuming that the male-female proportions have remained constant, that would work out as 654 boys and 557 girls, killed by 678 women and 533 men.

In Britain the situation is less clear-cut. One can say with certainty that rates of child homicide are—like all other forms of killing—far lower on this side of the Atlantic: In 1990 a total of 79 British children under the age of sixteen were victims of homicide. Even allowing for differences in population, that still indicates a homicide rate that is 3.4 times as high in the United States as Britain.

That said, the single most dangerous age that any citizen of Great Britain can be in terms of murder risk is less than one year old. In fact, a baby is nearly four times more likely to be murdered than the average British citizen. Thirty babies were killed in 1990, which represents a rate of forty-four offenses per million population within that age range, compared to twelve homicides per million in the population as a whole. Of those babies, exactly half were male and half female. If, however, one looks at all the cases of infanticide in the period 1980–1990, the average distribution of victims is 57 percent male and 43 percent female.

The relative figures for victims, therefore, are roughly comparable with American findings. One cannot, however, say anything about the perpetrators of these crimes, for a surprising, but fascinating reason. In the years 1980–1990, 293 children aged less than one year old were victims of infanticide in Britain. Yet only 42 suspects were charged with infanticide in the same period. What happened to all the others? After all, allowing for those cases in which the child was attacked by both its parents, one would expect well over 300 people to be charged. There can surely be relatively few cases of unsolved infanticide.

In the years 1989–90, the discrepancy was particularly marked. There were fifty victims and only one suspect brought to court—a clear-up rate of 2 percent, which, even by the present wretched standards of police incompetence, could hardly be described as satisfactory.

Could it be that the legal system simply finds it intolerable to contemplate female perpetrators? The notion of a mother who kills her own child is profoundly horrifying. These days we talk about postnatal depression, or baby blues, as a means of explaining acts that are otherwise inconceivable. Yet, purely by virtue of the intimacy of their relationship, the stress imposed on the mother, the poverty in which many young mothers are forced to live, and the amount of time that mother and child spend together, it would not seem unreasonable to suppose that the majority of small babies are killed by their mothers. Unfortunately, as with so many other social phenomena, the numbers dry up once men stop being the bad guys. It's almost as if the specter of violent or abusive women is so threatening to society, right across the political spectrum, that we have to deny their very existence for fear of the damage that they would do to our image of womanhood.

PATTERNS OF PREJUDICE

What can we conclude, then, about the way in which child abuse, both sexual and nonsexual, is reported? And what should it tell us, particularly those of us who, as men, stand accused of these terrible crimes? Well . . .

The accepted feminist orthodoxy is that all abusers are male. The less accepted, but still widespread, view is that all males are potential abusers. (For abusers, read rapists, sexual harassers, violent spouses, etc.) This orthodoxy is offensive and grossly prejudicial. It is also inaccurate.

A denial of reality by political extremists on the one hand, and judicial fogeys on the other, distorts debate, social policy, and legal action.

Male victims of abuse (ditto domestic violence, harassment, etc.) are terrified of coming forward for fear of facing disbelief and contempt in equal proportions. They feel unmanned and humiliated by their experiences. They are not allowed to be victims.

Once accurate statistics are made available, it becomes clear that the situation is much more evenly balanced than had previously been believed. In other words, men and women are equally capable of committing acts of evil.

No government money or interest is given to men as victims. Nor is there any interest in academic research into their situation.

Given men's unwillingness to discuss such subjects in public, combined with the prejudice encountered by those men who do speak out, it often takes action by female journalists and therapists to bring an issue out into the open. The recognition of men's issues now depends on moderate women setting out an open-minded agenda.

Men need a network of support and—with the exception of the gay community, which has been forced to organize in order to survive—they haven't got it. Nothing will change until men are prepared to shed their inhibitions and their fear of female disapproval and get their act together. It is not fair either to blame women or to depend upon them. Not if you want to be a real grown-up.

Until men are prepared to stand up and be counted, and until they are willing to take action to fight for principles in which they believe and issues that affect them, they stand a severe risk of being left behind by a tide of social legislation that runs directly contrary to their interests and their human rights. Burdened as they are by accusations of their inherent moral and sexual deficiencies, they are at their weakest in the areas that mean most to them as individuals.

But those women who believe that they are doing their sisters a service by attacking and undermining men could not be more wrong. For if we are to produce men and women capable of living healthy, nonviolent lives, men have got to be trusted and Dad must be let back into the family home.

CHAPTER 9

Absent Fathers, Violent Sons

Although the vast majority of public—as opposed to domestic—acts of violence are committed by men, there is an important qualifying adjective that has to be included: The men in question are young. Once he is past thirty, a man is far, far less likely to mug, rob, or rape, let alone riot or loot. So the question arises: What makes a boy turn to crime? To which the answer is, Well, how long have you got?

Some factors appear to be predetermined. Testosterone does seem to have a significant impact on young children's general aggressiveness, impatience, and predisposition to rough-and-tumble. But that does not mean to say that those characteristics will necessarily be translated into actual violence or antisocial behavior. Even when the evidence appears straightforward, final judgments are very much a matter of interpretation.

For example, boys who suffer from a metabolic disorder known as Imperato McGinley tend to be born with very low levels of testosterone and small sex organs. Many are even thought to be girls, and are brought up as such until puberty, when their testosterone is, as it were, kickstarted and they develop as normal men. At this point, despite their feminine conditioning, they often behave in an aggressively masculine and sometimes criminal manner. From this one might conclude that testosterone will cause bad behavior, irrespective of conditioning. Or then again, one might decide that these teenagers were merely overreacting against their feminine upbringing and attempting to assert themselves as men.

Other physiological conditions that are more common in males than females, and more common again in criminal than noncriminal males, include hyperactivity, learning disorders, mild forms of autism, and mental retardation. These conditions, however, are not evenly distributed throughout society, but are skewed toward the poor. This is because poor mothers are much more likely to suffer from bad diet, alcoholism, or drug addiction than their middle-class sisters and, as a consequence, the babies that they produce are less healthy.

Then there are the pervasive influences of the general culture in which children grow up, and the pressure of the peer groups within which they move. The vast majority of all crime—particularly small-scale car thefts, burglaries, and muggings—are carried out by youngsters in their teens (or even preteens) and early twenties. This is an age at which young males are desperate to prove their masculinity, an age at which they define masculinity in terms of being tough, or hard, and an age at which they are profoundly influenced by the opinions of their peers. As a consequence, young men en masse will often behave in ways that few of them would consider if they were alone.

Even then, however, there are reasons for violence that seem impossible to pin down. During the 1992 European Football Championships, the infamous English soccer fans once again ran riot, causing havoc in peaceful Swedish towns and shaming their nation. Yet Scottish fans, who come from a country that is ruled by the same government, speaks the same language, and has roughly similar levels of general violence and criminality, were so good-humored and charming that their hosts presented their representatives with a special award. What was the difference?

Whatever the reason, it is not enough to blame it on maleness, pure and simple: There always has to be something else. Traditionalists use phrases like "lack of moral fiber" or "loss of discipline," which suggest that the problem can be solved by the reintroduction of standards that they believe were maintained in days gone by—a belief which looks decidedly questionable if one looks at rates of crime and violence in nineteenth-century cities.

For most liberal commentators looking at social disorder, that "something else" is poverty. We have already seen how the wealth and well-being of the mother can affect her children's predisposition to crime. Then there are the simple facts of deprivation, both financial and cultural, that bear down upon the members of the so-called "underclass." Dependent on welfare, deprived of traditional social networks by supposedly progressive housing schemes, and torn apart by drugs and violence, the people of the inner cities are society's guilty secret.

But poverty cannot be the only factor. After all, many English football hooligans have good jobs: They need them in order to have the money to follow their club or national side all over the world. And then again, many people who are poor are not in any way delinquent. Perhaps the most important common denominator lies elsewhere.

Increasingly, researchers are coming forward who place the blame for antisocial behavior on criteria that go beyond the simple effects of financial deprivation. In the United States, current rates of divorce and illegitimacy suggest that 51 percent of all children will grow up without a father living permanently under the same roof. David Blankenhorn, president of the Institute for American Values in New York, told the London *Times*, "Fatherlessness is the engine that drives many of our worst social problems. The most important predictor of juvenile delinquency is not race or income, it is the absence of a father. For teenage pregnancy it is the same story. Young fatherless women are twice as likely to get pregnant outside of marriage. The explosion of juvenile crime and teenage pregnancy tracks the increase in fatherless homes with eerie precision."

In Britain, some 60 percent of all boys from highly disadvantaged backgrounds will end up with a criminal record. So what stops the other 40 percent? Since 1947, the Newcastle Thousand Family Survey has been examining cycles of disadvantage in the same family groups. Reporting on the survey's findings for the London *Guardian*, writer Liz Hodgkinson revealed that "The overwhelming risk factors for young delinquent behaviour are a poor work record and alcoholism in the father. Parental criminality before the child's 10th birthday is also a major background factor . . . 40 per cent of sons of recidivist fathers are also persistent offenders . . . the ratio was the same with adoptive or step-fathers."

Other factors such as the number of children (first- and second-born children of small families were significantly less likely to be criminal), complications at birth, and childhood accidents (which might imply slipshod parenting) were also significant, as was the general ability of the mother to cope with her family. "The presence or absence of toys was not significant either way, but firm management and the ability to reason with children were protective. Mental resilience is far more important than social disadvantage."

In fact, "Social anarchy is directly related to the breakdown of family structure, personal responsibility and social order."

Except, of course, that no one from the Newcastle Thousand Family Survey, still less Liz Hodgkinson of the superliberal *Guardian*, said those last words, which are actually taken from a speech made by the then–Vice President Dan Quayle, shortly after the Los Angeles riots of 1992. Quayle went on, a couple of days later, to make his infamous remarks about Murphy Brown's baby, which, should anyone need reminding, ran: "It doesn't help matters when prime-time TV has Murphy Brown mocking the importance of fathers by bearing a child and calling it just another lifestyle choice."

Coming from the man who once addressed the United Negro College Fund (motto: A mind is a terrible thing to waste) with the words, "What a waste it is to lose one's mind—or not to have a mind. How true that is," who announced, "I didn't live in this century," and who could not spell *potato,* this seemed to be yet one more tragic example of congenital foot-in-mouth disease. Pundits on both sides of the Atlantic united in condemning Quayle, both for his repellent opinions and his political insensitivity. As it happened, however, Quayle's public approval ratings rose somewhat after his remarks. But that wasn't the most amazing thing about the whole incident. The most amazing thing was . . . Dan Quayle may just have been right.

WHY DADDY MATTERS

The relationship between fathers and sons is one of the great unspoken issues in men's lives. So much is left unsaid and so many misunderstandings created, purely for want of the ability to communicate with one another.

I remember sitting in a London cinema watching the movie *Field of Dreams,* in which Kevin Costner stars as a man who is convinced that he has to build a baseball field in his own backyard. One of the central themes of the film is the way in which men so rarely tell their fathers how much they love them, so that the father's death leaves all the tensions in their relationship unresolved. I am not ashamed to say that I wept almost continuously through the second half of the film. And, judging by the sniffs and snuffles emanating from the men (but not, interestingly enough, the women) around me, I was by no means the only one. By targeting the pain caused by all that is left unsaid in the struggle between fathers and sons, the producers of *Field of Dreams* had created the first male tearjerker.

As I researched this book and talked to men about their lives, their feelings about their own fathers would often emerge. Fathers set an example, to be emulated or, in many cases, to be challenged and denied. On one occasion I was talking to two workers in the American men's movement. I asked them what had moved them to become interested in men's issues. One replied that he had been so inspired by his father's love that he became determined to ensure that as many of his fellow men as possible were made aware of the redemptive power of positive, unrepressed emotions. The other said that he had been abused. He just wanted to do everything he could to prevent the same fate befalling anyone else.

So fathers were the markers against which we measured ourselves. But the particular significance of the father as a determinant of antisocial behavior was not something I had remotely anticipated, however obvious it seems to me now. When it came to male perversity and violence, I merely had a general view that it would be in everyone's interests—male and female—to try to find out why so many men, particularly young men, behaved in the way they do. To put it crudely: If there were fewer fucked-up men, there might also be fewer beaten-up women.

Yet wherever I went, experts from a wide range of fields kept making the similar points about the importance of paternity as a formative influence. A well-balanced man—just like a well-balanced woman—has to be taught how to channel his energies, many of which are potentially destructive, along constructive paths. Only another man can enable him to do this and that man should, if at all possible, be his father. To return once again to the *Star Wars* trilogy, Luke Skywalker is guided by elderly men to choose the light Force, rather than the dark. Luke depends on Obi-Wan Kenobe and Yoda for his lessons. His problems arise because he has been deserted by his father, who turns out to be Darth Vader, the ultimate abusive parent.

What has *Star Wars* got to do with life on earth? Well, in *Boys Will Be Boys*, Myriam Medzian asserts, "Major nurturant paternal involvement in child-rearing would play an important role in reducing male violence. It would signal the end to adherence to the masculine mystique and would lead to significant improvements in mothers' behaviour towards their sons."

Women have a strong self-interest in promoting successful fatherhood. Good fathers, producing healthy sons, are women's best hope of diminishing the dangers they face from abusive or violent men. In his book *Body Consciousness*, published in 1973, Seymour Fischer, then professor of psychiatry at the Upstate Medical Center of the State University of New York, Syracuse, discussed the idea that violence in young men is a way of reestablishing a long-threatened or repressed sense of masculinity.

He wrote as follows: "Cross-cultural studies . . . [have shown that] boys who have been relatively close to their mothers and distant from their fathers and who, therefore, have had a limited opportunity to learn directly about the 'feel' of being masculine, have a strong tendency during adolescence to engage in hostile, predatory behavior as a way of announcing that they are, indeed, of the male species. It is well-known, too, that male delinquency comes with an unusual frequency from broken homes in which there is no visible father and where almost all of the primary socialization experiences have been with women."

Of course, maternal smothering is by no means the only way in which a boy's masculinity can be distorted to the point at which, as an adult, he feels impelled to rape or murder women. A father who is present, but abusive, is just as bad as a father who is absent. The key point is that extreme acts of violence or sexual perversion are not functions of masculinity per se, but of its distortion or suppression. It would be foolish, of course, to suggest that one will ever create a world that is free from psychosis or parental abuse. Nor do I have anything but praise for educational reformers who attempt to wean boys away from violence by showing them the satisfaction that can be derived from behavior that is nonconfrontational. Boys who learn to resolve conflicts by negotiation, rather than force, are learning useful lessons indeed.

But any educationalists who seek to cut down on sex-attacks and crimes of assault by attempting to undermine the very idea of masculinity or to feminize young boys will find that their policies have precisely the opposite effect. Well-balanced men, who are secure and confident in their masculinity, are far less likely to harm women than men who are insecure or resentful. Boys will be boys whatever we do: The question is, what kind of boys do you want them to be?

As the British criminologist Patricia Morgan puts it in a 1983 paper for the Social Affairs Unit entitled *Feminist Attempts to Sack Father—A Case of Unfair Dismissal,* "There is something pathetic and perverse about demands for rape crisis centres, security bolts and self-defence classes from those doing their best to promote the very social conditions which necessitate such services."

Even if one forgets about extreme examples of criminal or antisocial behavior and just considers the happiness of the child, the case for fatherhood is still very strong. In 1984, an article in the *British Journal of Developmental Psychology* by P. S. Fry and Anat Scher examined "The effects of father absence on a child's achievement motivation, ego-strength and locus-of-control orientation: a five-year longitudinal study." In plain language, they spent five years researching a group of kids to see whether the loss or absence of a father made any difference to their self-esteem, achievement levels, educational aspirations, ambition, loneliness, and/or self-centeredness.

The authors noted that much earlier research had maintained that a father's absence from the home made no difference to a child's achievements. But they added a word of caution, taken from a 1979 article in *American Psychologist* called "Divorce—a Child's Perspective," which cautioned that "In the current eagerness to demonstrate that single parent families headed by mothers can provide a salutory environment for raising children, and that the presence of fathers is not essential for normal development in children, there has been a tendency to overlook the contribution of the father to family functioning."

Certainly, as far as Fry and Scher were concerned, the evidence in Dad's favor was overwhelming: "The adverse effects associated with father absence are evident fairly early in the development of children and are cumulative over time. . . . The father's presence and his involvement in children prior to and during the years of formal education may make a significant contribution to a positive and healthy personality development."

They found that father presence increases a child's ego strength and self-esteem, while father absence decreases it. This effect is even more pronounced in boys than in girls, and this is particularly the case in the teenage years. A boy who is blessed with a supportive, present father will become more confident and secure during his teens. A boy who is deprived of that relationship will decline during the same period. Fry and Scher state that "Fatherless boys have less confidence in their ability to shape positive or negative experiences. [The father's] prolonged absence has the effect of locking boys, more so than girls, within their own ego-centered insecurities. . . .

"It is conceivable that long-term father absence and the resulting lack of involvement in the child may result in such ego-strength and self-esteem deficits as lack of self-confidence and lack of personal adequacy in the child, and a continuing sense of social alienation and self-centeredness."

That sounds like a recipe for the creation of maladjusted, potentially violent young men, and indeed the authors conclude, "A judicial or social policy which impedes, rather than facilitates father-child interactions and relationships is likely to aggravate the adverse effects which parental deprivation has on the children's personality development."

In many, many cases, the negative effects of single parenthood upon a child's development are no fault of the mother. It is, for example, not a woman's fault if she is poor. In 1991, 14 percent of Americans lived in female-headed, single-parent households. But these people comprised about 50 percent of all Americans living below the poverty threshold. Nor can a woman be blamed for her inability to do the impossible and provide a same-sex role model for a young male. But even if the mother is not to blame, the society in which she lives may well be culpable.

In other words, if you create a system that places a significant financial premium on single parenthood by insisting that a range of social security payments are available only to unmarried, unpartnered mothers; if you give men little chance if any of maintaining satisfactory relationships with their children after divorce; if you frame legislation solely in terms of the punishment of men who have reneged on their financial responsibilities without giving them corresponding personal rights; if you leave men embittered and embattled in the face of the system's indifference to their needs—if you do all these things, as society presently does, then the result will not be greater fairness and harmony, but more bitterness, more hostility, and a great deal more violence, much of it directed at women.

THE CARING MONKEY

A number of immediate objections arise. Men, one might say, do not have the natural child-rearing instinct that is innate in women. This, however, is an argument into which one should proceed with extreme caution. Suppose, for example, that it were true. Would it not imply, then, that women should stay at home and exercise their instincts as exclusive, full-time caregivers? After all, with so much of their minds taken up with maternal affairs, there could not be much left over for professional matters.

The evidence, however, does not suggest that the parenting instinct is exclusive to women. It would be surprising if there was not a natural tendency for mothers to have extremely strong feelings toward the children to whom they have given birth, and there is—as we have seen— evidence to suggest that women's brains are designed to assist them to raise children; but that does not mean that men cannot feel deeply about their offspring, too.

What is certain is that—in this case as in so many others—any differences that are present naturally are greatly enhanced by the way we rear our children. Little girls are observably more interested in fantasizing about babies, marriage, and homemaking than little boys. But much of this is due to the efforts that are made to turn boys away from forms of play that could be thought of as sissified. Both sexes play with dolls, but girls play house with Barbie while boys play war with Action Man. One of the reasons that boys ask for Action Man may be that they want to play with dolls, but are terrified of seeming like sissies: A doll that acts out acceptably macho fantasies of war is an allowable substitute.

There is a biological parallel for male nurturing. In his book *A Question of Sex*, the British psychologist Dr. John Nicholson reports on experiments carried out with rhesus monkeys. The male monkey is usually indifferent to his young, and may even attack and kill them. But researchers gradually exposed male monkeys to the presence of motherless baby monkeys, with the following results:

> The baby monkey . . . approached the adult and tried to cling to him. At first, he was repulsed angrily, but after a while the adult began to groom him—an important ice-breaker in the social life of rhesus monkeys—and from then on the two became steadily more attached to one another. In fact, they became closer than most rhesus mothers and their children, and remained so long after the time when young monkeys usually break with their mothers and start to lead an independent life. Their relationship was not the same as that of the typical rhesus mother and child—

they went in for more rough-and-tumble play than female monkeys will tolerate—but the younger monkey developed into a perfectly normal adult male and remained on excellent terms with his foster-father.

Research on humans suggests that men, like monkeys, tend to give their children more active stimulation and play with them in a more physical way than do mothers. But there is nothing to suggest that males are any less capable of caring for children should the need or desire arise.

At the Germantown Friends school, a Quaker institution in Philadelphia, a program called Education for Parenting has been running since 1979 (it has since been taken up by a further nine schools in ghetto areas of the city). From their first year, pupils spend time with babies, brought into school by their parents, charting their progress and discussing it in class. They will even take responsibility for a particular baby and act as its caretaker for a few hours a week. Children learn about their own capacity for emotional involvement and the pleasure that brings. There is little difference between the aptitudes of the boy and girl pupils.

Maybe not, but surely, our skeptic might say, men who are allowed too close to children may very well abuse them. There is some force to this argument. A tiny minority of male teachers, like some female childcare workers, may be drawn to their profession by the opportunities it offers for sexual activity, but among fathers there is evidence to suggest that active parents are actually less likely to abuse their children.

Myriam Medzian cites research conducted at the University of Utah by Hilda and Seymour Parker. "The Parkers did a comparative study of fifty-six men who were known to have sexually abused their minor daughters and fifty-four men with no known child sexual abuse in their backgrounds. They found a very significant correlation between lack of involvement in child care and nurturance, and child abuse."

The Parker study reinforced previous findings which suggested that, in general, stepfathers were much more likely to abuse children than natural fathers. But those stepfathers who had been actively involved in nurturing their stepdaughters were no more likely than blood relatives to abuse them subsequently. The Parkers conclude that "If primary child care were shared more equally by men and women, one basis for . . . the sexual exploitation of females might be eliminated."

There is a fairly straightforward rationale for the behavior the Parkers uncovered. Abuse is often a substitute for a more natural relationship, either with the mother or the child. But a man who has spent time with his child, who has loved it and cared for it, is far less likely to want or need to betray that relationship. Not only has he invested too much of himself and his time, but he will also have received the emotional satis-faction that seems so clearly to be lacking in the lives of abusive parents.

Even if we accept this, one final objection arises. Surely any boy who is raised by his father will be all the more deeply inculcated in the evils of machismo and the patriarchy. Isn't he likely to behave in a way that is even more harmful to women?

This might well be an opinion put forward by the more extremist, separatist elements of the feminist movement. And there are plenty of educators and political theorists who might, I suspect, be seduced by the prospect of converting young men to a more ideologically sound, feminine mode of behavior.

This point of view is fatally misguided and the reason for that is very simple. By definition, any man who nurtures his child is bound to be a man whose masculinity is not compromised by gestures of overt sensitivity or gentleness. A man who cares for his baby may do so in a way that is more physically robust than a woman might employ, but he will still be overwhelmed by love for his child. If that child is a boy, he will look to his father for information about how a man should be. If the father is absent, the boy may create an exaggerated, overaggressive masculinity of his own. If the father is distant or abusive, the boy will learn from that, too. But if the father is loving, the boy will learn that masculinity and tenderness are not mutually exclusive and will carry that knowledge for-ward into his own adult life.

I do not need research to tell me this. I learned it from my own father. Looking around at my friends, I see it in them too. I know few men of my generation who do not regard fatherhood as the most magical part of their lives. Lord knows it can be tiring, not to mention expensive, and there are times when the burden of responsibility weighs heavily on one's shoulders. But the thrill of rediscovering through one's children feelings of unfettered love that have lain repressed in one's soul since childhood far outweighs any possible cost.

It would, in every way, be a benefit to us all if fatherhood were looked upon as something to be treasured. In a perfect world, boys would be raised from birth with the expectation that being a parent would be one of the central experiences of their lives. When they became fathers they would find that it was a state that was honored, both by custom and by law. The result would be happier children, adults at peace with themselves, and a marked reduction in violence and malice, on the part of women as well as men.

So why, then, does society act in such a way as to ensure that none of these good things can ever occur?

THE PATRIARCHAL CONSPIRACY

The image of the adoring, attentive father is rapidly becoming a media cliché. Glossy magazines are full to the brim with movie star dads and their celebrity babies. Jack's got one, Warren's got one, Arnie's got one, and so have both the Bruces—Willis and Springsteen. Mel's got half a dozen. Forget cars and girls—the hottest accessory a guy can have these days is a child.

But men who become fathers receive wildly mixed and confusing signals about the validity of their role. On the one hand they are exhorted to help out as much as they can with every stage of the process, from prebirth breathing classes and attendance at labor, through to the final dirty diaper. On the other, they are assaulted by scare stories about their "potential" abusiveness, generated by social services and social sciences that have accepted as gospel truth the idea that patriarchy—the institution of fatherhood—is the root of all evil. Meanwhile the cover of *Newsweek* screams out: "DEADBEAT DADS. WANTED FOR FAILURE TO PAY CHILD SUPPORT."

The modern father is ranked somewhere between a surrogate mother and a household drudge. His job is to change diapers, wash dishes, and watch the kids. Parenting is presented as a genderless exercise in which Dad just tags along wherever Mom may lead. Because however fashionable fatherhood may be as a lifestyle choice, as a political issue it is little more than another stick with which to beat men.

In an earlier chapter, I described how the idea of the patriarchy as an oppressive class defines men as an inherently violent and evil group. The word patriarchy is derived from the Latin word *pater*, or father, and thus (for those who believe in the whole thing to begin with) fatherhood is the living embodiment of patriarchal power. Writers such as Kate Millett and Beatrix Campbell have consistently sought to portray the family as an institution created and imposed by men as a means of controlling female reproduction and colonizing women as individuals.

Dr. Rosalind Miles is the British feminist and founder of the Centre for Women's Studies at Coventry Polytechnic whose remarks about "the penis rampant" were mentioned earlier. In her book *The Women's History of the World,* she describes how the world's first societies were matriarchies, in which the ruling deity was the great Goddess and women were, at the very least, equal with men. She quotes Marilyn French: "In the beginning was the Mother."

But, she says, "Male pride rose to take up the challenge of female power; and launching the sex war that was to divide sex and societies for millennia to come, man sought to assert his manhood through the death and destruction of all that had made woman the Great Mother, Goddess, warrior and queen." Miles believes that the rise of monotheistic (or single-god) religions marked the shift in power between the genders. "As phallomania swept the world, male godhead found a new measurement in lost maidenhead; Zeus, king of the immortals, demonstrated his superiority by the numbers of young women he raped."

With God the Father came the patriarchy and "a system in which women are excluded by divine warrant from everything that counts, for ever. . . . A summary of the disabilities imposed upon women in the name of these false gods fatuously posturing as loving fathers can hardly do justice to their crippling nature or extent."

Miles goes on to claim that women were stripped of any choice in marriage; denied security within marriage; forced to live within marriage; victimized by patriarchal laws; and stripped of their humanity. Many readers might find her opinions to be bizarre, a sort of mirror image to the Family Values espoused by right-wing religious fundamentalists, and this form of extreme feminism is often seen as an irrelevance to everyday life. "Why do you worry about these people?" one is often asked. As my sister—herself a former postgraduate anthropologist—remarked to me, "No one cares about the patriarchy anymore."

Except that they do. Or, more to the point, the few people who care, care very much. In the same way that fundamentalism has an influence upon Republican politics that is related to the zeal and determination of its supporters, rather than the degree to which they represent the opinions of average Americans, so the politics of patriarchy infect great expanses of academic, political, and public life. The very fact that legislation can be proposed that assumes a priori that men are to blame for the poverty of divorced spouses, or that men carry out all acts of domestic violence, testifies to the success that antifatherhood campaigners have had in poisoning the role of men as fathers.

My personal belief is that one should look on feminist notions of the patriarchy, not as scientific explanations of genuine phenomena, but as forms of conspiracy theory. In other words, the patriarchy can be made to stand for whatever you want it to. If you're looking for an enemy, or if you suffer from the delusion that everything in the world is rotten and you want a reason why, then the patriarchy is the perfect solution. Why bother blaming society's problems on freemasons, or the Elders of Zion, or the Communist plot to take over the world, when you can blame it on the patriarchy?

Of course, you can't see the patriarchy. You can't touch the patriarchy. But it's there. For those who believe, it is responsible for all the world's greatest sins. In fact, it can only be a matter of time before some lecturer in women's studies staggers out of a backwoods university, clutching a copy of the Zapruder film and claiming she can see the patriarchy standing on the Grassy Knoll.

One might note, in passing, the profound irony underlying the feminist obsession with the supposed powers of patriarchy, which is that two of its most celebrated priestesses, Gloria Steinem and Germaine Greer, were childhood victims, not of the oppressive nature of fatherhood, but of its absence. Dr. Greer wrote a book, *Daddy We Hardly Knew You,* as her attempt to uncover the truth about her father, while Ms. Steinem was left to tend to her sick and mentally unbalanced mother alone after her father deserted the family when she was ten years old. These two fascinating women have between them done as much to shape the second half of this century as any male politician. Might their joint obsession with patriarchy's alleged wrongdoing arise from their childhood devastation? Are they just two examples of the pain caused by an absent father?

There are, of course, other ways of looking at the organization of the family. In a 1983 paper published by the Royal Anthropological Institute entitled *Rules and the Emergence of Human Society,* the anthropologist Meyer Fortes puts forward a very different view. He argues that the family is the basic unit of social order since it introduces the concept of nonbiological rules and of commitment between individuals. Within this unit, the father's role is not oppressive, but altruistic. He is asked to look after children whom he does not know for certain to be his own. Fatherhood is a suspension of his own self-interests for the greater good.

In conversation with me, the criminologist Patricia Morgan asked the question, "If you destroy the family, you go back . . . to what?" She further pointed out the human need for affiliation. We need to know who we are and to whom we are linked both vertically from one generation to another, and horizontally across the same generation. Take away the father and you take away half the affiliative possibilities: half the uncles, aunts, grandparents, and cousins. "That negates the notion of human society," she concludes.

DEADBEAT DADS

However benevolent the family may be, one can state with a fair degree of certainty that the notion of the evil father is embedded deep within the social practice and legislation of the state. At every stage in the process of fatherhood, a man's rights are consistently undermined, while his obligations are reinforced.

Moreover, a man's status in regard to his offspring is constantly shifting. At one moment he is considered responsible, at another he is not. His rights are equally evanescent: here one minute, gone the next.

The issue of abortion illustrates my point. For what it is worth, I cannot escape a personal conviction that abortion is wrong, but I accept that it has to be legal. Whatever the law says, pregnancies are going to be terminated: That process should not be encouraged as long as there is any other possible course of action, but if it must happen it is best that the procedure be carried out by qualified doctors working in good conditions. It serves no moral or practical end to have women dying as the result of backstreet butchery.

If I have an argument with the pro-choice lobby it arises from its assumption that the abortion debate should be conducted entirely in terms of the woman's reproductive rights. Of course, these are absolutely crucial, but they are not the only issue at stake. Any pregnancy (and thus any termination) involves three participants: the mother, the father, and the fetus. It seems to me to be ironic that the very women who most loudly proclaim their exclusive right to decide on the survival of their babies are the first to proclaim the duty of a man to pay for those babies should they decide to give birth.

I am not asking for men to have a veto on abortion decisions. All I am saying is that men are either involved, or they are not. Reproduction cannot be a shared endeavor at one moment and purely an issue of women's bodies at another. Personally, I would hope that, wherever possible (and clearly there will be many occasions in which it is not), a man's involvement should at least be acknowledged. If he is going to foot the bill, he should at least be allowed to look at the menu. Because the moment that the baby is born, the man whose opinions or wishes were so insignificant just a few short weeks ago is now thought to be so important that he should bear a near-permanent commitment to the child's financial well-being.

Suppose, however, that the father is one of the 27 percent of all American parents who is not married at the time of the birth. In many states he will have no automatic right whatever to make or even share in any decisions concerning the child at all, even if he can establish that he is the child's father. Yet the Family Support Act of 1988 enshrines a father's obligation to pay toward his child's upbringing according to predetermined guidelines, and empowers states to collect that money or to arrest him if he fails to pony up.

Now, anyone who campaigns for fathers' rights has to accept their responsibilities. If you believe, as I do, that fathers are essential to their children's upbringing, then you must accept that fathers have a duty to provide both moral and financial support. Clearly there are many men who fail in this regard, but the evidence does not suggest that nonpaying fathers are quite the curse that they are made out to be.

According to the Bureau of the Census, approximately 21 percent of single mothers who were entitled to financial support received no money whatsoever. More than 63 percent received all or part of the money due them. The remainder had been awarded support that was not yet due for payment. There is no inherently male indifference that makes fathers uniquely unwilling to provide for their children. As *Newsweek* reported, in its May 1992 cover story on "Deadbeat Dads," "Fifteen percent of custodial parents are now men, and mothers in those cases have an equally dismal record of supporting their children."

But how dismal is it? Collection rates fluctuate up and down in direct relationship to the state of the economy. They were relatively low at the beginning of the 1980s, rose with the prosperity of the middle years of that decade, and declined again as the recession hit. Many men who refuse to pay are simply unable to do so.

In the words of Roger F. Gay, a Texas research consultant who has submitted evidence to the U.S. House of Representatives Ways and Means Committee, "Surveys of mother-recipients under-report the actual rate of payment. After accounting for unemployment, Braver et al. ['Non-Custodial Parent's Report on Child Support Payments,' *Family Relations,* April 1991] found that divorced fathers who are fully employed have traditionally paid well without income witholding and other hardline tactics; between 80 per cent (as reported by mothers) and 100 per cent (as reported by fathers) of what is ordered. Taking the reporting bias into account, we can see that the rate of unemployment, or alternatively the general poverty rate for the nation goes a long way to account for the rate of non-payment of court-ordered child support."

Gay argues that the sums spent on the enforcement of child support orders far exceed the amount recouped and that there has been no appreciable increase in income among the women who were the Family Support Act's intended beneficiaries. He suggests that the money would be much better spent enabling the unemployed to find the work that would increase their living standards, and comments, "There are many who do not believe that getting tough with poor people will significantly improve the national unemployment figures or access to educational and training opportunities."

What has happened here, surely, is that ideological extremism, which denigrates the role and moral standing of the father, has coincided with bureaucratic convenience, which seeks to feather government nests while avoiding genuine issues of poverty and discrimination. Hence the creation of a bogeyman called the deadbeat dad—a fitting partner for that other scapegoat for legislative failure, the welfare mother.

The solution to both problems lies not in passing legislation that treats people as criminals, even if they are not, but in facing up to a much tougher challenge, which is to create a society that encourages people to act as responsible, loving parents, and rewards them for doing so. Tax dollars spent on helping poor couples to bring up children decently would reduce violence, improve those children's educational and professional prospects beyond all recognition, and pay back ten times over in savings in lives and money. How would you rather spend your taxes, fighting crime, or preventing that crime from occurring in the first place?

MY DADDY, THE GOOK

When, in the mid-1960s, the U.S. armed services set about the wholesale devastation of Vietnam and its population, they did everything they could to convince themselves that the destruction of millions of acres per annum of rain forest or agricultural land, the tens of thousands of dead, the hundreds of thousands of wounded, and the millions of refugees were not actually real. A language of military euphemism, of "attrition," "discreet bursts," and "friendly fire" evolved whose chief purpose was to disguise, rather than describe, the truth. General William Westmoreland, for example, once justified the bombing, shelling, and napalming of civilians because "it deprives the enemy of the population." That it also deprived the population of its life was not, for him, a significant issue.

Regular soldiers, airmen, and marines did the killing that generals like Westmoreland had ordered. They tried to persuade themselves that gooks (or dinks, or slants, or zips, or any of the other derogatory terms used to describe the indigenous population) didn't feel the same way about life as honest, God-fearing Americans. If a few baby gooks went up in flames, well, Mom and Pop Gook just made a bunch more. Now, readers should be aware that when I use the word *gook* I do so in the full knowledge that it is repellent. Because there are times when, reading some of the things that are written about men, I wonder whether some people don't think of us as gooks as well.

So many assumptions about male behavior, whether in the texts of feminist academics or the pages of women's magazines, seem to presuppose a man's emotional indifference or anaesthesia. You can slap a man in the face and he won't be hurt . . . because he's a gook. You can harass a man at work and he won't mind . . . because he's a gook. You can kick him out of a house that he has paid for, which is filled with his family, his memories, and his possessions and that's okay . . . because he's a gook. And gooks don't have feelings like everyone else. Do they?

People need to pretend that their opponents are less than human in order to justify their actions against them. How could you bomb or napalm Vietnamese civilians if they were actually the same as you? They *had* to be gooks. How can a man hit or rape a woman if she is a sensitive human being? In his mind, she *must* be a bitch or a whore. How can a radical feminist say that all men are bastards, or rapists, or child abusers if, for one moment, she allows herself to think that they might be caring husbands, or loving fathers? If she is to maintain her anger, she needs to see men in the worst possible light. They're all the same. They're gooks.

Getting back to fatherhood, the presumption behind legislation aimed against nonpaying fathers is that they are heartless brutes who refuse to do their duty. But what if a father cannot pay? Or what if he is witholding payment as a last, desperate attempt to force his ex-wife to grant him some contact with his children? Why should we assume that he cannot be as badly wounded as she is?

For every man who uses money as a weapon against his ex-wife, there is a woman who uses the children as a weapon against her ex-husband. This has nothing to do with the awfulness of men or women, and everything to do with the depths to which the human soul will sink once an old lover becomes an enemy. Now, over the past year or two I have been conducting an informal, nonscientific poll. I ask friends or colleagues who have children to imagine a situation in which a stranger gave them a choice: "Have sex with me, or I'll take your children away from you forever." Then I ask them, what would they do?

I have never yet met a parent of either sex who would not rather be raped than lose their kids. This suggests, in a crude and unsubtle way, I admit, that the trauma of sexual assault—though terrible—is not quite as horrendous as the trauma caused by the loss of one's children. So, let's look at the legal consequences of those two acts. Any man who assaults a woman runs the risk of severe punishment under the criminal law. Any woman who denies a man access to his own children runs . . . no risk whatsoever.

Somehow, the all-powerful patriarchy appears to have had a bit of an oversight when it comes to the protection of paternity itself. Most heterosexual men can expect to become fathers at some point in their lives. Of these, 27 percent at current rates will have babies out of wedlock. As we have already seen, they have no automatic rights over their children. Of those who marry, at least 40 percent can expect to be divorced at least once. After noncontested divorces, roughly 90 percent of all children live with their mother—usually in the family house, which the father may very well have paid for, but been forced to vacate. After contested divorces, the figure rises to 95 percent. Roughly half of all children of divorced parents lose contact with their natural fathers within two years of the divorce.

Two-thirds of all fathers (i.e. 27 percent plus most of 40 percent) can expect either to be denied joint control of their children by virtue of their extramarital status, or to lose it as a result of divorce. And an absolute minimum of 20 percent of all fathers (and probably a great many more, since I have not included any extramarital parents in this calculation) will, at some stage in their children's early lives, be permanently separated from their own flesh and blood.

It would, I know, be absurdly idealistic to suppose that many men would actually choose to consider the alternative option, which is to be their children's full-time caregiver. But even so, I have spoken to enough divorced men to know that many of them feel bitterly hard done-by as a result of their experiences and they are deeply wounded by the loss of their paternal role. They invariably note that while women in search of increased alimony can usually count on free representation supplied by the state, they enjoy no such benefits when attempting to enforce their visitation rights, or trying to reduce payments as a result of loss of income. This atmosphere of inequality does not help women in the long run. It merely makes men desperate. And desperate men do crazy things.

In August 1991, the FBI arrested an Englishman called Bernie Downes in Philadelphia. He had fled there with his young daughter after kidnapping her from his former partner's London house. Downes, a small, lightly built social worker with no record of violent behavior, had been so frustrated by court decisions depriving him of meaningful contact with his child that he had taken the law into his own hands.

After a massive manhunt, during which the British police claimed that he was both dangerous and mentally unstable (a claim for which there was no genuine evidence), Downes was jailed for four years. His actions, which involved forcing his way into the house where his daughter was living, and tying her mother to her bed with electric cable, were undoubtedly criminal, but they were a perfect demonstration of what happens when men are driven to the breaking point. The stories that follow involve British men, but they might just as well have happened in America: In both countries, legislative procedures and public attitudes are similar, as are their consequences.

"Mark" is a TV executive who forcibly abducted his child from his ex-wife's house. "I had not seen my children for about six months, despite a court order allowing me to see them every other weekend. I had no assistance at all from the police or the court system in enforcing the order. They had no enthusiasm at all. They'd say, 'It's a waste of time.' Eventually I ran out of patience. I went along at the correct time one weekend with a witness and enforced the access order myself.

"I used minimum force, but I had to break down the door to collect my children. She had said they weren't in the house, but I knew they were there. I could hear them. I went off, had a nice weekend with them, and returned them very politely at the end of the weekend. I was promptly arrested and thrown in jail."

Mark claims that while he was there, the police offered him bail on condition that he agree never to see his children again. "I felt that was wrong, so I refused," he says. "If I had agreed to that, I would have lost access forever."

In the end, although Mark was charged with kidnapping, the judge found in his favor and even ordered his wife to obey the original access order on pain of imprisonment. Yet he remains angry about his treatment. "I'm fairly certain that if I hadn't made a fuss I would never have seen my kids again. I was forced into the position of breaking the law because of lack of support from the system."

For other fathers, the consequences of abducting their children are entirely negative. In May 1989, "Chris" tired of a routine that allowed him to see his son for six hours every three weeks. One weekend, he did not return the boy, but took him for a fortnight's holiday in the Mediterranean. On his return he was arrested at the airport. The police took him and his son into a small room, where they told Chris that his ex-wife and her new partner were waiting to take the boy away. "He was holding on to me and screaming, 'Daddy, daddy,' " says Chris. Since then he has seen his son for a total of four hours. Their last meeting was in October 1989.

Chris has paid a heavy price for that fortnight abroad. The police have arrested him on several occasions, believing that he may be about to kidnap his son again or take violent action against his ex-wife, both of which charges he strongly denies. He finds it impossible to create new relationships with women: None of them, he says, can stand the strain imposed by the struggle for his son.

Chris claims, "I have been described by the courts as obsessive. But if you want to win these cases you have to be. Most fathers lose contact. It's the sheer strain. I am fighting for the right of my child to a proper relationship with a father who loves him and I don't let anything get in the way. People like me are not going to be treated like child abusers. We have done nothing wrong."

His paternal feelings are clearly sincere. But there's no denying that they are inextricably bound up with the conflict between him and his former wife. He claims she has turned the boy against him, even tearing up pictures he has sent to remind the child of his father. For his part, he admits, "My attitude towards my ex-wife won't change. My hatred is even stronger than it was five years ago. I'm damned if I'm going to let her off the hook."

When asked why he kidnapped his child, he replies, "Thinking of another man playing Happy Families with my child really got to me. I wanted my ex-wife to know what it was like to be away from your child for that length of time."

Lucy Jaffe works for Reunite, a charity that helps the parents of the 1,200 children abducted from Britain every year. She believes that the traditional tabloid description of "tug-of-love" cases misses the point: "Tug-of-love is an absolute misnomer. It's tug-of-hate. Mainly what comes across to us is that these are relationships that have gone wrong and people are trying to hurt each other through their children."

Anne-Marie Hutchinson, a lawyer who specializes in family law and who sits on a parliamentary working party on abducted children, remarks that "There is a school of thought that says abduction is a form of abuse. If you love a child, one of the worst things you can do is to remove it in circumstances the child doesn't understand."

Ironically, the child may end up blaming the wrong parent for what has happened, as Lucy Jaffe explains: "The little psychological evidence that has been produced suggests that the child feels abandoned by the nonabducting parent and feels very angry. We've had reports of children coming back home and hitting the parent they're coming back to."

The fact remains, however, that many divorced or separated parents are driven to a point where they consider abducting their own children. The fathers involved seem united in their contempt and bitterness. They live in a world of affidavits and *ex parte* judgments, of rumors and allegations that can deny a man all access to his child, no matter what evidence he presents. All unite in attacking the enormous sums of money that can be wasted as cases drag on across the years.

Yet the collapse of the family is a curse that can hurt both former partners equally badly, as Lucy Jaffe points out: "Families are a refuge and the fragmentation is terrible. A man can end up living in a bed-sit [studio apartment] on his own and the isolation of that is appalling. Meanwhile the woman is under immense pressure being a single parent alone with the kids, perhaps on a low income, trying to get out to work—maybe the child support didn't get through. It's a quagmire. We are just not prepared, structurally, for the number of divorces that are happening."

Meanwhile, the malice continues. Ron Brake works as a volunteer for the men's organization Families Need Fathers in the west of England. His files are filled with cases of men who have been left bankrupt and homeless as a result of their fight for more contact with their children. "The judges just laugh at you," he says. In one case with which he is familiar, a father had succeeded in getting the care and control of his daughter, who was eleven. One weekend, he left her with her mother for a routine visit. When he returned to pick her up and take her home, he was met by a team of police and social workers, who arrested him and charged him with sexually abusing the child.

Medical examination and interviews established that there was no truth to the allegations, which had been made by the mother, and the case was dropped. By then, however, the child had been placed in foster care. In a subsequent court case, the judge ruled that the girl should live with her mother. When she said that she did not wish to do so, but wanted to return to her father, the judge insisted that she be put back into foster care, where she remains. "The judge's mind was made up before the court case," claims Brake. "He believed that a child should be with its mother and that was it."

As long as judges continue to hold these opinions, no matter what the law may say, fathers will continue to feel resentful. And some of them may just end up deciding that, if the law can't help them, they'll find another method that can—whatever the cost of that may be.

CHAPTER 10
The Skynner Interview

The research for this book took me from Hollywood to the Australian bush. My study shelves are groaning with the files of newspaper and magazine cuttings, the books, the videos, the interview tapes, and the notebooks that mark the process that led, for better or for worse, to the words you are reading now. But of all the people I met, or read about, or to whom I spoke, the most inspirational was Dr. Robin Skynner.

Although not known to the general public in America, he is familiar to Britons as the coauthor, with the comedian and film star John Cleese, of the best-sellers *Families, and How to Survive Them* and *Life, and How to Survive It*. Those books are presented as a series of dialogues in which Skynner, who is a prominent psychiatrist, guides Cleese toward a better understanding of the dynamics of human behavior. To academics, he is also highly regarded as the author of the textbook *One Flesh, Separate Persons: Principles of Family and Marital Psychotherapy*. Now seventy, he has retired from his work as a family therapist, but he still writes and talks about the inner workings of the human mind with warmth, understanding, and, I believe, great wisdom.

What the plain text does not tell you about the conversation that follows is the tone in which it was spoken. Skynner's most shocking remarks—shocking, that is, to people whose ideology would prevent their considering the possible truth of what he says—were made with a smile and often a chuckle. If he seems on occasion to contravene the rules about what may or may not be said in politically correct society, then that is simply because the decades he has spent observing the way people actually are may contradict some theories about the way they ought to be. Given the choice between Skynner's kindly, tolerant, and open-minded humanity and the bitter dogmatism of the politically correct, I know where my sympathies lie.

I do not agree with all of Skynner's observations. As previous chapters will have made clear, I am not certain that males are, necessarily, more violent than females. Nevertheless, I print our conversation at length because it seems to me to sum up much of what has been discussed up to now in this book and to point the way toward a more positive consideration of what can be done to reevaluate and redefine the position of men in society. I must apologize to Messrs. Skynner and Cleese for aping the pattern of their work and for being such a clumsy interlocutor. I hope they will forgive my impertinence.

The interview took place one morning in December 1991 at Dr. Skynner's North London flat. Once coffee had been brewed and poured, I asked Skynner about the differences between men and women. To what extent were they inherent, as opposed to being conditioned?

SKYNNER: It's a most difficult area in that the more you try to find differences and to pursue them to some clear kind of conclusion, the more everything slips through your fingers and you're left with almost nothing very definite. And yet at the same time we know that there is an enormous difference that is somehow so difficult to pin down.

There are a number of things to say about it. The first thing is that because biological influence is very important and isn't black or white, and because social conditioning is not only variable but often reversed, so boys are brought up to be girls and vice versa, you get this huge overlap, whereby anything you can say about men that is true in the average sense is not true about some men and it is true about some women.

The second thing is that it's hard to disentangle basic biological influence and social conditioning so that no one quite knows how much is which. And finally, you can't trust anybody and we can't trust ourselves. It's not that people are deliberately deceitful—although some are, many are—but that people get committed to a particular position about gender, as they do about politics, and everything gets unconsciously fitted into it. So we don't know what to make of evidence. We have to distrust even apparently basic physical studies, where they claim to have measured things and found statistical differences.

For example, in the textbook I wrote, I had a whole chapter on gender differences. One crucial bit of evidence was that John Money at Johns Hopkins Hospital in Baltimore had studied two twin boys who both had been circumcised early on and due to some accident the penis of one had been destroyed. . . .

[Author's note: In the case referred to, the child was operated on and given a sex-change. "She" was then brought up as a girl and appeared, according to all the evidence, to be happy and completely normal, behaving exactly as a typical girl would be expected to do. This case was referred to repeatedly by writers attempting to put forward the nurture rather than nature argument for sex differentation.]

SKYNNER: I couldn't get around that. I thought, that's the clincher if it's true. I couldn't really believe it. On the other hand I had to believe it, this was a prestigious institution. But the BBC heard about it and made a program called *Open Secret* and they contacted Money and what had happened was that this family had moved to another area and had come into contact—because of problems with their daughter, quote, unquote—with a local child psychiatric team. The BBC interviewed the team about this child and showed drawings that the child had made and the opinion of these people was that the child was very disturbed. Now that's typical of different views that are genuinely held.

That leads us on to what genetic differences are [here Dr. Skynner quoted from *One Flesh, Separate Persons*]. "[Girls who received abnormal doses of male hormones before birth], but who had all been brought up as females with early correction of any anatomical abnormalities, displayed many statistically significant differences from matched female controls. They tended to be tomboys; were highly active physically; showed a lack of satisfaction with female roles, choosing male rather than female playmates, wearing slacks rather than skirts and rejecting preening, perfume and hairstyling. They played with toy cars and guns rather than dolls, and demonstrated a lack of interest in looking after babies and an absence of fantasies about marriage, pregnancy and motherhood, being more interested in a career instead.

"The exact counterparts to these syndromes do not exist. Although male hormones produce a masculine pattern, the female pattern does not need the presence of female hormones but occurs in the absence of male influence. However, genetic males [deprived of male hormones] show many physical and psychological features more usual in a female. Besides physical feminisation, they are likely to show a preference for marriage and homecraft instead of a career, as well as fantasies about raising a family, playing with dolls and other toys usually associated with girls; strong interest in infant care and contentment with the female role, preferring female clothing."

It's very hard to get away from the fact that there's some physical thing operating there. You've got to go to stuff like that where as far as you know the social conditioning was the same and the only difference is physical.

THOMAS: One of the things that bothers me is the degree to which we limit male behavior. It starts very young, with the way that boys are taught about what is and is not manly. But perhaps we have to do that, because masculinity is so tenuous that it has to be clearly defined . . .

SKYNNER: The boy has extra things to do and more things can go wrong . . .

THOMAS: Like violence, for example.

SKYNNER: If you look at the physical differences, you end up with one indisputable fact that everyone agrees about and that is the enormous difference due to different levels of the male sex hormone. Men are naturally and normally and properly, biologically designed to be more aggressive and more competitive and all the other things which follow from that. Therefore, they are more violent when they are *uncontrollably* aggressive. So if some people are going to go around hitting other people or inflicting pain and injury it's more likely to be men, simply because of that.

THOMAS: There are plenty of women who batter men.

SKYNNER: Yes, but what I'm saying is that there's more of that particular energy in men. Other things being equal, men are going to show more instances and more magnitude of aggression than women do, simply because of that natural difference. Now, whether it takes a violent form in either sex is something else.

THOMAS: If men have more aggressive energy in a negative sense, are they more likely to have it in a positive sense too?

SKYNNER: Sure, yes, yes. What I'm saying is that the aggression is normal. It's supposed to be there. It's necessary and it can't be got rid of. It shouldn't be got rid of. But the important question is, why is it harnessed in a constructive version in some instances where it serves the community and serves the family and protects the women, and why in other cases is it directed at society? It's an enormously important difference. A lot of the feminists talk as if aggression itself was a bad thing, which is absolute nonsense. It's a good thing.

THOMAS: How do you educate or condition boys so that you get the good side of their aggression without getting the bad side?

SKYNNER: To say that you want the good things, but you don't want the bad things, may not be possible or even desirable. Maybe one has to have the bad things before one gets the good things. If the bad things are uncontrolled, unharnessed aggression and the good things are socially channeled aggression, then obviously you have to have one before you can have the other. You might have to go through a wild stage in which you behave badly and go around screwing girls and not caring about it and misbehaving, before you come to a point where that begins to be influenced by, and guided and contained by other emotions, like meeting girls you're really crazy about and having babies and so on.

THOMAS: So Shakespeare was right: You have to be the wild Prince Hal before you can be Henry V?

SKYNNER: Absolutely. So I'm not sure it's even a desirable way to approach the subject to think of having good things without having bad things. They may both be necessary.

THOMAS: That sounds as if all those Victorian ideas about making young men play football to work off their surplus energy and aggression may well be true after all.

SKYNNER: That's right. If you've got a lot of wild Young Turks who insist on smashing everything up, then being in the army and driving tanks may be just right for them. Or, when that doesn't exist, then other things may be needed like adventure courses or things which challenge them. That's necessary for men.

THOMAS: Most British boys are now being educated in a system that sets out to be noncompetitive, nonsporting. All the things that are natural to those boys are now thought to be macho and therefore a bad thing. So perhaps, instead of working things out on the rugby pitch, they go joyriding in stolen cars and smashing up football stadiums instead.

SKYNNER: I think that that kind of approach of trying to stop these male, bad impulses in fact is almost bound to make them worse. They're just going to take more and more socially deviant and uncontrollable forms.

THOMAS: The other thing about the male upbringing is that boys learn not to get too close to anyone else. That surely leads to isolation and pain.

SKYNNER: It's a very bad beginning.

THOMAS: Exactly. So how do you keep the things about being male that are valuable, whilst getting rid of that terrible emotional deprivation?

SKYNNER: I went through all that. It's what I'm interested in and it's very central to me. It's all about the missing father, including my father, and trying to find answers to that. . . . Can I tell you about the first men's group I attended? Because the key to it must be in something like that. The summer before last, John Cleese and I were invited to speak at the American Family Therapy Association, which is a gathering of teachers in that field.

About three hundred people were there and Robert Bly was also to speak at the same time. It was no accident that John and I and Bly were invited together. It all happened because women had got in charge of the event, so they invited men to come and speak in a way that the men had previously felt that women wouldn't like. That was interesting in itself, the idea that the men were so frightened of the women's disapproval that the *women* had to be in control before men's issues were addressed. So . . . we listened to Bly, got to know him a bit, and had dinner with him.

At the end of the conference there was a men's group. It was the first time that they had ever arranged one. The women have had a very powerful, strong group for ten to fifteen years and it shows. They're an amazingly talented, lively bunch and they had the men on the ropes for a long time—they didn't know what was happening to them. Finally a lot of young people convened this men's group. There was no leader, just these three or four younger men who arranged the room and suggested that we should go round the room and talk about ourselves.

We spent the morning doing that—I went along and there were quite a few men there, I suppose about twenty percent of the men attending the conference (this year, when they had the group for a second time, I gather about forty percent of the men turned up to it). First of all, I didn't know what kind of men would be there. But in fact there were a lot of people I knew about and respected— leading American figures. We spent the morning going round the room and each person would spend about five minutes saying why he was there. And the feeling in the room was incredible, so powerful.

What puzzled me was why it was happening now and why I hadn't been able to do this nearly seventy years earlier. What was the difference? Of course Bly had been giving the talk earlier, so that message was in the air and he had been talking about it . . . but the depth of feeling and the openness and frankness with which the men spoke was staggering, and many of them were weeping. And in all this, the main thing was the lack of relationship with their father.

I was about three-quarters of the way around the room and was listening to what was being said and feeling that when this gets to me I'm not going to be able to avoid weeping. And then just before it got to me, about two places before, someone mentioned the word "joy." I don't know how it came into this conversation, but that kind of opened up my feelings in a different way. I realized that what I wanted to weep about was not sorrow, or the lack of my father, but joy that it was possible to have this kind of experience.

This was a transforming experience because I realized that we don't need our fathers. It doesn't matter what our fathers were like. What's getting in the way is something to do with the fact that you felt you could only get that kind of affirmation from your father when you were a little boy. And if you didn't get it then, you would never get it at all because you would never have that kind of relationship again. And it was quite clear that you could have it at any time. It was a totally transforming experience.

THOMAS: Do you think you need some kind of mentor?

SKYNNER: Bly says this and it also happened in the couples groups that my wife and I ran together before she died about four years ago. We ran them for about fifteen years. And in those groups, the men change in the same way. It was something to do with me being there and giving permission. It was as if a spell was broken. That's the only way I can put it.

THOMAS: It's funny you should talk about joy. I've done lots of market research on various publications and one of the things that has most struck me, when you watch and listen to groups of men talking, is that there's a point in a man's life when the joy leaves it. Up until their mid-twenties, guys are up for anything. They're full of confidence. They'll take risks and they'll experiment with things that are new. But at some point the shutters come down. The concept of fun leaves them. It's as if once a man has a marriage and a mortgage he doesn't dare let fun enter into his life for fear that it will tell him there's a better way of living. That doesn't seem to happen to women in quite the same way.

SKYNNER: Women have children and they get enormous fun and enjoyment out of their kids. Also women get together and have a lot of fun there too. For men, certainly my experience was that you feel you're getting older and older and you're at your oldest when you're about forty-five. After that you start getting younger again, if that's any comfort! I've been getting younger and younger since about that age, when the mortgage and the school fees . . .

THOMAS: There has to be a better way of doing it. The sense of obligation can be so crushing.

SKYNNER: The question is, would men feel like that if they had better relations with other men? I don't know the answer, but it must lie in this experience I've had. Later on, I went to a Bly weekend here in England. It was very interesting and even entertaining, but I'd got all I wanted from the first one. It was as if I had been touched by a magic wand. Someone had said, ''You're not in a glass box, even though you thought you were all your life." Now, if the whole bloody thing can be dispelled at the age of nearly seventy by sitting in a room for one morning with thirty men and no one telling you what to do, then surely there must be some way of not setting up that thing in the first place and that's what I'm interested in.

THOMAS: Speaking of Robert Bly, what was your view of *Iron John*?

SKYNNER: I had very mixed feelings about it. I think Bly's got it absolutely right, but when he talks about it, I think the kind of language he uses and the kind of psychologizing he does makes me feel very unhappy. He's understood things from his own experience and his group work, and if he just said that, then you couldn't fault it. But when he tries to justify everything in terms of anthropology and myth and his kind of psychological explanations I think he runs the risk of people saying that a lot of this is very dubious.

THOMAS: In other words, his intuition is more accurate than his science.

SKYNNER: Well, it's a very valuable book, but it's unfortunate in the way that it's been written.

THOMAS: Why was the reception in this country so hostile to *Iron John*? I could understand the anger from the women critics—that's just a knee-jerk reaction. But the men were just as bad. I mean, sure, the book has many faults, but the response was out of all proportion: They seemed so desperate not to admit any sense of need.

SKYNNER: The impression I had was that there was a tremendous fear of homosexuality, much more than I had realized, and they were reacting with that. Homophobia is very prevalent amongst men. . . . One thing that I remember that might be interesting in relation to that . . . many years ago, when they were developing various forms of training in the U.S.A. to help doctors and psychologists to be more at ease with people who had sexual problems, my wife and I arranged for a day's training modeled on the way American medical schools were doing it. This was to show a whole lot of very explicit films with normal intercourse, homosexual intercourse, lesbian intercourse, and so on, on several screens at the same time, a kind of flooding experience, and then have a group discussion afterwards.

One thing which came out was a lot of talk among men about homosexuality and their awkwardness about homosexuality. What became clear as the discussion went on was that the reason non-homosexual men are frightened of homosexuality is that they're frightened that women will be jealous of them getting together.

That, I think, makes sense in terms of boys' being fearful of joining their fathers and really forming good relationships with them and pushing their mothers aside, provoking their mother's jealousy because she won't let them go. I think it's about that. And it makes absolute sense therefore that the more fear there is of that particular issue, of mothers' jealousy, the more men are going to react to the idea of men's groups or the men's movement in a similar way.

THOMAS: Jealousy explains something that has puzzled me, which is why when women get together it's an act of consciousness-raising and sisterhood, but when men get together it's an act of sexism and exclusion. One of the other things that has baffled me is the sort of self-defined, willed victimization you get among some women, who aren't victims at all, but who want to be seen as victims of someone else's oppression—male oppression—and blame all their problems on that.

SKYNNER: The women's movement has basically been positive. But the fact is that when people do that they are showing a very great deal of immaturity. The way you deal with that, I think, is to see that it is a normal way for people who are emotionally immature and less healthy to operate. If you see that, you see it for what it is.

THOMAS: Are you saying that the archetypal militant feminist woman is emotionally delinquent?

SKYNNER: Yes, I am, in the sense that they are using very immature psychological mechanisms: "It's all your fault. It's Daddy's fault. It's not my fault." That's distorting reality and not taking responsibility. It is blaming others rather than accepting your own limitations and faults. It is immaturity. And that needs to be said steadily, repeatedly, and without any quarter.

THOMAS: But the idea that men, as a whole, oppress women, as a whole, is very widespread. Just look at the argument that's going on over date-rape. People are trying to define almost any act of sex which takes place without the woman's explicit consent as rape. If the woman gets drunk and he sleeps with her that's rape. If he says he loves her, but he doesn't really, that's rape.

SKYNNER: You sound as though you're taking it seriously.

THOMAS: Well, it is serious.

SKYNNER: It's serious in the fact that it's being taken seriously by a wide body of opinion, including a lot of men. It's become the fashion. People are actually taken in by this. But it is not something that should be taken seriously. It is absurd.

THOMAS: You're not disputing that a violent and forcible act of sex is a crime.

SKYNNER: Absolutely not. No, I'm all for proper safeguards and pro-
visions which will encourage and arouse feelings of healthy
respect for the law in people who are thinking of abusing confidence and trust. I'm all for that. But the actual way in which the
problem is being presented is absolutely terrible.

THOMAS: From conversations I've had, I think a lot of women feel
angry about that, too.

SKYNNER: So they should. It's stupid, childish, it belittles and degrades
women.

THOMAS: Well, it defines them as helpless children.

SKYNNER: I don't think it should be taken seriously. One has to make
one's voice heard. More men need to say this is rubbish.

THOMAS: People under forty have no experience of anything other
than feminism. It's a bit like growing up in Czechoslovakia, or
somewhere, when people had no experience of anything other than
communism. How do you set about reacquiring masculine self-
confidence when men are being made to feel guilty by association
with a wave of criminal activity?

SKYNNER: When you talk about it you obviously do take it seriously
because you've grown up with it, but it's so ridiculous I can't give
it room in my brain. It's absurd. Once you start arguing about
whether you're persecuting people, when it's absolute nonsense,
you're lost.

THOMAS: Whenever I talk or write about this sort of subject, there's
often some flak in the papers, but I always get incredibly positive
mail. One of the things that is clear from it all is that the New Man,
whoever he may be, doesn't seem to be working out well for
anybody.

SKYNNER: Can I tell you why this is? I'd like to tell you something
about the main experience that my understanding is coming from
because it's more useful than just coming to conclusions. My views
were formed through having been one of the first people in this
country to start working with families seen together. And what
immediately struck me when I began doing that was the importance
of the father. In case after case, more than half the cases, the
problem seemed to be one not so much of children who were
inhibited or fearful, but children who were uncontrolled. They were
all over the place, not getting on with their work and generally
not structured or organized, with no self-discipline.

In all those families the father was not playing a full part. The
mother had usually taken over his role as well as her own. It was
impossible to say whether the mother had pushed him out or he
had opted out. It was a double thing, they were both responsible.

But if you got the father to come back in and take a more active role, the problem would often be solved in a week or two. Whereas dealing with the mother and child alone could take two years with not much change. We saw these miraculous results from reintroducing the father and usually getting him to take a more authoritative role, creating structure and ordering limits.

You may say, what was the justification for that? The justification for that was that the children asked for it and the wives asked for it. We'd talk about the problem and then in the end I'd say, well, what do you think we should do about it? What do you think Daddy's contribution is? And they'd say, he's too soft, he lets us get away with it.

So I'd go on to him and he would say that when he tried to do anything, she'd say he'd been too hard on them. And the children would always say, well you should do it anyway. The mother would usually agree that, even though she would appear to want to protect her role and stop him being the heavy father, nevertheless, she really wanted him not to let her stop him. So the message both from the children and the mother was that he should be a man.

THOMAS: How did you establish that this was what was really going on?

SKYNNER: I worked with my wife and we'd have forty couples a week come and see us, so we'd see a lot of people. Now, the pattern we saw was almost standard, over and over again with hardly any deviations, some variations, but no major differences.

To start with, it was clear that the man had a problem because she was more powerful and her power came from the fact that he was seeking mothering from her. He wanted her to be a mother to him as well as a wife. Although she resented this, at the same time she didn't want to give up the power this gave her. It kept him under control, both by the fact that she was giving him dog biscuits, as it were, by nurturing him, and also by the fact that by not challenging him on his dependence she could keep him feeling inadequate without knowing quite why. He had the feeling she knew something about him that she could tell the world about. She knew about the little boy inside him that he was keeping hidden.

THOMAS: "Men are such little boys" . . . you hear that all the time.

SKYNNER: That's how they would start. The woman would usually come when she had had a baby. The woman was no longer willing to have two babies and the man resented the fact that he wasn't getting any attention. So he had gone off and had an affair or was tuned out sexually, or whatever. That was often the crisis, it could be other things. So they had come into a negative relationship. The woman was angry with the man for not supporting her as she felt he should be doing, since she had to support the child, and the man was angry that she didn't love him anymore and often the sexual relationship went wrong.

Now, what could we do about it? What we found we had to do was to encourage the woman to be much stronger in her attacks. In other words, she was pulling her punches, because although she was angry and dissatisfied, at the same time to challenge him that he wasn't behaving like a man might make him rise to the occasion and become one, in which case, we later saw, she would have to change and would lose her power.

Anyway, what would happen is that my wife became particularly attuned to egging women on and I would pick the poor chap up, dust him down, and send him back in with some fatherly encouragement. The strength of the arguments would intensify with great shouting matches until at a certain point the worm would turn and he would be driven to a point where he couldn't bear it any longer and he would fight back. There would often be a brief episode of violence. He would hit her or she would hit him or throw plates. And at that point they would then suddenly become equal. Their sex would improve because it became exciting at that point and he would be a match for her. And that was the pattern we saw all the way through.

THOMAS: I've known of cases in which the woman would needle the man, almost daring him to hit her.

SKYNNER: Often it's not sustained. She then backs off and she keeps the advantage. This business of going silent or being hurt, that's a process of manipulation, which has to be disregarded. It always puzzled me why women were so fearful of going for the man's balls, really saying, look, you're not a man, I despise you. And if you asked them they'd say well that would be like castrating him, like taking his manhood away. But [that attitude] in itself takes his manhood away, because if you treat someone as if he hasn't got any balls he starts wondering what it is he hasn't got, whereas if she goes for his balls he has to fight for them.

THOMAS: He rediscovers them.

SKYNNER: That's right. The inhibition in women about doing that is enormous. I came to think in the end that the reason for it was that if they really challenge the man totally and he responds, he then becomes free. He then can fight back and she then may lose him, she hasn't got him under her control. And also he can then challenge her and she has to really become a woman once he becomes a man.

THOMAS: I can see that that might be frightening, but at the same time, it's what we're all trying to achieve. It's liberating, too.

SKYNNER: Yes. I asked my wife once, I said, why is it you want us to go after you so hard and really pin you against the wall? And she said, well, can't you see? Very impatiently: *Can't you see?* It's obvious. When you do that we come into our own. We don't have to worry. We can use our energy and aggression and be what we really are and not worry about whether you can take it or not. We become totally free.

THOMAS: That reminds me of a remark made by a friend of mine. She said that men were so feeble that they wouldn't even tell her to shut up. She needed someone who was strong enough to handle anything she could throw at him.

SKYNNER: Now one other thing is if you expand that up to the social level, one has to question whether that's the point we are at. You see, maybe we need to have these immature, rather paranoid extreme feminists pushing the rules to such an extreme degree that the men finally say, this is just too much, and then come back and become real men.

THOMAS: It's funny how the same women's magazines that are always going on about sexual harassment and women at the workplace and goodness knows what else are also the first to run stories about how there are no real men anymore. Perhaps the answer lies in being more masculine, rather than less.

SKYNNER: Real women are never threatened by that. They love it if their men become more male.

CHAPTER 11

Ladies and Gentlemen of the Jury

The time has come for men to get used to the idea of thinking of themselves as a group with shared interests and coherent aims. I deeply regret the splintering of society, but as long as people are putting themselves into little boxes, each with its own, exclusive label, men are only being foolish and unfair to themselves not to play the game too. The men's movement, such as it is, originally developed as a splinter from the plank of feminism, and many of its early members accepted without question the Marxist-feminist notion of the oppressive patriarchy. Their aim, therefore, was to atone for the sins of the past by trying to do better in the future. And, by and large, the way in which they would do better was by becoming more female.

Since then, the Robert Bly school of hairy New Machismo has talked about putting men in touch with the repressed masculine selves that lie within. Read a few of the books of Bly's ilk and you'll discover that there's a regular cast of thousands nestled away inside your soul. There's the child within, the warrior, the priest, the wizard, the hairy man . . . they should get together and form a basketball team.

There's a lot of good stuff mixed up with all that mumbo-jumbo. And I know many men who have been helped by the teachings of Bly and men like him. But I don't believe that there's a warrior in me, or a wizard, or anyone else. Inside me, all you'll find is . . . me. I may be mixed up and we all may be mixed up. But men are no more mixed up than women, any more than the reverse is true. We're all human. We all live with the knowledge of our own fallibility and our own mortality. In the wee small hours of the morning we all feel alone and afraid. There really are no exceptions.

Some people say that the reason women are still in pain is not because they have had too much feminism, but because they haven't had enough. To me, that sounds a bit like saying the trouble with Russia was that it wasn't communist enough. Truth is, communism doesn't work, feminism doesn't work, and no ism you can think of works, because the world and the people in it are much too complicated to be reduced to a set of simple formulae.

It is, however, true to say that we've only gone halfway down the road to sexual equality. And now it's men who need to be liberated.

As matters stand, we have removed all the legal prejudices against women, without touching the ones against men. Or, to put it another way, we have said that women are the same as men when it suits them to be so, but different when it does not. At work, men and women are—in law, at any rate—equal. At home they are not. When a woman is an executive, she is exactly the same as a man. When she is a mother, she is not. When a woman wants an abortion, reproduction is entirely her own affair. When she wants child support, it suddenly becomes the man's responsibility.

I do not blame women for this state of affairs, even if I think that some feminist campaigners have added to the human pain that it has caused. Men's rights are men's responsibility. Men passed the laws that got them into this sorry state of affairs. Men should damn well change them.

The first thing that they can do to help themselves is to stop apologizing. There seems to be no middle way at the moment between the bastard and the wimp. For every man who attacks and degrades women, there's another one who's down on his knees saying he's sorry. A plague on both their houses.

British people, of both sexes, who go to live and work in America often comment upon the incredible anger of American women. There are a number of causes for this. In the first place, women in the States are still denied a number of straightforward, practical rights that are commonplace in Europe. The sex war has always been much more intense in the States, too: The struggle between the bullying man and the ball-busting woman has been as violent as every other American conflict. Then there's the traditional American belief in human perfectibility and, more than that, the sense that people have a right to be happy. Women are not happy, so they look for a reason why, and the obvious one is men. It does not seem to occur to anyone that happiness is not the lot of the average human being, whatever their gender.

But there's another major factor that lies behind women's rage: men's weakness. So cowed by feminism have decent American men become that they no longer dare argue back at their female assailants. Ever since my conversation with Dr. Robin Skynner, I have been asking women I know for their opinions on the need for men to stand up for themselves.

One woman, with a six-figure salary, said to me, "I could never fall in love with a man who could not beat me in an argument." Another, less well paid, but equally intelligent and assertive, said, "There's nothing sexier than a man who disagrees with me."

These remarks did not mean that the women wanted to be subservient to their men, by any means. But they did want to feel that they were dealing with an equal whom they could respect. If everything they said was met with meek acquiescence, such respect would be impossible to achieve. Besides, disagreement—if expressed in terms that are not overly aggressive or offensive—is a sign of attention. Someone who has taken the trouble to form an opinion about something you have just said, even if it is a contrary one, has clearly been listening. And most women, like most men, like what they say to be heard.

Nothing is more infuriating than having an argument with someone who won't fight back, particularly if you know that they are going to go off and mutter insults behind your back. That is what is happening to the two sexes now. Women argue against men. The men either say nothing or give in to ensure a quiet life, but then they mutter misogynist jokes to their male friends in locker rooms or bars. Members of Parliament and Congress pass laws designed to appease women, and then go back to their clubs to complain. If I were a woman, and that was the treatment I was getting, I'd be angry too.

Above all, appeasement isn't attractive. A friend who lives in New York recently told me that she had started a new relationship with a man there. At first everything was fine. They went out on a few dates and had a good time. Gradually they won each other's trust. One thing led to another, and then finally they went to bed together for the first time. Everything was looking great until, just at the very moment when they were about to make love, the man paused, turned to my friend and said, "I want you to know that I am only here to serve you."

She didn't know whether to laugh . . . or puke. Perhaps the man thought that this display of abject self-subjugation would gain the approval of a woman who, he assumed, would see him as nothing more than an instrument for her pleasure. Perhaps this is what his past lovers had demanded.

My friend, however, was horrified. She did not want to go to bed with a man who was, as she put it, ashamed of his own cock. She wanted them both to have a good time and take pleasure in each other's sexuality. Quite apart from anything else, she did not particularly want the burden of his expectations. His desire to serve her was, in a way, a demand that she must be satisfied. This was certainly not what she had in mind when she thought of sexual equality.

I genuinely believe—and this book is a testament to that belief—that one of the best things that men can do to help their relationships with women is to stand up for the things in which they believe. This does not imply any need for hostility. On the contrary, I think that if men spoke out, they might get rid of some of the frustration and anger that cause the hatred so many of them obviously feel toward the other sex. First, of course, they've got to work out what those things that they believe in might be.

One of the most striking things about the men I have met while researching issues such as domestic violence and child custody is how many of the victims are middle-class professionals. All their lives they have operated on the assumption that the world was run by men like them, for men like them. Suddenly they discover that they are only half right. Men like them do indeed sit in government or on court benches, but in some respects at least, it doesn't make a damn bit of difference.

So they sit like clowns who've just had a custard pie slapped right in the kisser. They're dumbfounded. "There's nothing we can do," they say.

Yes there is. They can do what women did, and continue to do—they can get out into the streets and march. If they want a campaign, here's one with which to start. It should be an offense for a parent—any parent, regardless of sex—deliberately to deny their children contact with another parent or close relative who has a right to such contact. If, as I have suggested, it is true that the psychological harm done by a vicious former spouse can be as great as that done by an acquaintance rapist, then is it unreasonable to expect there to be a similar legal sanction against the act?

Here's another suggestion: Anyone of either sex who makes false allegations of sexual abuse or physical violence against their partner or colleague should be liable to severe criminal penalties. Precisely because the crimes involved are considered to be so heinous, it is vitally important that the innocent are not wrongfully accused. As matters stand, accusation is often just another form of abuse.

If the men's movement still felt energetic once these measures had been achieved, it might turn its attention to the representation of men in the media. On television, as in newspapers and magazines, negative generalizations about men are put forward by people who would rather die than make a sexist remark about women. But if it is offensive to generalize and joke about one sex, then it cannot be acceptable to be rude and contemptuous about the other. Either we should let everyone say whatever they want, irrespective of hurt feelings, or we should apply standards equally. That's the point about equality: It isn't a buffet menu. You can't pick and choose between the bits that are tasty and the bits that are tough. It's an all-or-nothing deal.

Men must have the guts to tell the self-appointed representatives of womanhood: If you want to share in the benefits of masculinity, you can share in some of the crap that comes with it, too. If you're enough of a grown-up to run the country, you're also enough of a grown-up to live with the consequences of your own actions. If you hit us, we feel it. If you kick us out of our houses, we feel that too. And if you take away our kids, we are destroyed. Those things are wrong. They are as wrong as the terrible things that men do to women. So we should treat them in the same way.

Men and women should accept and appreciate their differences without having to fight like children over who is the best or the worst. If there were more equality, then we wouldn't do quite as much harm to one another in the first place.

Children who grew up with a loving father are happier, do better at school, get better jobs, have fewer teenage pregnancies, and are less of a burden on the state. Women who are supported by a loving partner are less tired, feel less resentment, and can spare more of themselves for themselves, and for everyone else. People who don't drive themselves crazy working for dollars and pounds which they are then going to waste on nannies, school fees, and consumer toys they don't really need can live lives that have room for a little peace of mind.

When I was a boy, my mother taught me that men and women were equal. Take away the conditioning, and we would, in fact, turn out to be exactly the same. Looking at my two younger sisters, I'm not sure that I ever quite believed that last bit then, any more than I do today. But I had no doubt that women were as capable and intelligent as men, and that men could be as loving and caring as women. As far as I could see, my mum was seriously clever, my dad was really kind. I had no trouble at all with the notion of equality, then or now.

The way I learned it, we were all trying to create a world in which the liberation of both sexes would act to everyone's benefit. A new world order would arise in which men and women would be equal partners as workmates, friends, and lovers. The sun would shine, children would be happy, and glorious formations of flying pigs would wave benevolently at the fairies frolicking at the bottom of the garden.

We all know now that it didn't work. The pigs are as earthbound as ever. The conflict between men and women has become a sexual civil war. But it was still a nice idea. We could at least try to get a little of the way toward it. And the contribution that men make toward that ideal is to stop being bullies on the one hand, guilt-ridden apologists on the other.

Meanwhile, those campaigners who accuse us of being bad by definition, those propagandists who maintain that all men are violent and all violence is male, and even those well-meaning young women who assume—as who would not after the sexual politics of the past twenty-five years?—that right is on their side must come to terms with the fact that life is not that simple. Neither sex has the monopoly on virtue or vice versa. Men do not wear the black hats, nor women the white. We are all of us fallible souls decked out in shades of gray. As a man I stand accused of violence, aggression, oppression, and destructiveness. Members of the jury, I plead: not guilty.

BIBLIOGRAPHY

The following is a brief selection of the works that have informed, inspired, and occasionally irritated me (sometimes all at once) during the writing of this book. It should not be taken as a comprehensive guide: These are merely the eccentric choices of one individual reader.

Atallah, Naim. *Women*. London: Quartet, 1987.

Beard, Henry, and Cerf, Christopher. *The Official Politically Correct Dictionary and Handbook*. New York: Villard Books, 1992.

Bishop, Amanda, and Pannell, Rebecca. *All Men Are Bastards*. London: Pan, 1991.

Blackwood, Margaret. *The Monstrous Regiment: A Book of Aphorisms*. London: Andre Deutsch, 1990.

Bly, Robert. *Iron John: A Book About Men*. Reading, Mass.: Addison-Wesley, 1990.

Bray, Madge. *Poppies on the Rubbish Heap: Sexual Abuse, the Child's Voice*. Edinburgh: Canongate Press, 1991.

Brownmiller, Susan. *Against Our Will: Men, Women and Rape*. New York: Simon & Schuster, 1975.

Burgess, Jane K. *The Single-Again Man*. Lexington, Mass.: Lexington Books, 1988.

Bywater, Michael. *The Chronicles of Bargepole, the Man Who Wouldn't Be Gagged*. London: Jonathan Cape, 1992.

Chinweizu. *Anatomy of Female Power*. Lagos, Nigeria: Pero Press, 1990.

Corneau, Guy. *Absent Fathers, Lost Sons: The Search for Masculine Identity*. Boston: Shambhala Publications, 1991.

Coward, Rosalind. *Female Desire: Women's Sexuality Today*. London: Paladin Books, 1984.

———. *Our Treacherous Hearts: Why Women Let Men Get Their Way*. London: Faber & Faber, 1992.

Davidson, Neil. *Boys Will Be . . . ? Sex Education and Young Men.* London: Bedford Square Press, 1990.

Dworkin, Andrea. *Letters from a War-Zone: Writing, 1976–87.* London: Secker & Warburg, 1988.

Fallowell, Duncan, and Ashley, April. *April Ashley's Odyssey.* London: Jonathan Cape, 1982.

Faludi, Susan. *Backlash: The Undeclared War Against Women.* New York: Crown Publishers, 1991.

Feirstein, Bruce. *Real Men Don't Eat Quiche.* New York: Pocket Books, 1982.

Fischer, Seymour. *Body Consciousness: You Are What You Feel.* Englewood Cliffs, N.J.: Prentice Hall, 1973.

Friday, Nancy. *Women on Top: How Real Life Has Changed Women's Sexual Fantasies.* London: Hutchinson, 1991.

Friedan, Betty. *The Feminine Mystique.* New York: Dell Publishing, 1964.

———. *It Changed My Life: Writings on the Women's Movement.* New York: Random House, 1976.

Gaute, J.H.H., and Odell, Robin. *The Murderers' Who's Who: 150 Years of Notorious Murder Cases.* London: George G. Harrap & Co., 1979.

Goldberg, Herb. *The Hazards of Being Male.* New York: New American Library, 1977.

———. *The New Male: From Macho to Sensitive, but Still All Male.* New York: William Morrow & Co., 1979.

Goldman, William. *Adventures in the Screen Trade.* London: Macdonald & Co., 1984.

Greer, Germaine. *The Female Eunuch.* London: MacGibbon & Kee, 1970.

Hebdidge, Dick. *Subculture: The Meaning of Style.* London: Methuen, 1979.

Herr, Michael. *Dispatches.* New York: Alfred A. Knopf, 1977.

Hite, Shere. *Women as Revolutionary Agents of Change: The Hite Reports, 1972–1993.* London: Bloomsbury, 1993.

Hudson, Liam, and Jacot, Bernadine. *The Way Men Think—Intellect, Intimacy and the Erotic Imagination.* New Haven, Conn.: Yale University Press, 1991.

Hunter, Mic (ed.). *The Sexually Abused Male.* Vol. 1, *Prevalence, Impact and Treatment.* Lexington, Mass.: Lexington Books, 1990.

Keen, Sam. *Fire in the Belly: On Being a Man.* London: Piatkus, 1991.

Kent, Nicholas. *Naked Hollywood: Money, Power and the Movies.* London: BBC Books, 1991.

Lapham, Lewis H. *Money and Class in America: Notes on the Civil Religion.* London: Picador, 1989.

Lasch, Christopher. *The Culture of Narcissism: American Life in an Age of Diminishing Expectations.* New York: W. W. Norton, 1979.

Lyndon, Neil. *No More Sex War: The Failures of Feminism.* London: Sinclair-Stevenson, 1992.

Magid, Ken, and McKelvey, Carole A. *High Risk: Children Without a Conscience.* New York: Bantam Books, 1987.

Markham, Ursula. *Women Under Pressure: A Practical Guide for Today's Woman.* Dorset, England: Element Books, 1990.

Medzian, Myriam. *Boys Will Be Boys: Breaking the Link Between Masculinity and Violence.* New York: Doubleday, 1991.

Metcalfe, Andy, and Humphries, Martin (eds.). *The Sexuality of Men.* London: Pluto Press, 1985.

Miles, Rosalind. *The Women's History of the World.* London: Michael Joseph, 1988.

Millett, Kate. *Sexual Politics.* London: Virago, 1985.

Mills, Jane. *Womanwords.* London: Virago, 1991.

Morris, Jan. *Conundrum.* London: Faber & Faber, 1974.

Mulvagh, Jane. *The Vogue History of Twentieth-Century Fashion.* New York: Viking, 1988.

Nicholson, John. *A Question of Sex: The Difference Between Men and Women.* London: Fontana, 1979.

Paglia, Camille. *Sexual Personae: Art and Decadence from Nefertiti to Emily Dickinson.* New Haven, Conn.: Yale University Press, 1990.

Pizzey, Erin, and Shapiro, Jeff. *Prone to Violence.* London: Hamlyn Paperbacks, 1982.

Polhemus, Ted (ed.). *Social Aspects of the Human Body.* Middlesex, England: Penguin, 1978.

Popcorn, Faith. *The Popcorn Report: Revolutionary Trend Predictions for Marketing in the Nineties.* New York: Doubleday, 1991.

Pronger, Brian. *The Arena of Masculinity: Sports, Homosexuality and the Meaning of Sex.* London: Gay Men's Press, 1990.

Roberts, Yvonne. *Mad About Women: Can There Ever Be Fair Play Between the Sexes?* London: Virago, 1992.

Rowbotham, Sheila. *Woman's Consciousness, Man's World.* Middlesex, England: Penguin, 1983.

Segal, Lynne. *Slow Motion: Changing Masculinities, Changing Men.* London: Virago, 1990.

Sheehan, Neil. *A Bright, Shining Lie: John Paul Vann and America in Vietnam.* New York: Random House, 1988.

Skynner, Robin. *One Flesh, Separate Persons.* London: Constable, 1976.

———, and Cleese, John. *Families and How to Survive Them.* London: Methuen, 1983.

Smith, Joan. *Misogynies.* London: Faber & Faber, 1989.

Steinem, Gloria. *Revolution from Within: A Book of Self-esteem.* London: Bloomsbury, 1992.

Stibbs, Anne. *Like a Fish Needs a Bicycle.* London: Market House Books, 1992.

Tannen, Deborah. *You Just Don't Understand: Women and Men in Conversation.* New York: William Morrow & Co., 1990.

Theweleit, Klaus. *Male Fantasies.* Vols. I and II. London: Polity Press, 1979.

Trevelyan, G. M. *A Shortened History of England.* London: Longmans, Green & Co., 1942.

Tula (Caroline Cossey). *I Am a Woman.* London: Sphere Books, 1982.

Tysoe, Maryon. *Love Isn't Quite Enough: The Psychology of Male-Female Relationships.* London: Fontana, 1992.

U.S. Bureau of the Census. *Statistical Abstract of the United States.* Washington, D.C.: U.S. Government Printing Office, 1991.

Warner, Marina. *The Mermaids in the Basement.* London: Chatto & Windus, 1993.

Wilson, Gordon. *The Third Sex: The Genders of the Species.* London: Taprobane, 1990.

Wolf, Naomi. *The Beauty Myth: How Images of Beauty Are Used Against Women.* New York: William Morrow & Co., 1991.

Wolfe, Tom. *The Purple Decades.* New York: Farrar, Straus & Giroux, 1982.

York, Peter. *Modern Times.* London: William Heinemann, 1984.